SCAPEGOATS

SCAPEGOATS

A Defense of Kimmel and Short at Pearl Harbor

Edward L. Beach, Capt., USN (Ret.)

Naval Institute Press
Annapolis, Maryland

A CIP record for this book is available from the Library of Congress

Printed in the United States of America on acid-free paper ∞

9 8 7 6 5 4 3 2
First printing

To Husband Kimmel's three sons,
Manning, Thomas, and Edward,
who, like him, dedicated their lives
to the service of their country,
and have not ever let him down.

. . . Men seek to avoid being deceived less than they seek to avoid being injured by deception. They detest illusion not so much as the noxious consequences of certain types of illusion. In a similar, limited sense, men also want the truth; they welcome the agreeable, life-sustaining consequences of truth, are indifferent toward pure knowledge that brings no consequences, and *are downright hostile toward possibly damaging and destructive truths* [emphasis added].

—Friedrich W. Nietzsche, "On Truth and Falsehood in the Extra-Moral Sense" *("Ueber Wahrheit und Lüge im aussermorealischen Sinne,"* 1873).

Contents

Acknowledgments

The author wishes to acknowledge the thousands of American citizens who have studied deeply into the origins of World War II and agree with the conclusions here set forth. May their dedication to the right course of action bear fruit at last.

SCAPEGOATS

1

What This Book Is About, and Why It's Needed

The story told by this book is half a century old. Were it not central to a pivotal event in world history there would be no need to tell it yet once again—but it's basic to the sequence of events that drove the United States into the greatest war of man's time on earth. The weight of the United States turned the tide of that war and preserved the world from an extraordinary, cold-blooded, killing tyranny that was without parallel in history. Ever since the moment of U.S. entry into World War II, however, there has been controversy over how it came about in the face of determined opposition from an articulate majority in both Congress and the public at large.

This was through a sudden and unexpected attack, from an unexpected direction, and in tremendous force. It was made by Japan, a nation not yet involved in Hitler's war, on a Sunday morning during a time of peace, on our major Pacific base, and it was well behind the lines of our farthest extension to the west. An enraged America wreaked an appalling revenge on Japan for this surprise attack but has never come to grips with the question of who was responsible, if anyone, for the unawareness of our troops and naval forces in Hawaii.

Since it is now known that we could break into Japan's diplomatic codes and had been doing so for some time, how could we have been caught so embarrassingly unalert at Pearl Harbor? To answer this it is first necessary to set aside everything in the deluge of detail except what bears directly on the subject. It is a confusing and complicated matter. The sheer immensity of the material is overwhelming. Investigators and historians have had to go over thousands—tens of thousands—hundreds of thousands of pages of testimony and personal narrative. Much of the data we see today was under such heavy security when it was fresh that its accuracy half a century later is doubtful. To this must be added political considerations. The motives of the participants are suspect: self-interest was not impossible; deliberate falsehood, for government secrecy or some other reason, not impossible either.

It is also important to go over everything from the points of view of the men on the spot at the time.

Now, however, half a century after the event, most of all this has been brought out. Magic (our code-breaking ability) has been exposed, and so have some of the political facts, so that others can be guessed at. It is time we put aside the superfluous and concentrated on the significant. This is not an impossible task, but it cannot be done by a politically closed mind.

The story of Pearl Harbor has been so fully written about in all possible ways, in both fiction and nonfiction, and shown visually as well, that it is almost insulting to the American public to inflict yet another rendition upon it. The necessity arises because the perception among serious students of the event differs from the "official" explanation, and the reputation of our country regarding the human rights of the officials blamed for being caught by surprise is besmirched. The facts are clear to all researchers; the discord lies only in their interpretation by the public, compounded by our refusal to believe that our investigative bodies might not have acted impartially and fairly. As will be shown, because of the elevated status of the principals, that faith has in this instance been betrayed.

This is not, however, to castigate the national leaders involved. The problems they faced were among the greatest ever to befall this country, and their resolution of them will remain one of its finest hours. No one who has seen the memorials to D-Day in France—the rows upon rows of white crosses and six-pointed stars, each standing for a human life extinguished in the cause of beating back an unacceptable tyranny—can ever doubt that. Nor can anyone who has walked through the Holocaust Museum, on Raoul Wallenberg Place in Washington, D.C., evermore hold that defeat of the despicable depravity embodied in Nazi tyranny was not a mandate upon us all.

In the briefest exposition, Prime Minister Winston Churchill of embattled England, joined by President Franklin D. Roosevelt and his administration, preserved human freedom in the face of the most abhorrent despotism seen by civilized mankind. Yet America Firsters of the time believed anything would be better than a war, and the majority of the U.S. population, in 1941 understandably opposed to war, emotionally closed its collective mind to the unbelievable trauma being inflicted on Europe. It argued that this was not our problem, that it need not affect us, that Hitler and his successors would most likely turn benign after overwhelming half the world, that in any case *that* problem need not be faced until it arose.

Arrayed against this was the argument, gradually espoused by more and more Americans as the realities of the European situation became more evident, that Hitler was coming close to winning the war in Europe, would soon conquer Russia, and that his next target would be the Western Hemisphere. This would be a calamity that should be prevented at all costs. However, as Roosevelt's conviction grew that U.S. entry into the war against Nazi Germany could not be avoided, his understanding of the tremendous political strength of the isolationist feeling grew likewise. Before our country could become part of the world crusade against Nazism, this had to be overcome. But Nazi Germany, victorious so far, was determined to avoid including the United States among its battlefield enemies, at least for the present. Roosevelt's reelection campaign for his unprecedented third term had emphasized that his active neutrality policy, which he described as "all aid short of war," was succeeding in its avowed purpose of denying victory in Europe to the Nazi war machine. He had stressed unremittingly, however, that no matter what, he would avoid U.S. entry into active war, and that this would in fact not be necessary: "I will say it agayne, and agayne, and agayne! Your sons are not going to be sent to fight in any foreign wars!" Later on he added the phrase "unless we are attacked."

But even as he said it, Roosevelt knew that this was not true. It was only rhetoric in the heat of an unprecedented third-term presidential campaign, intended to reassure voters that his continuance in office would continue the policies that avoided full involvement in the war against Hitler. Such statements were a political necessity that could not be evaded, but in his heart he knew them to be false.

If ever a leader painted himself into a corner, Franklin D. Roosevelt did just that in 1940. He knew it as he did it, and he and his party were convinced the election would be lost if he did not do it.

Pearl Harbor wiped away all the antiwar arguments. Secretary of War Henry L. Stimson's diaries note that despite the stunning cost in lives and damage to our armed forces, the attack brought a feeling of tremendous relief to everyone close to Roosevelt. Churchill is quoted as saying that he "slept the sleep of the saved and thankful." For all involved, the dilemma under which they had been laboring for a year was resolved.

The isolationist contingent of our society, whose motto was simply "America First," was diverse. It included idealists who held that we should solve our own problems before taking on those of others; hard-working people who tilled their own ground or minded their own businesses; opposition politicians who grabbed any issue to confront the party in power; other politicians who were most concerned with their inward-looking constituents, knowing that on them depended their continuance in office; and parents who feared for their children. For the most part, there can be no criticism of their motives, but they had become a one-issue party over a situation they did not fully understand. In the march of human events there are some forces that move relentlessly, and they were caught in one.

The America Firsters, like all other Americans, would go all out to win the war that had brutally seized them. Like all Americans, they set themselves to cope with the realities, and the world knows how that came out.

However, they retained a deep anger against those whom they saw as responsible for turning on its head their cherished outlook that war could be avoided. Most of the anger was directed at the Japanese, in particular against Admiral Yamamoto and Prime Minister Tojo, but some of it turned into unreasoning fury against any leaders on our side who could be seen as having failed in their obligation to prevent the surprise.

Roosevelt, the consummately successful politician of his time, probably understood better than anyone how inevitable was this fury, and how imperative it was that someone be named to receive the blame.

This emotional change in national outlook, combined with the shock to our pride, brought about, as Roosevelt understood it might, an almost pathological search for someone to blame for allowing it to happen. He needed scapegoats, if for no other reason than to allow him to carry on the war. Upon Adm. Husband E. Kimmel, commander in chief of the U.S. Fleet (CINCUS—pronounced as one word, "SINKus," never "sink us"), and Lt. Gen. Walter C. Short, commander of the Hawaiian Department of our army, instantly named by official action of the U.S. government (the Roberts Commission Report) as culpable since they were in military command where the most dramatic blow fell, therefore landed the weight of national obloquy.

Kimmel and Short were easy to charge with fault and, possessed of no powerful political connections, had no way to fight back. They could not mount a defense against the charges since this would have forced disclosure of secret information vitally important to the war effort. Specifically, they would have had to disclose the abilities of our code-breakers, whose extraordinary success remained highly secret for decades afterward. Ironically, neither Kimmel nor Short knew how much information had been available, nor how closely it had been at the heart of their predicament, until near the end of the war. But in the euphoria of victory and the complicated Cold War aftermath, most of the public had no further interest in the two discredited leaders, remembering only vestiges of the details, forgetting the hatred it had levied on them, uneasily feeling that to absolve them was to lay the blame on the legendary president who had brought the country successfully through this terrible war and, almost like Lincoln, died in the moment of victory.

In a sense, the shortsighted isolationist argument was continued in a different form, never mind its illogic: If Pearl Harbor had not happened, our nation might have been able to stay out of World War II and avoid its terrible cost; or tautologically, if we had not been caught by surprise, the cost in lives and damage would have been less. The instant success of the surprise attack could therefore only have been due to neglect of some kind on our side. Admiral Kimmel and General Short should have expected such an attack and had the navy and army at battle stations on that balmy Sunday morning. They were guilty as charged. Leaving the onus on them was easier than pushing it higher up. For those who held uneasy feelings about what this did to our national obligation to justice, there was another answer stemming from an inaccurate understanding of military tradition. Some people really believed that to the commander of a defeated military force must always go blame for the defeat.

There was some hope that things would finally be put right at the fiftieth anniversary of the attack, but not all of the necessary factors were in place. There was still lingering doubt, due partly to disinterest in resurrecting a discreditable national memory. The anniversary was commemorated and went into the record with this loose end still hanging loose, an indictment of our leaders of that long past time that need not still be there.

This is, therefore, not the usual book about history. It lacks the fundamental virtue of chronology, since it is entirely focused on a single point in time. The author has not discovered new material. All the material is already there, available to overflowing, researched and compiled by hundreds of others. While we may still seek a "smoking gun," to apply a modern term that did not exist then, there are few primary sources cited in this book. Where there is need to make reference, the reader will note that in almost every case the reference is to some other research, someone else's work, a committee report, some book or paper written by someone else. What *is* new is an effort to redirect the deluge of information and show how simple justice to the memories of our long-gone and truly heroic victims at Pearl Harbor—all 2,403 of them, in all services—requires that the stain of official blame be cleansed. The honor of the United States has needed this for many years.

A standard method of disparagement is to coin disdainful, innuendo-laden catchphrases with which to refer to that which it is desired to disparage. So it is with the term "revisionist," these days taken to refer to anyone who does not agree with accepted historical accounts. There is nothing wrong with revising an inaccuracy, or a falsehood, with the truth, which may not come to light for some years after the event, and that's what makes the study of history so fascinating. As these words are written, for example, the *Washington Times* of 2 August 1994 carries an article, dateline London, with the headline, "Churchill not tipped on Dec. 7"—showing that even at this late date there is unease, and anticipation of possible new information, on the subject. This short article, as reproduced in Washington, notes that its source is a 1945 "History of Britain's Naval Intelligence Division, released last week," thus implying still more to come.

In concentrating on the wrong done to the commanders of our Pearl Harbor forces, my purpose is not to revise history, or to rewrite it, but to reinterpret it. Were the awesome personalities of President Franklin D. Roosevelt and Gen. George C. Marshall not involved, it is my conviction that the events leading to the Japanese attack on Pearl Harbor would long since have been seen in their true light. The blame leveled, in the heat of that tragic day, upon our two unfortunate commanders there would no longer be part of the historical record.

This might even have happened during their lifetimes, while they might still have been able, personally, to savor the vindication. But President Roosevelt, who might conceivably have been moved to exercise the compassion that only he could give (though this is pure speculation), died too soon. For the rest of us there was too much involved in the national dilemma Japan settled so dramatically at Pearl Harbor.

However, I cannot overlook our faith that our standards and outlooks are the right ones. We of the United States believe ourselves blessed with a standard of government and justice for the individual that transcends all previous standards. We believe our system works, in the main, as we would wish it to, but we also know that eternal vigilance is the price of the liberty and freedom we enjoy. Where it seems injustice has been done, even if there can be no recompense to the individuals thus defamed, the greater obligation is to the system that should not have been allowed to do the injury and that can, at the least, rescue itself from past error.

The honor of our nation is involved in this issue more than in any other. In this controversy, misunderstanding and injustice cry together for correction. The role of the president of the United States in marshaling our national will to fight the destructive forces Hitler had unleashed should be better appreciated. National compassion for persons wrongly used by circumstances far beyond their control, and in which they had no part, should finally be exercised, late though it now may be.

2

The American Situation Before the War

The beginning of the climactic event known in historical shorthand as "Pearl Harbor" took place long before 7 December 1941. There are some who would place it late in 1940, aboard Adm. Isoroku Yamamoto's flagship, HIJMS *Nagato,* when Yamamoto assembled his staff and instructed them to begin the planning and logistic arrangements. It may also be said to have started earlier that year, when the United States made the basic decision that the line of our vital interest lay west of the Philippines.

People devoted to the idea of the long unbroken line of historical continuity will say it began in 1904, when Adm. Heihachiro Togo attacked the Russian fleet at its Pacific base at Port Arthur in advance of a declaration of war (and thereby directly caused it). Russia never recovered from this initial setback. Captured Port Arthur near the city of Dairen, at the foot of the Kwan-Tung Peninsula in Manchuria, commanding the Gulf of Chihli and the sea approaches to China's capital of Beijing (Peking), was ceded to Japan by the Portsmouth, New Hampshire, Peace Treaty, which was mediated by President Theodore Roosevelt and gained him the Nobel Prize for Peace.

The Japanese, incidentally, never fully forgave Theodore Roosevelt for bringing an end to the war with Russia before Japan had realized all the fruits of its stunning success. In Japan's view the peace was premature.

In 1940, when we placed our perimeter of national interest on the western side of the Philippines, we were (at least theoretically) increasing our impact on sea area that Japan considered its own proper sphere of influence, just as Czarist Russia had done by establishing a base at Port Arthur. We had heretofore considered Honolulu, specifically Pearl Harbor, our fleet base on the island of Oahu in Hawaii, to be our Pacific outpost, notwithstanding our annexation of the Philippine Islands, thousands of miles to the west, after the Spanish-American War of 1898. Since we had committed ourselves to the ultimate independence of the Philippines, we did not then consider them as being within our defensive perimeter.

Although we had long maintained an Asiatic fleet with headquarters in the Philippines and knew we might have to fight to maintain control of these distant islands, the concept that they lay within any sort of boundary of our own was entirely anomalous.

In 1898 we had also acquired from Spain the small island of Guam in the Marianas, and in 1899 American Samoa, farther south, by agreement with Britain and Germany; but these had not added one way or another to our concept of where lay the boundary of our Far East hegemony. Somehow that question had never been addressed.

All this changed in 1940 when, by unilateral decision but supported by embattled England, President Franklin D. Roosevelt declared the periphery of U.S. national interests to be much farther west, anchored on the Philippines. No one consulted Japan about it. Making this decision just at this time would seem to have been somewhat unusual, given the state of the world in 1940, but the fact was that Great Britain, once known as the "guardian" of the Far East, was delighted, and Prime Minister Winston Churchill himself may have suggested it. It was founded, apparently, on the concept of long-range bombers, specifically the new and truly formidable B-17s, based in Luzon and able to deliver devastating attack anywhere within a circle of a thousand miles. To implement a strategy based on long-range bombing (miscalled "deterrent strategy" by some), plans were drawn to station heavy forces of these new aircraft in the Philippines.

Were we truly isolationist in outlook, we should not have gone beyond previous boundaries to look for more lands and more ocean areas to be concerned about. No one in America, however, thought much about this purely conceptual change, as it then seemed to be.

This particular decision had far-reaching consequences. Pearl Harbor was no longer on the front lines, its defense no longer something that would come to instant mind at the thought of war in the Pacific. Instead, protection of that far-distant, somewhat theoretical line on the far side of the Philippines began to claim more and more attention. Gen. Douglas MacArthur, retired from the U.S. Army and now serving as field marshal of the Philippine Army, found himself (willingly) called back to active duty in the rank of lieutenant general in command of U.S. Forces Far East, soon to be promoted back to four-star general. He was given extra funding for troops and promised more, as well as more reinforcements from the United States. He made impressive plans for a Philippine Army of more than one hundred thousand soldiers and for much enlarged U.S. forces as well. He also argued for greatly increasing the air power under his command, citing the Philippines as being well placed for holding Japan in check should that nation begin heading to the south.

John Costello, in his brilliantly researched *Days of Infamy* (New York: Pocket Books, 1994), lays this out with great care and in superb detail. MacArthur's ideas for military expansion in the Philippines were more on paper than in the flesh, more theoretical than real, but they did achieve some success. His forces were increased, and more aircraft, specifically more of our newly developed long-range B-17 bombers, were promised. One of our extraordinary Purple machines, able to decipher Japanese diplomatic codes and produce Magic, was assigned to Station "Cast" ("cast" was the phonetic word at that time for the letter *c*). *C,* or Cast, stood for Corregidor, just as "Hypo," or the letter *H,* signified Honolulu. Cast, with necessary operating personnel, was hidden in one of the tunnels on Corregidor, while Hypo, later famous under Cdr. Joe Rochefort because of its inspired performance in detecting and code-breaking the Battle of Midway preliminaries, operated from the rigidly guarded basement of a large building in the navy yard at Honolulu.

Everything about Purple, even the knowledge that it existed, or that it produced Magic—also a secret code word—was under the tightest security classification. The instrument was kept hidden, and its operators were the most close-mouthed people in military service. No one with any awareness of Purple, or Magic, could be risked to capture by the enemy; so the people working at Station Cast, with their top-secret device, were quietly spirited away after the outbreak of the war.

A Purple machine had originally been designated for Pearl Harbor also. "In return for useful intelligence information," however, it was diverted to augment England's code-breaking capability at Bletchley Park. We had built eight Purple machines, intending four for Washington (two each for the army and navy), two for London, one for Manila, and one for Pearl Harbor. One of the two London machines went to the super-secret decoding agency at Bletchley Park, the other to the prime minister's underground war headquarters. Before delivery was made to Pearl Harbor, Bletchley Park requested a second machine, citing information it was sharing with Washington as justification and promising in return that we would get one of the English Enigma machines that could break the German codes. It seems that Gen. George C. Marshall authorized the switch, and the evidence is that Vice Adm. Richmond Kelly Turner, in his self-arrogated role as the navy's chief intelligence arbiter, made the decision as to which of the originally proposed recipients on our side would be blocked out.

Bletchley got its second Purple machine, but English codebreakers unexpectedly cited an unlooked-for set of regulations that barred them from completing their side of the bargain. The result was that of our eight Purple machines, four remained in Washington, three went to England, and one went to Station Cast in Manila. Another machine could have been quickly built and sent to Pearl Harbor, but no effort was made to do this. The whole thing was so secret that the Pearl Harbor commanders had no idea a Purple machine had been scheduled for them and later diverted. They did not, in fact, even know such an instrument existed. As Adm. Harold R. Stark testified after the war, everyone knowing of it, or on the distribution list for Magic, was required to sign a supersecret oath never to divulge anything about the machine, or about Magic, or even guardedly talk about anything resulting from or connected with it to anyone under any circumstances for the rest of his or her life.

Adm. Husband E. Kimmel and Lt. Gen. Walter C. Short had been pledged in writing by their respective chiefs of service that all information pertaining to their posts, from whatever source, would be sent them as soon as received in Washington. Kimmel made a special trip to Washington in June for the purpose of handing directly to Admiral Stark, the chief of naval operations (CNO), a strongly worded letter specifically requesting this, and received in return Stark's categorical assurance that it would positively be done. Kimmel's and Short's communications centers early on did in fact receive a considerable amount of such information, some identified as having come from intercepted messages. This was reassurance to both that the commitment was being honored as promised. They had no way, however, of discovering whether they were in truth receiving all they should have been getting. For this they had to depend on the promises of their superiors, as was proper.

But Kimmel and Short were not informed that since their posts were now well inside the defensive perimeter, it had not been thought necessary for them either to have a Magic machine or to be able to decide for themselves whether any particular message bore on their areas of responsibility. Unknown to them, over time, the dispatches from Washington gradually diminished in immediacy. The relatively chatty personal letters from Stark to Kimmel gradually reflected less and less of the growing crisis in the nation's capital. They were, in other words, "cut out of the loop"—and, as is usual in such circumstances, were not even aware of it.

Though Kimmel and Short were kept uninformed of the diplomatic preliminaries, it is now evident that no immediate forewarning could have changed the course of events on 7 December 1941. We might have avoided an embarrassing *tactical* surprise but not the *strategic* surprise. That was inevitable because of the condition of our forces. We were vulnerable regardless of anything we might have done at that late date because we had neglected to build up our military forces in the face of obvious danger. Both army and navy had been allowed for years to remain essentially stagnant while Europe marched implacably toward a new world war and Japan began its conquest of China.

As the emergency in Europe unfolded, our war production, late-starting as it was, was gradually put into high gear; but nearly all we produced went to Europe, specifically to beleaguered England. In addition, because of the steady increase in ships needed in the Atlantic, our Pacific Fleet had been steadily reduced in force—"robbed," Kimmel would have said—to send needed ships through the Panama Canal to the other ocean. The remaining ships, already inferior in numbers and in offensive power to those of the Japanese fleet, were far below the antiaircraft standards reported necessary by our observers in Europe. And we had only two effective aircraft carriers (the third Pacific carrier was in overhaul), compared to the six in the Japanese strike force (thank God our carriers were far from Pearl!—they were the principal targets of the attack, by Yamamoto's express direction).

The purpose of all naval bases is to replenish, repair, and protect warships during their necessary in-port periods. Ships cannot remain indefinitely at sea, nor indefinitely on alert against attack. From time to time they must "stand down," pass under the protection of the base from which they operate, and be relieved of an impossible permanent burden. But the land-based antiaircraft defenses of our vaunted stronghold on Oahu were pitifully inadequate as measured by experience in Europe, and we had done nothing, despite the prayerful recommendations of our Hawaii commanders, to bring them up to minimum standard. Even our ability to maintain surveillance of the ocean area around Hawaii, to give warning of hostile approach by sea or by air, was inadequate.

All the flyable army and navy patrol aircraft in Hawaii totaled only one-sixth of the number required to guarantee detection of unannounced ships and aircraft.

Adequate numbers of these specialized aircraft were already in full production; but nearly all of that production, in the neighborhood of two thousand planes as of the time of the attack, had gone to England, whose need was considered by Washington to be greater than Pearl Harbor's.

Refusal to admit a fact does not alter it. The main reason why Pearl Harbor and our Pacific Fleet were not ready for war on 7 December 1941 was that, despite being touted as impregnable, Pearl Harbor's defenses had never been adequate, nor its support capability good enough, to maintain our fleet. Adm. James O. Richardson, Kimmel's predecessor in command, had been summarily fired from his post for having been too forceful in his requests for improvements, and for having presented the problem too often to President Roosevelt. For years, too few of the necessities of successful sea war had been provided that fleet of which we were so proud, and lately planes, ammunition, fuel—even a goodly percentage of its best ships—had been diverted. It was, realistically, only the shell of what we in America thought it was.

For years we had adhered to Mahan's principle that the fleet should never be divided lest an enemy, even though not equal in total force, succeed in confronting each of its separated parts with a superior force. This was one of the principal reasons why we built the Panama Canal. Since the end of World War I Japan had been seen as the greatest maritime threat, and the U.S. Fleet had by consequence been based in the Pacific, at Long Beach, California, where adequate support facilities existed or were within easy reach. Its commander bore the title of commander in chief, U.S. Fleet (CINCUS), as had his predecessors for many years. The Atlantic Fleet, by contrast, had been created only recently, by upgrading the previous Atlantic Squadron in recognition of the growing menace on the other side of that ocean. At the same time, because of the emergency in Europe, most of the armament and munitions our factories produced went to our allies and friends there, while the new Atlantic Fleet received the bulk, in all categories, of our remaining prewar production. The U.S. Fleet, higher rated in theory than the Atlantic Fleet, however, still consisted mostly of World War I–type battleships that, through long habit, were thought of as the essence of "the fleet"—and were spoken of in this way. To our prewar navy, these great old battlewagons *were* the U.S. Fleet, and by extension the "real navy." Only a few forward-looking people saw them as obsolescent, lacking in speed and anti-aircraft capability, not modernized as they should have been, not suited to the realities of modern war at sea. These battleships, and the officers and men serving them so faithfully and pridefully, might have done well in 1916 at the Battle of Jutland, but they were not up for the game in 1941. All the same, they trained hard and worked hard, for their admiral, Kimmel, demanded it; but even they, when they thought about it—in the little time they had left to think during the unceasing rounds of exercises—must have realized that they had been left behind, that their abilities with their fine but old ships were no longer adequate.

It took the jolt of Pearl Harbor to bring this home, but it is nevertheless noteworthy that during our two years of buildup to war our "battle line" got nothing in terms of practical attention from Washington. It was almost as though some sixth sense of its actual uselessness for its designed purpose had infiltrated the subconsciousnesses of the decision makers there.

It had become an incongruous situation. CINCUS, by his charter, was the senior of all the fleet commanders, nominally in command of all our afloat forces. His consultation and approval were supposedly prerequisites to any big movements of "forces afloat," particularly as they concerned strategy and readiness. But with the creation of the Atlantic Fleet, decisions as to allocation of ships, aircraft, and weapons, all of them greatly affecting the U.S. Fleet, began to be made in Washington without even notification of the same being sent to CINCUS. This gradually increasing lack of information and consultation had been one of Richardson's principal complaints, and his resistance to the situation was one of the reasons, possibly even the primary one, for his removal. When Kimmel took charge as CINCUS he fully understood the growing separation of the two portions of the U.S. Fleet and knew that he was responsible only for the Pacific portion thereof.

In most cases Kimmel received, without forewarning, only the bare directive to transfer certain ships—for example, the recently overhauled Battleship Division Three, consisting of the *Mississippi, Idaho,* and *New Mexico,* arguably the best of his battlewagons because recently modernized—to the Atlantic to support the forces sent to Iceland. The carrier *Yorktown* was requisitioned a little later, and the *Wasp,* due to transit the Panama Canal and join the Pacific Fleet, was held in the Atlantic and employed in the support of Malta, in the Mediterranean. A still bigger, because less noticeable, problem was the quiet, unannounced diversion of promised resources such as long-range patrol planes. The CNO had unequivocally assured Kimmel that 100 additional PBY-5 Catalinas would quickly be sent (not the 250 he had so urgently asked for), but they never arrived. Not one was even put in motion toward Hawaii, while many hundreds, in the meantime, went to England.

Of none of this was CINCUS informed. At some point Kimmel should have raised a loud and indignant fuss over the official neglect of his forces, but again, it was precisely this that had led to the abrupt removal of his predecessor. His job, he knew well, was to do the best he could with what he was given, relying on the superior awareness of his superiors in Washington to parcel out scarce resources in the best possible way.

What he did do, during his tenure as CINCUS, was to train strenuously to carry out the latest version of the Pacific Fleet war plan, while at the same time urgently listing his fleet's deficiencies and pleading for the equipment it needed: more aircraft carriers, to compare better with Japan's ten; sufficient patrol aircraft to permit a proper continuous air patrol of the sea approaches to Oahu; antiaircraft weapons and ammunition, in which his fleet was terribly deficient, according to closely studied reports from England's Royal Navy; fuel in enough quantity to permit prolonged operations; fleet oilers to enable the ships to refuel at sea instead of being forced to return to port to hook up directly to the tank farm; provision ships for the same reason; more destroyers for fleet escort; and more antisubmarine vessels.

Kimmel certainly had good reason for trying to move Washington to correct his fleet's deficiencies. A Pacific war was definitely in the wind. In 1931 Japan had invaded Manchuria and set up the puppet kingdom of Manchukuo—the so-called "China Incident." In 1937 occurred the Rape of Nanking, and the world was horrified. Fighting had continued in China since then, but in 1941 Japan was undoubtedly on the move, its target clearly the Far East: French Indo-China, the Dutch East Indies, perhaps the Philippines. Pearl Harbor was not, however, a likely objective of attack, being far behind our defensive perimeter. Kimmel had received numerous letters and dispatches from Stark to that effect.

The glitch in this simplistic analysis appears now to have been Japan's Admiral Yamamoto, commander in chief of the Imperial Combined Fleet. The opposite number to Kimmel, Yamamoto felt the U.S. Fleet had to be neutralized before it could embark on its long-studied War Plan Orange, or one of its derivatives, to interfere with Japan's Greater East Asia Co-Prosperity Sphere. He had carefully studied the histories and the personalities of his potential antagonists and felt he knew them as well as the circumstances permitted. Kimmel, Yamamoto had discovered, was a hard-working man who trained his fleet tirelessly and could be depended on to act aggressively in carrying out the U.S. Navy's war plans. A war with America would bring the U.S. Fleet to sea in battle array, which Yamamoto would, of course, have to meet, to the probable detriment of Japan's planned campaign in its primary area of interest, the East China and South China Seas on down to Singapore and the Dutch East Indies. A quickly executed attack, to pin down the U.S. Fleet before it go could forward with its latest version of Orange, Yamamoto felt, would permit his Combined Fleet to carry out its own mission essentially free of interference.

A well-planned surprise attack is one of the most basic of military operations, and hardest to defeat because, by definition, the defenders are not ready. A major portion of the planning is always devoted to preserving the element of surprise. The defeat of the Maginot Line, the invasion of Normandy in 1944, the Iraqi invasion of Kuwait in 1990 are all examples.

In 1940 and 1941 the nation as a whole wanted at all costs to stay out of the fighting in Europe and China, and the president justified sending arms and supplies to England by saying that it would enable us to avoid engaging in the war directly. By and large, Americans believed this argument because they wanted to. Although few could predict just how this was supposed to work, with tiny England the only remaining bastion of freedom in all of Europe, the idea promised an easy way out of what everyone perceived as a growing world catastrophe. To the unthinking—or to those who did not want to think about it—Roosevelt's policy was a panacea.

Our policy makers, while issuing encouraging announcements, knew the truth to be the contrary. The situation was 1916 all over again. But how to change America's antiwar mind-set? The war in Europe directly affected only a small part of our citizenry. It was, in fact, economically beneficial to us, although no one in our isolationist wing had yet explained how a conquered England would pay for all the help we had sent. (As we found out after the war, the ultimately victorious England could not do so either.) By late 1940 the United Kingdom had nearly exhausted its dollar and gold reserves and fought the rest of the war on credit. (So, in effect, did the banker, the United States. The debt may finally be paid off by greatly increased inflation, and the only hope is that this may take place slowly enough that it will not be ruinous.)

The war had, however, ended the Great Depression. It had sent an enormous amount of profitable work our way. The status quo, from a short-sighted perspective, was fine. How could the president change the collective mind of the U.S. citizenry?

With Magic in his bag of tricks, Roosevelt began to look for ways to bring the United States to a wholehearted national commitment to victory. At the same time, naturally enough, he continued to insist that his only objectives were to keep Japan from enlarging its war with China in the Far East and to support England in its war against Hitler.

In 1937 Japanese aircraft attacked and sank our Yangtze River gunboat *Panay*—an inexcusable "accident of misidentification" for which Japan apologized and paid indemnity. This did not cause the United States to take more than passing notice, for the *Panay* was after all only a small and unimportant warship. Four years later, however, as narrated by Rear Adm. Kemp Tolley in *Cruise of the* Lanikai (Annapolis: Naval Institute Press, 1973, reprinted 1994 by the Admiral Nimitz Foundation), three small ships, one of them Adm. Thomas C. Hart's officially assigned yacht, the USS *Isabel,* and two even smaller schooners, the latter made "warships" overnight by explicit orders of the White House, were directed to certain positions in the path of Japan's expected advance to the south. Tolley was skipper of one of them, the *Lanikai,* and was convinced (Admiral Hart, commander in chief of the U.S. Asiatic Fleet, later told him, "Yes, you were bait!") that Roosevelt's intent was to present the advancing Japanese fleet with another *Panay* that might, this time, become a *causus belli* in support of our European friends.

Parenthetically, the first part of Tolley's book is something of a surprise. It has little to do with the *Lanikai's* escape from the Japanese but is instead a thoughtful analysis of Roosevelt's diplomatic offensive, which many historians believe induced Japan to enter World War II. Tolley stops short of suggesting that the president had advance knowledge of Pearl Harbor but leaves no doubt that he caused Japan's entry into the war and knew half a day in advance that Japan was about to implement some desperate sort of contingency plan with which to begin it.

3

Roosevelt and Churchill and the Emergency in Europe

In 1933 a megalomaniac named Adolf Hitler took command in Germany and began gearing his nation for a war to avenge the unfair peace imposed at Versailles after World War I. But he moved too fast. In 1939, when he set up a fictitious border incident as an excuse to send his mechanized cavalry to destroy Poland's heroic but outclassed horse cavalry, England and France finally faced up to the unpleasant reality they had been avoiding.

The Treaty of Versailles, imposing ruinous terms on an only partly defeated Germany, had brought a madman to its helm. The failure of England and France to act sooner, when Hitler might have been stopped at relatively small cost, would now cost them dearly—but not so much as it would surely cost a few years later, if indeed it would be possible to stop him at all. Even so, by the end of 1940, after little more than a year of war, France, Holland, Belgium, Norway, and all of Central Europe had fallen to the German war machine. Italy was entirely under German domination, and thanks to German submarines and air power, England's survival was in serious doubt.

When the war began in Europe, President Roosevelt, nearing the end of his second term of office, began a series of conversations over the transatlantic telephone with Winston Churchill, newly installed as prime minister of England. Initially only professing concern, Roosevelt's attitude gradually shifted toward being more and more supportive of England as its fortunes waned. By 1941, few citizens really understood (though some did, particularly members of the armed forces involved) the true extent to which our help for Britain already exceeded the limitations of neutrality as stated in both international and our own law. None, perhaps not even Roosevelt's closest advisers, knew how far he had gone in his promises to Churchill, and we still do not know.

"Lend Lease," the transfer of fifty old destroyers from our navy to that of England to bolster its anti–U-boat campaign, and a Declaration of Neutrality encompassing gradually more of the Atlantic Ocean until fully half of it was declared officially under our aegis and prohibited to U-boats, were among the measures he put in place. But we paid no attention to our own area limitation. Roosevelt issued a "shoot on sight" order, anywhere in that ocean, to our Atlantic antisubmarine craft. Since mid-1940, we had been convoying ships filled with war necessities—munitions, aircraft, provisions, fuel—nearly all the way to England, in many cases turning them over to hard-pressed British navy escorts only a day or so away from their shores. England's damaged warships were being repaired in American navy yards, their crews welcomed as heroes of a war against a common foe.

It cannot be stated exactly when Roosevelt's interest in England turned to active worry. This must have happened over time, in 1940, perhaps coincident with the placement of our perimeter of interest beyond the Philippines.

During 1940 and 1941 Roosevelt and Churchill became more and more concerned over the war in Europe. German soldiers seemed invincible, and German air power nearly the same. The Royal Navy was all that stood between England and destruction, and the convoy of vital necessities from America had become England's lifeblood. Somewhere in their deliberations, the question of how to get America into the war on the side of England must have become paramount.

In the meantime, although Japan and Germany were on opposite sides of the world and had little in common, other than tyrannical governments and an intent to conquer weaker neighbors, in September 1940 they negotiated a treaty of alliance. With the pro forma inclusion of Italy, this became known as the Tripartite Treaty, and it soon appeared that it might present an avenue by which the United States could get into the European war—at the expense of fighting Japan at the same time.

There is no proof positive that this idea occurred full-blown to either Roosevelt or Churchill, or to anyone working for them, but as with so much that was done by these two masters of public policy and intrigue, the final motivation has to be inferred from the final fact. This entire period of world history was one of the highest risk. It is illogical to suggest that leaders of important nations could carry out any long-range plan, in which so much depended on the actions of other nations, without serious and lengthy consultation with friends and allies.

The fairest thing that can be said is that everyone involved was churning about in a swirling maelstrom of enmities, ideas, and perceptions. Their basic purposes can be seen clearly, however, even though their actions at any given time might appear directionless or contradictory. As Roberta Wohlstetter explains in *Pearl Harbor: Warning and Decision* (Stanford: Stanford University Press, 1962), how any individual deals with the confusion resulting from the kind of information overload Roosevelt, Churchill, and their advisers were getting is best understood by studying his or her orientation. That factor alone will bring consistency.

The scenario for the "back door" approach to getting the United States into the European war is this: Nearly all Japan's fuel oil came through the United States and was paid for by funds on deposit in the United States. If fuel were to be cut off, Japan would either have to give up the war against China or find fuel elsewhere. The oil fields of the Netherlands East Indies and British Borneo were right at hand but in July of 1941 were closed to Japan because of disapproval of its "Greater East Asia" policies. Holland had long since been occupied by Germany, and the Dutch royal family was in hiding in Britain, but there was hope of restoration if and when Germany was defeated. Any attack by powerful Japan upon weak Dutch defenses in Java could result only one way, and that very quickly, but besides involving England as an ally of the Netherlands this would also seriously threaten Australia. As England's ally in the Far East, and therefore Australia's also, America would have to weigh into that potential battle. According to the Tripartite Treaty, Germany would then enter the war alongside Japan, and since the Philippines lay directly in the Japanese path to the south, Japan would probably attack them too. The European war would have been converted into a true world war, and we would automatically become full allies of England in the Atlantic as well as in the Pacific.

The flaw in this reasoning is that Hitler was not known for honoring treaty obligations, and Japan might choose to limit its risks, and costs, by at least temporarily bypassing the Philippines. Japan had not joined the fight against Soviet Russia, thus demonstrating one of the limitations of its alliance with Germany. Japan had received assurances (according to Capt. Tracy Kittredge, USNR (Ret.), until 1953 a member of the historical section of our Joint Chiefs of Staff Secretariat) that Germany and Italy would fight on its side in the event of war, but Japan saw no need to consult with its Axis allies before initiating war itself. Quite the reverse, for Japan felt, probably rightly, that making its plans known in advance to either Germany or Italy would involve unwarranted risk of their being detected or betrayed.

Germany already had ample cause for war with the United States because of our disregard of the obligations of strict neutrality, but Hitler had clearly indicated his intention to avoid this, at least for the time being. It is hardly likely that Roosevelt could have expected Hitler to change this policy because of our involvement in a Pacific war with Japan. Our president played the hand dealt him as well as he was able, was as much caught by the developing circumstances as anyone, and managed more than most to stay ahead of the game.

The positive side of the coin is that enlargement of the European war into a world war with Japan as an Axis member would almost certainly put the United States in the fray against Hitler, a point agreed to by most historians despite the somewhat murky path. A shooting war between Axis members and our close friends and allies, Australia in particular, in such close proximity to the Philippines and our Asiatic Fleet, could hardly result otherwise. But time was also important, in that it was obviously in Nazi Germany's interest to delay this expansion of the war until the issue in Europe had been resolved. There are knowledgeable persons who feel England was in less serious straits than represented; others believe the situation was, indeed, desperate. It is a question that may never be conclusively answered, but this is less important, at this stage, than how the situation was handled in 1941.

The evidence suggests that in 1941 Roosevelt was convinced that immediate aid for embattled Britain was important. It is also apparent that without some supervening cause he could not be sure of congressional support for a declaration of war against Germany. Since no one close to Roosevelt at that time ever explained the point, and no records have been found, historians have had only the actions taken by all concerned to guess at what their purpose must have been.

Some would-be isolationists, advancing this scenario, bitterly accuse Roosevelt of conspiring with Churchill to get the United States into the war. Lost sight of, in all the argument and invective over who was "guilty" (and of what), is that any "back door" scenario leaves Hitler with the initiative and therefore cannot qualify as a successful conspiracy. For four days after Pearl Harbor, Roosevelt and Churchill, and their inner circles, anxiously awaited what Hitler would do. Would he declare war, or would he not? We know that Hitler's advisers argued that involvement of the United States in all-out war in the Pacific was entirely to Germany's advantage, that our support of England could only thereby be reduced. Some people, this author among them, for a long time felt that Hitler's declaration of war on the United States at this juncture was the greatest mistake of his career, greater even than the attack on Soviet Russia in June 1941.

Kittredge changed that thinking, in part at least, by a thoughtful article in the July 1955 issue of the U.S. Naval Institute *Proceedings*. Immediately after confirmation of the Japanese attack, according to Kittredge, Grand Admiral Erich Raeder, Hitler's navy chief, arguing it was now no longer possible for the Allies to prevent a total German victory in 1943, surfaced a closely held proposal to establish a holding line in Russia, free as many as one hundred divisions for redeployment against England, then campaign for victory over England in 1942 and Russia by 1943.

On 9 December Hitler was briefed. He approved several directives to this end, including the temporary shift to a holding posture in Russia, but he held back approval of Raeder's plan for declaration of war with the United States, which the admiral also proposed on the ground that U.S. "gross disregard of neutrality [had reached the point where] an open declaration of war cannot make any appreciable difference."

Later on that same day, Roosevelt said in a nationwide broadcast,

> We know that Germany and Japan are conducting their military and naval operations with a joint plan. . . . Germany and Italy consider themselves at war with the United States without even bothering about a formal declaration. The United States hopes to remove the Japanese threat—but victory over Japan would be of little value if the rest of the world is ruled by Hitler and Mussolini. . . .

Kittredge goes on to say that Raeder's views "were largely reflected, often in the same words, in Hitler's speech to the Reichstag on December 11. . . ." Despite the apparent preponderance of opinion that the German declaration of war on the United States was one of Hitler's greatest errors, "His judgment was now impaired by grandiosity and defensive manic omnipotence," says one psychoanalyst with solid claims to being also a historian; but against this must be noted another historian's comment that "there were no oral or written dissents from this decision on the part of Germany's political, diplomatic, or military leaders." The probability is that Hitler made two errors at this moment of history: the first was in deciding not to redeploy the one hundred divisions from east to west, and the second was in going ahead with the declaration of war on the United States. He evidently thought our new concern with the faraway Pacific made this a good opportunity for him.

It is probably something about which we shall always be able to argue. Doubtless, in the Germany of 1941, opposition to Hitler could not be taken too far, but there can be no question that Hitler's refusal to deploy the one hundred divisions against England during 1942 was a major mistake and that most of his high command felt so at the time. Kittredge indicates that the German General Staff put less emphasis on the declaration of war than it did on an increased offensive against England and believed it had convinced the Führer. But Hitler, exercising his fabled "intuition," reversed himself, refused to consider the establishment of a defensive line in Russia, and, going so far as to remove his army commander in chief for protesting the change in strategic plan, put an end to all planning of this nature. Kittredge believes it was this decision, more than the declaration of war on America, that ultimately destroyed the Third Reich.

One wonders how much, if anything, Churchill may have known about German plans to shift those divisions. It is hard to conceive of any effective defense England could have mounted.

If by any chance Churchill had gotten an inkling through some supersecret, as yet unidentified agency, he undoubtedly would have pressed Roosevelt with every means at his command. Roosevelt would have fully appreciated the urgency. At this stage it is not likely that anything more will ever be discovered on this point, but one can be sure that had Churchill known, he certainly would have asked the president for help during the much heralded Atlantic Conference aboard the USS *Augusta* and HMS *Prince of Wales* in early August 1941 at Argentia, Newfoundland.

It had been the bleakest year of British history, with the most discouraging news. The German U-boats and the German army had Britain on the ropes. Churchill's appeals were becoming increasingly desperate. At Argentia, Churchill laid the emergency on the line: just as in 1916, when England had only enough food for a meager six weeks, the country was again nearing prostration, and for the same reason: Germany's unremitting submarine war against shipping. Food, of course, was not England's only need. It could not build the sinews of warfare fast enough to compete with the industrial power of Germany; but lack of food was the most dramatic shortcoming. Nearing the end of the tether, England could at best last but a few months longer. If Churchill and Roosevelt had heard reports of the proposed shift in German forces, the urgency of the predicament would only have been heightened.

Churchill's pleas, combined with Roosevelt's own growing appreciation of the true state of affairs in Europe, brought our president to the conviction that our active entry into the war in Europe was imperative, and that he must somehow get around the promises he had made only a few months before. This, as he well knew, was extremely dangerous political ground. Campaign assurances on a matter so fraught with popular emotion could not be disregarded so quickly. Roosevelt knew he could not simply "change his mind" on this issue.

It is hard to fault his analysis. He needed strong enough reasons for war to overturn the entrenched isolationists. Ideally, the Axis, or a member of it, would attack us so that he could shelter behind his newly minted corollary to his "agayne and agayne and agayne" speech.

Today it is customary to decry our isolationist wing, to group it with Prime Minister Neville Chamberlain of England, whose fatuous pronouncement "Peace in our time" is now viewed with derision. Contrary to today's outlook, isolationism in 1941 was a vibrant U.S. political trend, concentrated in the middle of the continent, its principal mouthpiece the widely circulated *Chicago Tribune*. "Colonel" Robert R. McCormick, owner and publisher, was known as one of the most extreme of the isolationists, sufficiently hostile to the administration (as cited by Kittredge, among others) to give full publicity to virtually treasonable information in hopes of damaging Roosevelt. Fervently believing in his ideas, a large group of our population dreaded the cost of war in lives and treasure and, like England and France a few years earlier, wanted passionately to think each of the successive aggressions by Hitler's Nazis would be the last. They believed Hitler would probably not want to get involved on our side of the Atlantic, and in all probability something would come up to assuage residual anger over our unneutral support of his enemies.

Possibly.

Although some argue that public opinion was already beginning to favor intervention in Europe, the clamor put up by the isolationists may have masked this change, for most historians believe Roosevelt was far ahead of the rest of the country in feeling the need for our entry into the war. What is not clear is how we could have gotten in it without some outstanding provocation—which Hitler seemed determined not to give us. There are some who think that by 1941 enough Americans had made up their minds about Hitler to make possible a viable request to Congress for a declaration of war. The reverse was more likely the case: the isolationist movement was so strong that, in the face of his campaign rhetoric, Roosevelt dared not test it.

The author adheres to the idea, implicit in another of the president's repeated statements, "They must strike the first blow," that his strategy was to force an Axis attack on the United States. This would galvanize the country's opposition to the Axis and support of the Allies. Then he would capitalize on our indignation over the attack to sweep aside any remaining opposition to our helping to eradicate the Axis threat worldwide.

The problems he faced at this juncture were three: First, though our war production had indeed greatly increased since September 1939, most of it had gone to help England. His professional leaders of the army and navy, General Marshall and Admiral Stark, had strongly pointed out our own unreadiness in light of British experience: insufficient modern weapons—aircraft and tanks in case of the army; too few warships, inadequate antiaircraft weapons in all of them, and far too little antisubmarine capability for the navy. For both services, there were insufficient trained personnel, despite continuance of the draft and an active recruiting campaign. Both service chiefs emphasized their need for three to six months of additional time to prepare for war.

Second, antithetical to the first, news from England was grim. Churchill was positive that delay in our entry into the war would spell doom for western civilization in Europe. The Battle of Britain, pretty much over in the final months of 1940, showed strong signs of rejuvenation, and its outcome was in doubt.

Third, it seemed that there was nothing America could do that would cause Germany to declare war on us. We had gone far beyond the prescriptions of neutrality, having actively rendered aid and comfort to the enemies of Germany. Our navy had engaged German naval forces surreptitiously and openly, had fired upon them, and had been shot back at. Obviously, Germany had not declared war because it did not suit Hitler to do so, but that he would do it when he was ready, we in the U.S. Navy had little doubt. The initiative was his, and he was exercising it in a negative sense. To those who feel that he might at some point have reversed this established pattern—always a possibility, of course—the only answer that can be given is that he had not, yet. Most likely he was waiting until victory over England was assured. There is strong evidence that Roosevelt and Churchill had little hope that Hitler would declare war any time soon against the United States, and still less that under the circumstances enough of the isolationist bloc would side with the administration to carry a vote for war through Congress.

It is a mistake to say that Roosevelt "conspired" to get the United States into the war "through the back door." These are pejorative terms loved by Roosevelt haters. But there is no question that he applied tremendous pressure on Japan and had an excellent, and secret, source of information (Magic) as to the effects of his policy. He also had strong assurances, though perhaps not conclusively so, that war by the United States with one member of the Axis meant war with the other two members as well. In an October diary entry, for example, Secretary of the Interior Harold L. Ickes noted, "For a long time I've believed our best entrance into the war would be [via] Japan . . . [which] will inevitably lead to war against Germany."

Thus Roosevelt, in 1941, could not help feeling he had very little choice left. He had to get into the war or see the demise of Britain. He had done his best to get the United States ready for war, but it was not yet ready, and probably would never be as ready as some professional military persons would like. Time had, however, run out. His only option lay in provoking the latest member of the Axis, not yet well tuned to Hitler's war policies, into making war on us.

"Plot" or not, this is exactly what happened.

Roosevelt was hated by many Americans (not all, of course) and for many reasons, among them his election to a third term. Most isolationists were Republican Party members, conservative in outlook, viscerally opposed to nearly all aspects of the liberal revolution he had wrought since 1933. Nothing he could have done in regard to the war in Europe would have pleased them. The unexplained probability that he might have known more about the imminence of war than was let on, the massive secrecy connected with all details of our intelligence activities, the apparent illogic of his diplomatic onslaught on Japan just when "common sense" should have dictated concentration on Nazi Germany, his known coziness with England's prime minister, himself famous for a Machiavellian turn of mind—all combined to indict Roosevelt as a "conspirator."

So be it, provided the user of the term realizes that it was a conspiracy only in the dictionary sense of being "a combining or working together" with one of our country's best national friends, and that it was done to preserve Western civilization. This it did, by forcefully eliminating one of the most malevolent tyrannies ever to disgrace the face of the earth. So far as this author is concerned, since this tyranny had already brought on total war, war was the only way to do away with it, and Roosevelt and Churchill were right in this judgment.

Japan's propaganda, in fact, claimed bitterly that it was the United States that had forced it to go to war. In light of the attack on Pearl Harbor, and the obvious long planning period that had been involved, this argument received very little credence in the United States. The fact is, however, that in the face of the growing emergency in England, beginning in 1940 our pressures on Japan had become continuously heavier. In Washington the top officials of the army and navy, Secretary of War Henry L. Stimson and Secretary of the Navy Frank Knox, and General Marshall and Admiral Stark, were arguing with the president to keep our commitments within bounds. This was, indeed, their publicly known position. Of their private, confidential discussions with Roosevelt, we have no real knowledge.

What is clear is that while we *appeared* to be trying to maintain peace in the Far East, we were *in fact* becoming steadily more intransigent with Japan and its "China policy," which amounted to conquest of that teeming but powerless country. It must be assumed that the individuals mentioned were fully cognizant of the divergence between the president's public statements and his actual policy. There may have been strong disagreements, but at some point they must have felt they had fully done their duty to advise the chief executive and from then on were obligated to carry out his directions.

Japan had been for years dependent upon the United States for both scrap steel and fuel, and despite our sympathy for China we placed no limitation on the export of either to Japan until the end of 1940. (My father's old cruiser, the USS *Memphis,* wrecked by a tsunami in 1916, was finally scrapped by a Japanese firm in 1937 and came back to us in the form of Japanese munitions and ships of war in 1941–45.) Coincident with our development of the ability to intercept and read Tokyo's top-secret diplomatic correspondence with its embassy in Washington was our active opposition to Japan's adventure in China, and we went to whatever lengths we could muster to deter it. Initially, deterrence appears to have been our true intent, to the extent that true intent can be determined from action. Somewhere in the creeping progress of deterring Japan from *continuing* its campaign against China, we shifted, perhaps subconsciously, into espousing China's cause and trying to force Japan out of territory it had already conquered. Partly this was in response to the atrocious manner of the occupation, to which American nature rebelled, but as our opposition grew, its political horizons grew likewise.

One of our moves was to restrict Japan's ability to procure war-making needs from us. First it was aviation fuel, then steel and iron scrap. Finally, late in July of 1941, we froze all of Japan's assets in the United States, thus totally closing off the supply of oil. This led to full-scale negotiations between the two countries, primarily over the oil, which Japan urgently needed, not only for its war effort but for its civilian economy too.

According to James Rusbridger and Eric Nave's *Betrayal at Pearl Harbor: How Churchill Lured Roosevelt into World War II* (New York: Simon & Schuster, 1992), the then prime minister of Japan, Prince Fumimaro Konoye, with his entire cabinet, evidently despairing of any success in the negotiations with the United States, in September gave the Japanese emperor a full-scale briefing of his plans for a simultaneous attack on British, U.S., and Dutch installations in the Far East. This the emperor, in a very "obtuse" manner understandable only to a Japanese court politician, did not approve.

However much one might disbelieve the Rusbridger-Nave argument as a whole, the one-time director of Naval History, Ronald H. Spector, in *Eagle Against the Sun* (New York: The Free Press, 1985), gives much the same story with less detail, noting only that Hirohito "unexpectedly broke his traditional silence . . . to read a poem on the theme of peace composed by his grandfather. . . ." John Costello, in *Days of Infamy,* quotes the poem in its entirety.

The result was tremendous loss of face by Konoye, and in October the fall of his cabinet. The world knew little or nothing of the reasons behind Konoye's fall from grace. (Just after the war ended he committed suicide, but not quite in the traditional Japanese style. He used poison.) His replacement in 1941 was Gen. Hideki Tojo of the Imperial Army General Staff, who had been minister of war under Konoye.

The American press viewed Tojo's appointment with dismay, principally because he was a general and therefore believed to be part of the military cabal that seemed actually to run Japan. His mission, we assumed, was to perfect Japan's war plans. There may have been some truth to this, but the fact appears to have been more subtle, if John Toland is to be believed. Toland, married to a

Japanese woman of a distinguished old family, wrote in *Infamy: Pearl Harbor and Its Aftermath* (New York: Doubleday, 1982) that Tojo's instructions from the emperor were to "go back to blank paper" so far as war with the United States was concerned, and that the new prime minister did his best to comply, refusing to be pushed into an aggressive posture until he had exhausted all possibilities for peace. Spector confirms this in *Eagle Against the Sun.* The powerful military party—it could surely be called that because of its exercise of political clout—was allowed nonetheless to continue with "contingency" preparations for war, considered to be Japan's last fallback option. Tojo probably felt he had the obligation to be able to go either way.

Yamamoto, as a matter of personal conviction apparently strongly opposed to war with the United States, might have been a better prime minister at this point than Tojo. But as commander of the Combined Imperial Fleet he was not in the chain of decision on war. If it came, it was his duty to be ready with his plans, as he was. He was, of course, aware that the U.S. Navy, in its War Plans Office in the Navy Department, had for years been studying war with Japan, and that its Naval War College in Newport had for years been war-gaming such a war. He had carefully examined everything the Imperial Navy knew about the conclusions reached and the plans made. Having also studied America's industrial potential, he felt that a knockout blow to our Pacific Fleet was essential to give Japan the maneuvering space it required in the Far East, provided that the business could be finished in six months to a year. To Premier Konoye he expressed this in the often quoted remark "If war comes I will give them hell for a year or a year and a half, but cannot answer for anything after that."

To the new cabinet under Tojo he was even firmer, with a new twist: in the event of war, he must be allowed to begin it with his Pearl Harbor attack. Yamamoto is known to have been an inveterate—and good—gambler. He was prone to high stakes and big chances, and often won through sheer bluff against players with less self-confidence. Having devoted his full effort to readying his plan, certain that a deeply discouraged America, more concerned with Europe than the Far East, would be willing to negotiate a cessation of hostilities and leave Japan its desired hegemony in the Far East, he would resign if the surprise attack was not approved. So says Hiroyuki Agawa in his definitive biography of Yamamoto, *The Reluctant Admiral* (Translated by John Bester. Tokyo and New York: Kodansha International Ltd., 1979).

Wohlstetter hits close to the mark with her appraisal of Japan's appreciation of American morale:

> Most unreal was their assumption that the United States, with ten times the military potential and a reputation for waging war until unconditional victory, would after a short struggle simply accept the annihilation of a considerable part of its air and naval forces and the whole of its power in the Far East.

On 4 November, Saburo Kurusu, holding the rank of ambassador, arrived in Washington as a special envoy to assist the regular ambassador, retired admiral Kichisaburo Nomura, with the negotiations for resumption of the oil exports Japan so urgently required. He brought with him two proposals, known as "A" and "B," in both of which Japan proposed some minor concessions to end the logjam, and either one of which, it was hoped, might bring forth somewhat equivalent American concessions upon which negotiations could continue.

Nomura, blessed with only a moderate command of English, would have been a good choice as ambassador had the conditions been anywhere near normal. He was a retired admiral of the Imperial Navy, innocently diffident in personality, intellectually honest. He had been the naval attaché to Washington, was well liked by Americans, and reciprocated the good feeling. Admiral Richardson, in *On the Treadmill to Pearl Harbor,* describes him as "intelligent and friendly." Had he not been ambassador at that precise moment, he would have been remembered as a popular and competent envoy. In the situation in which he found himself, however, he was well beyond his depth, and both he and Tokyo knew it. Apparently he welcomed the arrival of Kurusu, and the two worked well together. It has been suggested that Nomura's poor English may have been responsible for some misunderstanding in Washington, but there is no indication that slowness of comprehension was a factor in the negotiations as they developed during this critical time. The most accomplished linguist could not have deflected the massive forces that were converging.

On 5 November Magic decoded a message from Tokyo to its two ambassadors in Washington, informing them that some kind of accommodation must be signed by 25 November in order to "[save] the Japanese-U.S. relations from falling into a chaotic condition." Our Pacific commanders were not told of this. We now know, but did not then (despite contrary-wise ideas in certain quarters), that 25 November had been selected as the day the Pearl Harbor attack force, the *Kido Butai*, composed of Japan's six best aircraft carriers and supporting ships, was to depart from its last staging port in the Kurile Islands, Hitokappu Bay, and head east across the North Pacific for the launch point two hundred miles due north of Oahu.

Late in November 1941 Marshall (principally) convinced the president and the cabinet that Japan should be offered a three months' *modus vivendi,* essentially a return to the pre–oil embargo time, while thoughts jelled and passions cooled. There are those who believe the original suggestion for this came from Kurusu, possibly at the subtle suggestion of Tokyo, but since Kurusu had an American wife and is known to have been honestly striving for a successful termination of the negotiations, the idea may well have actually originated with him (or her). In support of this idea, there was a story current in Washington that Kurusu had quietly proposed the three-month hiatus at a private dinner party at the lovely Belin estate "EverMay" in Georgetown early in November. His co-ambassador, Nomura, was in full agreement.

As originally proposed, the *modus vivendi* would have benefited our side by giving us three months more to complete the buildup of MacArthur's forces in the Philippines and to reinforce our fleet antiaircraft defenses. For the Japanese it would have eased what were to them the intolerable restrictions we had placed on their search for empire in the Far East and, in combination with the Japanese ambassadors' proposals "A" and "B," might have been a basis for continued discussion of the fundamental problem. It would, however, have slowed the U.S. march into war against Hitler, and this might have been fatal for England.

The circumstances in which the *modus vivendi* proposal was blocked are interesting. On 25 November when Stimson, learning that Japanese naval forces were nearing the Kra Peninsula with the evident intent of making a landing in defiance of whatever peaceful purpose their ambassadors might have announced, informed the president, Roosevelt flashed into great anger—"rose right out of his chair!" as Stimson, in surprise at the strength of his reaction, put it—and immediately canceled all thought of the *modus vivendi.* Secretary of State Cordell Hull was directed to prepare an uncompromising position that Roosevelt roughed out on the spot in pencil, and this was what Hull delivered to the two ambassadors the next day, the twenty-sixth, when, in hopes of being able to follow up on proposals "A" or "B," they came in response to his summons. The formal note had ten points, abridged as follows:

1. A multilateral nonaggression pact with Britain, China, the Netherlands, the Soviet Union, and Thailand as additional signatories.
2. Respect for the territorial integrity of French Indo-China.
3. Japan to withdraw entirely from China and Indo-China.
4. United States and Japan to support the Nationalist Chinese Government (Chiang Kai-shek).
5. Elimination of extraterritorial rights in China stemming (particularly) from the Boxer Protocol of 1901.
6. Mutually advantageous trade agreement between Japan and the United States.
7. Mutual removal of freezing restrictions on Japanese funds in the United States and U.S. funds in Japan.
8. Stabilization of the dollar-yen rate.
9. Japan to abandon its agreement with the Axis powers.
10. Japan and the United States to "use their influence to cause other governments to adhere to" the political and economic principles herein set forth.

After reading the document, Kurusu asked if this was the U.S. reply to the Japanese proposals "A" or "B" that he had brought with him from Japan three weeks earlier or, speaking somewhat desperately, the *modus vivendi* he had "heard rumors" about. Hull's response that it was indeed the U.S. reply brought from Kurusu the comment that he could not see how his government could consider the paper except as an affront. Hull told them that it was now out of his hands.

It was this message that historians now credit with putting the final "go" signal on the surprise attack.

Roosevelt, so far as is shown by the public record, had been apparently of two minds up to this moment. Stimson was known to have long been urging the most stringent measures against Japan, even while officially arguing moderation. Marshall and Stark had been for an equal time publicly urging moderation in view of their services' general unreadiness for war. What all of them said in private is, of course, unknown.

Stimson's diary is not clear at this point either. On 26 November there were two messages to Roosevelt from Churchill, or possibly telephone conversations, and they may have influenced the president's decision. Japan's apparent movement toward the Malay Peninsula seems, by itself, hardly enough. It is known, however, that presidential support for the *modus vivendi* nevertheless vanished at that very moment, and there was no more public talk about unreadiness.

Japan's foreign office, as predicted by the ambassadors, considered the message of 26 November an unacceptable insult, and the chain of events leading to the surprise attack was nearly complete.

All of this points to a geopolitically naïve Japan, not seeing far beyond its own immediate problems and certainly not accustomed to the Byzantine maneuvering in Europe, possibly manipulated by Roosevelt into the war it had been planning for years as a contingency, but not for the immediate future.

From Japan's point of view, had we not suddenly taken so much interest in China there would have been no need to fight us. Had we gone along with the Greater East Asia Co-Prosperity Sphere, more properly the Japanese Empire of East Asia, Japan's contingency plans for war with America could have been laid aside for a more propitious time. Roosevelt's calculated policy simply forced Japan to show its hand at a moment that was premature for Japanese plans but, through a series of fortunate circumstances, not yet too late for Western Europe.

4

Magic

There is evidence that Churchill and Roosevelt may have received some uncertain indications possibly pointing to an attack on Pearl Harbor. Toland's book carried allegations of this, and Rusbridger and Nave went further; but all investigations have downplayed these as little more than rumors, and in the main, historians have given them little significance. There may someday appear a "smoking gun" in the shape of conclusive confirmation of one or more such rumors, but until that happens only revisionists will pay serious attention to any of them, while more comfortable scholars will decry yet another attempt to change history.

There were, all the same, certain things of proven existence, the "bomb plot" message of 24 September 1941, for example, that counsel for the defense of Kimmel or Short would assuredly have brought up in any court of law. So called because it divided Pearl Harbor into five subareas and asked for regular reports on the locations of "warships and aircraft carriers," this was a message sent in "consular" code to the Japanese consul in Honolulu, intended for an officer in the Imperial Japanese Navy posing as an official in the consulate. Delays in decryption prevented the Office of Naval Intelligence (ONI) in Washington from reading the message until early October, but it was then evaluated by some intelligence officers as the precursor of a possible air attack on the area of interest.

The director of Naval Intelligence, Capt. Allan G. Kirk, saw it as such and urged it be sent to Kimmel. So did Capt. Howard Bode, head of the foreign-intelligence section under Kirk. But then Rear Admiral Turner, director of Navy War Plans, angrily objected. Both were senior captains, experienced in intelligence, but they evidently pressed their case too strongly to suit "Terrible" Turner, who saw to it that both were summarily reassigned to posts far from ONI. Strangely, although this incident was part of the lore of Pearl Harbor and was frequently called "the battle of the second deck (of the Navy Department)"—or "the October Revolution," a reference to the date of the "bomb plot message" that was its cause— not one of the nine investigations of the disaster called Kirk or Bode as a witness. (Bode died in 1943, but Kirk had a distinguished career, including postwar ambassadorship to the U.S.S.R. and three other countries, attained the rank of full admiral, and must have carried some unusual memories to the grave with him twenty years later.)

The message was transmitted in the J-19 Consular Code, which was easier to break than either the Purple Diplomatic Code or the Naval General-Purpose Code, JN-25. For this reason it was assumed to carry messages of lesser importance and was relegated to a deferred decoding and translating status. Nonetheless, it had been broken and circulated to army and navy officials, and the White House, by 9 October 1941. It was followed by three additional instructions to the Honolulu consulate that were circulated prior to 7 December, and others not broken until after the attack. Rear Adm. Edwin T. Layton, who was fleet intelligence officer under both Kimmel and Adm. Chester W. Nimitz, tells this story fully in his book *And I Was There* (New York: William Morrow and Company, Inc., 1985), and it is also recited, equally fully but with less detail, by Toland. The wealth of specific information given by these two authors causes one to wonder how they could (both) be accused of speculation, conjecture, or "unconvincing revisionism," at least in this particular context and area. What they have to say is totally convincing—although, to be sure, Toland's inferred speculation that Captain Bode's later suicide may have been a result of either his contretemps with Turner at Main Navy in Washington (the principal Navy Department building on Constitution Avenue, built for World War I and taken down after World War II), or the criticism he may have received from Turner (who was in charge there) for an apparent failure of command at the Battle of Savo Island, can be explained in less sinister ways.

The "bomb plot" message has been quoted in full in a number of places and can be found most authoritatively on page 182 of the 1946 JCC (Joint Congressional Committee) Report, where it is followed by a lengthy discussion of its significance from the standpoints of both hindsight and foresight. Surprisingly, this passage concludes:

> It cannot be forgotten that a surprise attack by air on Pearl Harbor had been listed and understood, both in Washington and Hawaii, as the greatest danger to that base. We must assume that military men realized that in order to execute successfully such an attack the Japanese would necessarily need detailed information as to dispositions at the point of attack. It would seem to be a natural consequence that if Japan undertook an attack on Pearl Harbor she would seek to acquire such detailed

> information and in point of time as nearly as possible to the hour of such attempt.
>
> We are [however] unable to conclude that the [ship] berthing plan and related dispatches pointed directly to an attack on Pearl Harbor, nor are we able to conclude that the plan was a "bomb plot" in view of the evidence indicating that it was not such. We are of the opinion, however, that the berthing plan and related dispatches should have received careful consideration and created a serious question as to their significance. Since they indicated a particular interest in the Pacific Fleet's base this intelligence should have been appreciated and supplied the commander in chief of the Pacific Fleet and the commanding general of the Hawaiian Department for their assistance, along with other information and intelligence available to them, in making their estimate of the situation.

This passage reads as though the majority of the JCC wished to explain the message away, which it could not do. The significant thing is that not a word of this putative "bomb plot" message was transmitted to the persons most in need of knowing about it: the commanders of the base named in the message. The message itself stands alone as proof of crucially important dereliction in the nation's capital. The message(s) were received and were read by everyone in the chain of distribution (although some of them denied it under oath). An obligation devolved on every one of them to ensure that Admiral Kimmel and General Short were solidly and completely aware of precisely what had been sent. It is axiomatic that in wartime, or in tense conditions resembling war, the commanders at risk must be made aware of all factors affecting their commands. Commanders invariably react with indignation if they discover they have been kept uninformed.

The "bomb plot" message was definitely shown to the president and the other officials on the Magic distribution list. It even bore the translator's penciled notation "Very interesting," written by Lt. Cdr. Alwin D. Kramer. None of our other bases received comparable scrutiny. Yet, extraordinarily, Admiral Turner personally and viciously prevented any information about it from being sent to the Hawaiian commanders, whose primary base had actually been named in the message. Turner furthermore caused the two senior intelligence officers who had dared to propose sending such a message to be summarily relieved of their duties.

Had the CNO's failure to inform the Pearl Harbor commanders come before a duly constituted court of any kind, civilian or military, it would have been seen as strongly extenuating, and might even have constituted the basis for charges against him. In comparable civilian law, the Pearl Harbor commanders would have had a basis for a suit for damages.

To start at the true beginning of this extraordinary tale, it is necessary to understand how Washington, D.C., knew what it did in advance of the surprise attack. Therefore, we must understand Magic—where it came from, the reasons behind the adamant restrictions on information about it, and how it was used.

In 1940 our code-breaking capability was in its infancy, totally unsuspected by Japan. By mid-1941 it had been given the code name "Magic," and we could break some, but not all, of Japan's codes. We had, however, successfully invaded Japan's diplomatic codes, and the success was so great that the military services, practitioners of the art of code-breaking but woefully shorthanded in the persons with the necessary expertise, were directed to ignore all other codes and work only on "Purple," the diplomatic one. Sometime that year, partly in consequence of this sweeping directive, Roosevelt and his top advisers were informed that they could henceforth be provided, in real time, with the text of messages sent between Tokyo and its embassy in Washington: that is, they could be reading the secret encoded messages about as soon as the intended recipients could. It was a coup of the first magnitude.

Official recipients of Magic were the president, the secretaries of state, war, and navy (Hull, Stimson, and Knox), and the service chiefs (Army Chief of Staff Marshall and CNO Stark). One or two other officers not in the direct intelligence chain, notably high-handed Rear Admiral Turner, then building his power base in the Navy Department, were also aware of Magic, though as events marched on others were inevitably included. One of the primary concerns, nevertheless, was to keep knowledge of it at a minimum and eliminate all chance that persons aware of it might fall into the hands of the enemy.

We were also worried that demonstrating foreknowledge of supposedly secret enemy plans might endanger the source of this all-important information. We should not, for example, consistently concentrate superior forces at just the right place and time needed to defeat the enemy, for coincidences of this nature might raise suspicions. Of the many ways Japan might deal with the possibility that its codes had been invaded, the simplest and most naïve would have been to change codes immediately, and by doing this at an off-schedule time, alerting us that we had been found out. A more subtle reaction might have been to make no overt change at all but to begin using the compromised system for disinformation, or to send messages designed to discover whether or not cryptological invasion had actually occurred.

Cryptographers are traditionally alert for any signs that their systems have been compromised. From the code-breakers' point of view, once the enemy even suspects one of its codes has been violated, anything taken from the code or codes in question is no longer reliable, or at the minimum must be held highly suspect.

The code-breakers considered it a thousand times more difficult to invade a new system than for the originators to have created it in the first place. Unwise use of Magic thus might lead to its sudden demise, possibly forever but certainly for a very long time. We consequently went to tremendous lengths, at this early stage of our code-breaking capability, to keep everything about it as secret as possible.

The extreme emphasis on security seems a bit exaggerated today. To be valuable, intelligence must be wisely used, and we frequently did not pass vital information to those who had most need of it. Because of this, our forces—and at times civilians too—sometimes took losses it might have been possible to avoid. Democracies always find such losses difficult to explain to the survivors. It was invariably hard to judge which objective would be best served with any particular bit of intelligence, and it still is. The danger of compromising the source is a factor inherent in the use of intelligence at any time, something the British, with centuries of experience in European espionage, understood far better than we. Americans, for example, are always amazed to hear it suggested that the British high command may have deliberately allowed the terribly destructive raid on Coventry to happen when it could have evacuated the population or had fighter planes in place to intercept the bombers. It must be noted, however, that this interpretation of the controversy surrounding the bombing of Coventry is still shrouded in uncertainty. There was great loss of life and awful destruction. The cathedral is still maintained as it was destroyed, a monument to the terrible destructiveness of war, alongside the new and modern building replacing it. Did the British government deliberately accept this terrible raid to protect its sources of information? The British people, by and large, have agreed that they will never know the whole story and are probably glad not to know.

The war had been going on for some time in England, whereas Pearl Harbor was attacked during peacetime. So comparisons between Coventry and Pearl Harbor are not entirely fair. A more accurate appreciation of America's fortitude can be gained from our reaction to the horror of Tarawa, our first attack on a strongly defended Japanese base in the Pacific. The Japanese anticipated our coming. They had prepared their defenses well. This we knew, but the attack was necessary all the same, and we learned a very great deal from it. Like Coventry, it was a part of war, and there was nothing to do but accept it.

It is necessary to appreciate the foregoing to gain an insight into the extraordinary diplomatic power game Roosevelt embarked upon after the election, and the tremendous care with which he used his tools. Magic was fundamental to his entire foreign policy because, in poker parlance, it let him "look down Japan's throat." Magic gave the president information about Japanese plans and strategy at their very highest level, just as a similar capability, at the time code-named "Ultra," served the Allies against Hitler. In due course, probably not intentionally, "Ultra" came to be used to designate *any* "specially obtained" naval tactical information, such as the predicted locations of Japanese merchant or naval ships. It should not be confused with "Enigma," which was the German machine code used by the Reichsmarine and Luftwaffe. Parts of this machine, and the vitally important setup information, somehow detected or found by the Poles, were spirited out of Poland as that country fell to the Nazis. More setup information was found in a couple of German submarines as they sank, and the British from nearly the outset of the war were able to read some of Dönitz's communications with his U-boats.

On our side of the Atlantic, our code-breakers did the British one better, creating and building our own version of the Japanese Purple machine that was used for secret diplomatic messages, nearly always between the Foreign Ministry and its ambassadors. One of those machines may be seen today at the National Cryptologic Museum at the National Security Agency headquarters, Fort Meade, Maryland. Its product, the decoded Japanese diplomatic message traffic, was what was known as "Magic."

In addition to Purple, Japan had another, entirely different cryptographic system, the Naval General-Purpose Code JN-25, which was used for operational messages, and we had begun to make steady progress in breaking into this system also. In the U.S. code-breaking business there was, however, a steadily increasing demand for Purple from the president and the State Department. The military departments took what they could get, and this was considerable, but it was nowhere near what they might have gotten from JN-25, as we have recently discovered.

All the decoding units were desperately short of help. There simply were not enough trained people to do all the tasks. Communications intelligence, COMINT as it was called, had not yet attained importance and acceptance in the navy. Being an expert in gunnery, especially with the huge rifles carried in battleships, was considered to be far more useful, and important, than poring over papers in some locked and dingy room that, without very special precautions, could not even be cleaned. The pathetically few cryptanalysts the navy had (only fifty-three at one point; the army was no better off) were working eighteen to twenty hours a day, sometimes around the clock, and were simply overwhelmed by the steadily increasing numbers of messages they were asked to decode and convert to "exploitable"—that is, readable—text.

The result was inevitable. Purple, producing Magic, got all the attention the few analysts could give. JN-25 had to be put aside. Yet as postwar investigation showed, the attack on Pearl Harbor was clearly foretold in JN-25. Even Japan's ambassadors in Washington were kept in ignorance of the naval operational planning—but it was all there in the general-purpose code, where a rank amateur, only slightly naval-oriented, could have seen it.

Magic was, however, a tremendous success. Without Magic, our president could not have had the sure touch with which he led us through the war while wasting away from a debilitating illness that had no cure. But Magic, of incalculable value, was also extremely vulnerable. Men and women had sacrificed their lives to obtain only small portions of the extraordinary mosaic of logic and equipment that had gone into its creation, and more would do so to prevent even a small chance of its discovery by the enemy. Whether or not he knew specifically of Magic—we have no certainty of this either way—knowledge of our ability to break enemy codes was the reason why Capt. John Philip Cromwell chose to go down with his scuttled submarine as she took her final plunge. He deliberately chose death rather than risk divulging what he knew under torture or through the forcible administration of drugs.

There can be little question that the uncompromising ten-point ultimatum of 26 November 1941 that we had sent instead of the proposed *modus vivendi,* and Japan's fourteen-part message in reply, to which Magic had given us an unprecedented preview, made up the direct line that led to Pearl Harbor and our entry into World War II. Knowing in advance that the fourteen-part message was coming—through the interception and decryption of the so-called "pilot" message alerting the Japanese embassy to its imminent arrival—and through their work being quite aware of its significance, our code-breakers pounced on the separate parts the moment they began coming through the intercept radio. Although when fully assembled this message contained no declaration of war, it used strong language and specifically broke relations with the United States; and the "delivery" message, sixteenth in the actual sequence, directed that it be handed to our secretary of state at 1 P.M. on Sunday, long after the attacking planes had started on their way, half an hour before the first bomb was to fall.

The delivery message did not, obviously, say that bombs and torpedoes would fall at 1:30 P.M. Washington time (6:30 P.M. Greenwich Mean Time), but the urgent request to meet with the secretary of state at 1:00 P.M. Washington time could only mean, in the words of both Hull and Stimson (and as everyone who saw the messages and the delivery time noted), that Japan must be planning "some sort of devilment somewhere," probably at exactly that time. No one missed this. What *was* missed, partly because we had not yet learned how professionally accomplished the Imperial Japanese Navy really was, was that it would dare to send three-fourths of its entire aircraft-carrier force halfway across the Pacific, far inside the U.S. defensive perimeter, ready to expend everything it had on the biggest gamble Admiral Yamamoto had ever put together.

There is no evidence anyone, prior to the attack, brought up the idea that this message, largely paralleling the one sent to Moscow in 1904, might also have the same purpose: to square Japan, technically, with the law of nations. In 1904, the surprise attack on Port Arthur took place two days after delivery of the official diplomatic note terminating negotiations. In 1941, owing to the greatly increased speed of communications, Japan planned to reduce the two days to thirty minutes. But Murphy's Law stepped in: typing difficulties in the Japanese embassy in Washington prevented the ambassadors from delivering notice of the official break until nearly two hours after the attack began, instead of half an hour before it started. Thus the attack was made while negotiations were technically "still going on."

Of course, even with the "speed of communications," half an hour before or after the deadline made little difference unless by some extraordinary circumstance everyone had been poised to run to battle stations at a moment's notice—and all important lines of communication had been kept open for the instant relaying of orders. The attack was planned to take place early on a Sunday morning during a time of peace and had really begun on 25 November, when the secret task force had gotten under way. No hair-splitting argument about timing can change that obvious fact.

The sequence of events is important: On 5 November, the day after Kurusu's arrival in Washington, we decrypted a message from Tokyo to its two ambassadors:

> Because of various circumstances, it is absolutely necessary that all arrangements for the signing of this agreement be completed by the 25th of this month. I realize that this is a difficult order, but under the circumstances it is an unavoidable one. Please understand this thoroughly and tackle the problem of saving the Japanese-U.S. relations from falling into a chaotic condition. Do so with great determination and with unstinted effort, I beg of you.
>
> This information is to be kept strictly to yourself only.

On 19 November Magic decoded what became known as the "winds code" message, announcing that if diplomatic relations were cut off, certain words relating to weather would be added to the daily Japanese plain-language short-wave news broadcast. On hearing them, Japan's embassies were to destroy codes and secret documents. On our side, we welcomed the idea that the "winds code execute" might give us a few days of warning, seeing it as an alternate source that could be developed entirely free of Magic. So all stations, Pearl Harbor included, were directed to keep a close watch for the special words about weather. Although no official records can today be found of such a message having been detected, a number of operatives have sworn before Congress that they in fact did detect and report a "winds code execute" message. Capt. Laurance Frye Safford, the Navy's foremost cryptanalyst, testified positively that such a message, specifying war with the United States, was received on 4 December and routed to all officials on the list who were cleared to receive such information. When he later attempted to retrieve his files on this item, Safford found that the pertinent papers had been removed. George Morgenstern wrote in *Pearl Harbor: The Story of the Secret War* (New York: Devin-Adair

Co., 1947) that such records did at one time exist, but he believed they had been deliberately destroyed. Maj. Henry C. Clausen, sent out under Secretary Stimson's special direction to make a special investigation, for Stimson's use only, of the surprise-attack debacle, and Cdr. John F. Sonnett, his navy counterpart, working, however, not directly for the navy secretary but for Adm. Kent Hewitt and his inquiry of Pearl Harbor, both did their best to insinuate that Safford was "hallucinating," that there was no "winds code execute" message, nor had there ever been.

On 22 November Magic produced Tokyo's response to its Washington ambassadors' urgent request for more time (which we had decoded and read before it reached the Japanese Foreign Office). Tokyo extended the deadline, under strict and specific guidelines, until the twenty-ninth of the month. It is possible that Tokyo expected the *Kido Butai* to cross the international date line on this day, but Gordon W. Prange's backward plot of its actual movements shows it still several hundred miles west of the date line at noon on the twenty-ninth. Most likely Japan's Foreign Office simply played it safe. Agawa gives the departure from Hitokappu Bay as 26 November (25 November by the U.S. calendar) and says that on the sixth day out, 1 December [*sic*], the task force crossed the date line. At 2 P.M. "of that day" an imperial council was held, during which the entire plan of operations was reviewed and questions answered. "Thus the formal decision to declare war on the United States, Britain, and Holland was taken," says Agawa. (Prange wrote, "Although officially this conference decided on war, a brief look at the major Japanese forces in motion on that date suggests that the conflict had already begun in everything but name.") Agawa said that "the emperor himself sat silent throughout the meeting." The following day, 2 December by Japanese time but 1 December by ours, the entire Combined Fleet received a message in Yamamoto's name: "*Niitaka-yama nobore 1208* [Climb Mount Niitaka on December 8th (Tokyo date)]."

This message, of course, was not sent in the diplomatic code but in JN-25 and was repeated simultaneously on four different frequencies, one of them an "ultra-long-wave signal" that could be picked up by a submerged submarine. Had we been working as assiduously on JN-25 as we were on Purple it is almost a certainty that this message, bearing "urgent operational" priority, would have been intercepted and broken. The responsibility for this failure rests on the White House's insistence regarding the diplomatic code. A final refueling was accomplished on 6 (5) December in smooth seas, and the oilers departed. Ahead of the task force was another day of anxiety, and then Pearl Harbor.

According to the message extending the deadline, unless everything had been perfectly finished, to the dotting of the i's and the crossing of the t's, things were "automatically going to happen." In the plainest possible language Japan's ambassadors were being told that the twenty-ninth was the point of no return. Were the *Kido Butai* to be discovered even a few days before the date line, its mission would be obvious, its cover blown. There would be no misinterpretation of the purpose of a secret task force composed of Japan's six biggest and best aircraft carriers, two high-speed battleships secretly modernized to a top speed of nearly thirty knots, two new cruisers, and nine destroyers. Were the task force to be discovered east of the date line—or even only nearing it—war would certainly result—minus the advantage Yamamoto counted upon to let his fleet "run wild for a year to a year and a half."

On the twenty-sixth our time, the day after Japan's original deadline and coincidentally the day after the attack force set to sea but before it had reached its point of no return, we sent our ten-point ultimatum. Secretary Hull asked the two Japanese ambassadors to visit him in his office. There, instead of the expected *modus vivendi,* Hull handed the new paper to the astounded Kurusu and Nomura. Most important of its ten points was a formal demand that Japan stop aggression on the mainland of China. The next day, accompanied by Hull, the two Japanese ambassadors called on the American president to express their regret over the failure of the *modus vivendi* idea. According to Morgenstern, Roosevelt replied,

> We remain convinced that Japan's own best interests will not be served by following Hitlerism and courses of aggression, and that Japan's own best interests lie along the courses that we have outlined in the current conversations. If, however, Japan should unfortunately decide to follow Hitlerism and courses of aggression, we are convinced beyond any shadow of doubt that Japan will be the ultimate loser.

There was more to the conversation, of course, but this was the sternly stated gist of the American position on 26 November. On the twenty-ninth Hull told the British ambassador, Lord Halifax, that "the diplomatic part of our relations with Japan was virtually over, and the matter will now go to the officials of the Army and the Navy." He further informed Halifax that it would be

> a serious mistake . . . to make plans . . . without including the possibility that Japan may move suddenly and with every possible element of surprise . . . that their course of unlimited conquest . . . probably is a desperate gamble and requires the utmost boldness and risk.

This quotation was obviously included to show that Washington was very much aware of the Japanese propensity for sudden surprise attacks with which to initiate war. There is much more in the heavily annotated Morgenstern book. It includes many lengthy quotations from the principals involved, all of them footnoted.

Hull described the 26 November ten-point ultimatum to Stimson in the same words he used with Halifax, recorded in Stimson's diary as "I've washed my hands of it. Now it's up to you: the Army and the Navy!"

On 27 November differently worded "war warnings," specifying the probability of a Japanese amphibious expedition to Southeast Asia, were sent to the army and navy commanders in the Pacific. Originally intended to be strongly stated, the warnings were so modified by cautionary language about secrecy and upsetting the public that the most important thing about them, a sense of urgency, had been removed as though by evaporation. Several officers in both the army and navy protested the emasculation but were put down in no uncertain terms.

Kimmel received the following:

> THIS DESPATCH IS TO BE CONSIDERED A WAR WARNING X NEGOTIATIONS WITH JAPAN LOOKING TOWARD STABILIZATION OF CONDITIONS IN THE PACIFIC HAVE CEASED AND AN AGGRESSIVE MOVE BY JAPAN IS EXPECTED IN THE NEXT FEW DAYS X THE NUMBER AND EQUIPMENT OF JAPANESE TROOPS AND THE ORGANIZATION OF NAVAL TASK FORCES INDICATES AN AMPHIBIOUS EXPEDITION AGAINST EITHER THE PHILIPPINES THAI OR KRA PENINSULA OR POSSIBLY TOWARD BORNEO X EXECUTE AN APPROPRIATE DEFENSIVE DEPLOYMENT PREPARATORY TO CARRYING OUT THE TASKS ASSIGNED IN WPL [war plan] 46 X INFORM DISTRICT AND ARMY AUTHORITIES X A SIMILAR WARNING IS BEING SENT BY WAR DEPARTMENT X SPENAVO INFORM BRITISH X CONTINENTAL DISTRICTS GUAM SAMOA DIRECTED TAKE APPROPRIATE MEASURES AGAINST SABOTAGE X

Short received, over General Marshall's signature, War Department Message No. 472, which read as follows:

> NEGOTIATIONS WITH THE JAPANESE APPEAR TO BE TERMINATED TO ALL PRACTICAL PURPOSES WITH ONLY THE BAREST POSSIBILITIES THAT THE JAPANESE GOVERNMENT MIGHT COME BACK AND OFFER TO CONTINUE PERIOD JAPANESE FUTURE ACTION UNPREDICTABLE BUT HOSTILE ACTION POSSIBLE AT ANY MOMENT PERIOD IF HOSTILITIES CANNOT REPEAT CANNOT BE AVOIDED THE UNITED STATES DESIRES THAT JAPAN COMMIT THE FIRST OVERT ACT PERIOD THIS POLICY SHOULD NOT REPEAT NOT BE CONSTRUED AS RESTRICTING YOU TO A COURSE OF ACTION THAT MIGHT JEOPARDIZE YOUR DEFENSE PERIOD PRIOR TO HOSTILE ACTION YOU ARE DIRECTED TO UNDERTAKE SUCH RECONNAISSANCE AND OTHER MEASURES AS YOU DEEM NECESSARY BUT THESE MEASURES SHOULD BE CARRIED OUT SO AS NOT REPEAT NOT TO ALARM CIVIL POPULATION OR DISCLOSE INTENT PERIOD REPORT MEASURES TAKEN PERIOD SHOULD HOSTILITIES OCCUR YOU WILL CARRY OUT THE TASKS ASSIGNED IN RAINBOW FIVE SO FAR AS THEY PERTAIN TO JAPAN PERIOD LIMIT DISCUSSION OF THIS HIGHLY SECRET INFORMATION TO MINIMUM ESSENTIAL OFFICERS PERIOD

The very next day, 28 November, Short received a second warning message, No. 482, that read (as quoted by Prange in *At Dawn We Slept*)

> CRITICAL SITUATION DEMANDS THAT ALL PRECAUTIONS BE TAKEN IMMEDIATELY AGAINST SUBVERSIVE ACTIVITIES. . . . ALSO DESIRED THAT YOU INITIATE FORTHWITH ALL ADDITIONAL MEASURES NECESSARY TO PROVIDE FOR PROTECTION OF YOUR ESTABLISHMENTS, PROPERTY, AND EQUIPMENT AGAINST SABOTAGE, PROTECTION OF YOUR PERSONNEL AGAINST SUBVERSIVE PROPAGANDA AND PROTECTION OF ALL ACTIVITIES AGAINST ESPIONAGE. THIS DOES NOT REPEAT NOT MEAN THAT ANY ILLEGAL MEASURES ARE AUTHORIZED. PROTECTIVE MEASURES SHOULD BE CONFINED TO THOSE ESSENTIAL TO SECURITY, AVOIDING UNNECESSARY PUBLICITY AND ALARM. TO INSURE SPEED OF TRANSMISSION IDENTICAL TELEGRAMS BEING SENT TO ALL AIR STATIONS BUT THIS DOES NOT REPEAT NOT AFFECT YOUR RESPONSIBILITY UNDER EXISTING INSTRUCTIONS. ADAMS

Maj. Gen. Emory S. Adams was the adjutant general of the army, and as explained by Prange, he also signed a nearly identically worded message, bearing also the signature of Gen. Hap Arnold and sent to Maj. Gen. Frederick L. Martin, the army air corps chief at Honolulu who, like Short, also had his headquarters at Fort Shafter. Thus Fort Shafter received not one but three warning messages within a few hours, and all three of them strongly emphasized that any action taken was "not repeat not" to generate undue publicity or alarm.

On 27 November Kimmel likewise received three messages, but the other two dealt with the strange proposal that he send army fighter planes by aircraft carrier to Wake and Midway Islands, and that marine defense forces on these islands be reinforced with army troops. Within a few more hours General Short received similar instructions.

Washington's proposal to send half of Short's fighter planes to Wake and Midway by aircraft carrier, and to replace or reinforce the marine detachments at both places with army troops, brought Kimmel and Short into extensive staff conferences that lasted a week and produced strong objections on both sides, based mostly on technical difficulties ranging from inability ever to get the planes back to Hawaii (they could not fly that far over water and could not land aboard carriers, and there were no facilities in either place for loading them aboard) to the many unresolved command relationships and the unacceptable reduction in the defensive strengths of all three bases. The unusual request, coming so soon after the war-warning messages, produced a heavy diversion of staff attention, as Washington should have known it would, and resulted in a unanimous recommendation that the proposal be canceled.

It was. The idea went no further, but it effectively took attention precedence over the war warnings of 27 November and monopolized both army and navy staffs when they should have been concentrating on the war warnings. In short, the immediate necessity of composing a strongly worded, but tactful, reply to a most untimely order from Washington prevented staff planners in Hawaii from concentrating on their main jobs during the week before 7 December.

At this point Prange becomes particularly zealous in his criticism of the Pearl Harbor commanders, most notably Short. He goes into a grammatical and rhetorical analysis to point out that Short should have realized that the three nearly similar "war warnings" he had seen on 27–28 November were not the same at all, in spite of similar—in case of the last two, almost identical—wording. The first, sent over Marshall's signature but not composed by him (he was out of Washington on that day), did not in fact mention sabotage, and therefore Short should have carried out "reconnaissance and other measures" so long as he did not alarm anyone or disclose intent. Even a cursory reading of the three messages, however, shows them to have been so much alike in the sense of what they conveyed that Short was justified, regardless of their exact wording, in lumping them together in his mind. Besides, he had the immediate problem of composing a coherent answer to Washington's proposal to move aircraft and personnel to new posts.

As it turned out, the two commanders took the messages to be more of the routine warnings Pearl Harbor had been getting for more than a year. On 17 June 1940 Maj. Gen. Charles D. Herron, Short's predecessor, had been put on alert for a "trans-Pacific raid" but was also directed to avoid public hysteria or the curiosity of newspapers or alien agents. In January 1941 Ambassador Joseph Grew, in Japan, reported to Washington that the Peruvian minister had informed one of his staff members of a possible Japanese plan to attack Pearl Harbor. Stark thereupon wrote Kimmel, saying the report was a "rumor" in which he took no stock. In May Stark sent Kimmel a memorandum expressing concern over the political situation in the Pacific. In July Kimmel received five such intimations of concern, three by dispatch which could have been considered "war warnings." In August he received two, and in September one. On 16 October the resignation of the Konoye cabinet produced a dispatch with a true war warning, although that term was not used, but a letter from the CNO dated the next day greatly reduced its impact. And finally, on 24 November, all Pacific commanders except Guam (to be separately informed) received a dispatch that began, "Chances of favorable outcome of negotiations with Japan very doubtful. . . . a surprise aggressive movement in any direction including attack on Philippines or Guam is a possibility."

Kimmel and Short compared their respective messages of 27 November with those they had received during the previous several months, set up a lengthy staff conference to sort out the strange proposal to exchange marine and army planes and personnel, and agreed that Washington's principal concern, about which they had been warned, was potential sabotage and subversion resulting from possible war or aggressive action by Japan in the Far East. Both set up antisabotage procedures, and Short so informed Washington, as directed. Kimmel went further, directing "depth bombing" of all submarine contacts discovered in the fleet operating areas (previously they were only to be attacked if found within the three-mile limit), and not having been directed to "inform" Washington of his response to the 27 November warning, he merely sent a copy of his recent depth-bomb order.

Neither the War nor Navy Department indicated dissatisfaction with what had been done. Standard procedures in both services were satisfied, and the Pearl Harbor commanders chalked up one more "cry wolf!" exercise similar to the previous ones.

On the twenty-eighth Washington and Corregidor decrypted Foreign Minister Shigenori Togo's message to Kurusu and Nomura:

> Well, you two ambassadors have exerted superhuman efforts, but in spite of this the United States has gone ahead and presented this humiliating proposal. This was quite unexpected and extremely regrettable. The Imperial Government can by no means use it as a basis for negotiations. Therefore . . . in two or three days the negotiations will be de facto ruptured. This is inevitable. However, I do not wish you to give the impression that the negotiations are broken off. Merely say to them that you are awaiting instructions. . . .

On 30 November we read a message from Tokyo to its Berlin ambassador, that concluded

> Say very secretly to them [Chancellor Hitler and Foreign Minister Ribbentrop] that there is extreme danger that war may suddenly break out between the Anglo-Saxon nations and Japan through some clash of arms and add that the time of the breaking out of this war may come quicker than anyone dreams.

Nothing was sent to Hawaii apprising its commanders of these messages, but although this is not sure, MacArthur and Hart seem to have gotten the word. Hart, in any case, had made some preparations for this contingency in advance.

On 1 December we read a message addressed to Japan's ambassadors in Washington:

> The date set in my message . . . has come and gone and the situation continues to be increasingly critical. However, to prevent the United States from becoming unduly suspicious we have been advising the press and others that . . . the negotiations are continuing. . . .

The Pearl Harbor commanders were not made aware of this foreboding message either. Station Cast on Corregidor at the entrance to Manila Bay, however, possessing its own Purple machine, was able to provide General MacArthur and Admiral Hart with whatever its operatives, functioning in a vacuum as they were, were able to break. There is no positive information as to whether either MacArthur or Hart actually saw these messages, or the ones leading up to them, but the supposition must be that they did see something, despite MacArthur's extraordinary claim to Clausen, as revealed in *Pearl Harbor: Final Judgement* (New York: Crown Publishers, Inc., 1992), that none of the messages were shown to him. Hart, technically subordinate to MacArthur in the USAFFE, though of higher rank (MacArthur's four stars had not yet been restored), was not caught napping. Whether or not he had seen Magic, the well-observed Japanese convoys heading for the Malay Peninsula could have held but a single meaning for a professional naval officer.

It cannot, however, be similarly supposed that anyone outside Washington—with the possible exception of Churchill and his closest confidants in London—knew of our 26 November message to Japan, the one Tokyo called "this humiliating proposal," which foreclosed any possibility of further negotiations. But the top command in Washington knew of it. All of them had read every word.

No one could possibly read through the file as reproduced above and not understand that matters were proceeding rapidly to a head, that something very serious was about to happen, and that it was going to happen very soon. No one has denied that the tension increased dramatically in Washington during the ten days preceding 7 December, and that it was at its peak on the night of the sixth. Yet nothing whatsoever was done except for the "war warnings"—so titled but not so worded—sent ten days earlier.

All this time we had been accumulating thousands of messages in the JN-25 code and had even partially broken some of them, as Frederick D. Parker of the Center for Cryptologic History of the National Security Agency (NSA) carefully explains in *Pearl Harbor Revisited: United States Navy Communications Intelligence 1924–1941.* Published by NSA in 1994, this relatively thin monograph takes up the JN-25 controversy and explains in detail how the White House demand for total coverage of Magic preempted all the efforts of our code-breakers and resulted in the failure to break any of the 26,581 messages in the JN-25 code that had been intercepted by 7 December 1941. They were stored away—some of them partly broken but none sufficiently to be "exploitable"—until 1945 and were finally completely decoded and read in 1945–46, ironically while the Pearl Harbor Hearings of the JCC were in session.

But then, instead of being given publicity, they were again stored away until rediscovery in 1990. There is as yet no explanation for this train of events, but it is sure to generate a number of requests for one, for the entire Pearl Harbor attack is laid out there for the rankest amateur to take aboard. Even the most basic of questions, how we could simply have filed away this treasure-trove of information without breaking even a single message to gain an inkling of what it might contain, is unanswered. (A late development: As this manuscript was being prepared, it has come to light that some of the JN-25 messages were indeed broken and read, but there is still no explanation why no notice was taken of this tremendous source of critically important information.) Of all the JN-25 messages intercepted, 188 of them, if properly "exploited" in 1941, would have given positive warning of Japanese designs and even the actual composition of the *Kido Butai* as it approached the launch point due north of Oahu.

It is now tragically clear that the basic inadequacy of our code-breaking effort in 1940–1941, coupled with the insatiable thirst of the White House for the instantaneous breakdown of everything intercepted in the diplomatic code, forced our overworked code-breakers to concentrate all their efforts on Purple and set aside, at least for the time being, the equally important JN-25 messages. It was not as though a little more hard work on the part of the code-breakers might have enabled them to exploit JN-25 in addition to Purple. They simply could not do more than they were doing. They had been working long, impossible hours for months, in poor working conditions, and were overwhelmed by the hugely increased workload. Captain Safford, head of the code-breakers, and Lieutenant Commander Kramer, his top translator, to mention only two who were prominent in the navy, had long been working seven-day weeks and had often put in more than twenty-four hours steadily at their desks. Some weeks they were well over one hundred hours on the job, and their wives were in outright, open rebellion. Mrs. Safford became especially noted for her protectiveness of her husband.

From the vantage point of hindsight, it is a pity that someone in authority was not able to go to Admiral Turner and show him what we were missing because of the concentrated effort on Purple. Had it been possible to put in front of him even a single useful Japanese naval operational message he might have relented. But of all good ideas, this one would have had the least chance of getting anywhere. Not with a man like Turner in overall charge, for only after inspecting the message might he have changed his mind, and he was the type of hugely self-assured person who, secure in his own interpretations, would likely have refused even to look at it. This was, at least, his normally predictable behavior.

All the same, it is now evident that right here lies one of the biggest unexamined causes of our military surprise at Pearl Harbor and the Philippines. Our code-breakers, all of them military, were forced to leave strictly military code-breaking and work instead on the diplomatic Purple code, which Japan rigorously kept clean of anything relating to army or navy operations. The effort to break into JN-25 to the degree that it could be usefully exploited simply had to be abandoned because of greater priorities elsewhere.

On 2 December our Washington code-breakers intercepted a message directing all Japanese embassies worldwide, except the one in Berlin, to burn or otherwise totally destroy secret papers and classified libraries, codes, secret communications systems, and all but a single coding machine, which was, however, to be prepared for instant destruction. This in effect made the "winds code" moot, but the Pacific commanders were not informed of this important point. By previous order, their communications staffs were still wasting their time on maximum alert to detect a "winds code execute" signal that, according to the official account, never came, but after this day was not needed. We had all the information required, in Washington, to predict hostilities within days, if not hours.

On 3 December Admiral Kimmel received a message stating that the Japanese embassies in Washington, Hong Kong, Singapore, Batavia, Manila, and London had been ordered to "destroy Purple machine and most of their codes and ciphers." No one on Kimmel's staff understood the reference to Purple (Safford later claimed to have drafted the message, and somehow "Purple" slipped through), but fortunately an officer recently arrived from Washington was able to inform Kimmel's intelligence officer, Commander Layton, at risk of general court-martial had he been discovered revealing even this bit of not quite innocuous information, that Purple was the top-secret code name for a Japanese electric coding machine.

Safford's message read:

> 031855 TOKYO ONE DECEMBER ORDERED LONDON X HONGKONG X SINGAPORE AND MANILA TO DESTROY PURPLE MACHINE XX BATAVIA MACHINE ALREADY SENT TO TOKYO XX

DECEMBER SECOND WASHINGTON ALSO DIRECTED DESTROY PURPLE X ALL BUT ONE COPY OF OTHER SYSTEMS X AND ALL SECRET DOCUMENTS XX BRITISH ADMIRALTY TODAY REPORTS EMBASSY LONDON HAS COMPLIED

According to Tolley, who knew Safford well and had long talks with him, Safford once confided that the use of "Purple" was deliberate, not accidental: it was in fact an extracurricular and personally dangerous effort on his part to get a surreptitious warning to Kimmel.

Unfortunately, being all by itself with no supporting corroboration, Safford's "out-of-channels" message did not work as he had hoped. Kimmel and Layton noted that not all codes were to be destroyed, only some of them, and that since use of the code word "Purple" indicated the message was raw intelligence, according to the hard and fast rules they were trying to follow it was not to be talked about. They correctly felt it should probably not have been sent in that form and believed the intelligence evaluations both service branches had been receiving would surely soon reflect the same information in paraphrased language. From all this they also deduced that the action was precautionary, not in immediate anticipation of war, and that the army must be communicating the same news to General Short.

Short received no such notification, and no one on Kimmel's staff checked with the army. This was a failure of some magnitude on the part of Kimmel and his staff, though not of itself sufficient to support a charge of "dereliction of duty."

Brig. Gen. Sherman Miles, the army intelligence chief, knowing that Short had not been informed, on 5 December radioed Col. Kendall Fielder, Short's intelligence adviser, to "immediately contact Navy Cdr. Rochefort regarding Tokyo weather broadcasts." This was an unprecedented attempt to give Short a "heads-up" signal without crossing swords with Marshall, who alone was empowered to issue instructions to outlying army posts. Col. Rufus Bratton, second to Miles in army intelligence, claimed later to have suggested this most unusual effort to Miles in the hope that some of the urgency known to be affecting Rochefort would be conveyed. Obviously miscast in his intelligence role, Fielder did not carry out the order, even though it had come from his direct superior in intelligence.

Had Kimmel spoken with Short personally during the next three days, the two might have stretched the rules enough to develop some useful coordinated action. But the idea of using official channels to inform the army of this important bit of intelligence did not occur to Kimmel or anyone else. Layton describes how this happened on page 250 of *And I Was There*.

Not checking it with him was a bad decision. Here was a definite signal that something was afoot, and the Pearl Harbor commanders, not holding responsibility for intelligence (this point had been categorically made to them and everyone on their staffs), simply missed it. There was no indication that Pearl Harbor had been singled out for special attention, and from Washington's point of view the Japanese message therefore contained no problem for its commanders.

Parenthetically, Admiral Nimitz, when he succeeded to command of the Pacific Fleet, seemed to have some sixth sense that he might not be getting all the information floating around that might be useful to him. Much of it, even though generated right there in Pearl Harbor, was instead sent directly to ONI in Washington. He issued unmistakable orders, undoubtedly concocted in despairing post-attack hindsight between his intelligence officer, Layton, and Layton's good friend, Rochefort, chief of the 14th Naval District Communications Security Unit, that any information whatsoever that might affect the Pacific Fleet under his command was instantly to be made available to him in addition to anyone else Rochefort might be reporting it to. Similar orders, with the full authority of CINCPAC and CINCPACFLEET, were sent to all his outlying posts.

Because of this, Admiral Nimitz was stunningly successful in the two important battles that came his way so quickly: Coral Sea, five months after Pearl Harbor, and the Battle of Midway, not quite a month after that. Had such an understanding been in place in December 1941, there might have been a different story to tell about Pearl Harbor.

On 6 December Magic decrypted the following message from Japan's foreign minister in Tokyo to the ambassadors in Washington:

> 1. THE GOVERNMENT HAS DELIBERATED DEEPLY ON THE AMERICAN PROPOSAL OF THE 26TH OF NOVEMBER AND AS A RESULT WE HAVE DRAWN UP A MEMORANDUM FOR THE UNITED STATES CONTAINED IN MY SEPARATE MESSAGE #902 (IN ENGLISH).
>
> 2. THIS SEPARATE MESSAGE IS A VERY LONG ONE. I WILL SEND IT IN FOURTEEN PARTS AND I IMAGINE YOU WILL RECEIVE IT TOMORROW. HOWEVER, I AM NOT SURE. THE SIT-

UATION IS EXTREMELY DELICATE, AND WHEN YOU RECEIVE IT I WANT YOU PLEASE TO KEEP IT SECRET FOR THE TIME BEING.

3. CONCERNING THE TIME OF PRESENTING THIS MEMORANDUM TO THE UNITED STATES, I WILL WIRE YOU IN A SEPARATE MESSAGE. HOWEVER, I WANT YOU IN THE MEANTIME TO PUT IT IN A NICELY DRAFTED FORM AND MAKE EVERY PREPARATION TO PRESENT IT TO THE AMERICANS JUST AS SOON AS YOU RECEIVE INSTRUCTIONS.

This message became known to our "Magicians" as the "pilot" message and was later so referred to in all the investigations. Counting this preliminary message alerting the Japanese embassy in Washington, the fourteen parts of the basic communication, and the following "delivery" message, there were sixteen messages in all. As has already been stated, and can well be imagined, U.S. codebreaking resources went into full alert to detect, intercept, and decrypt these messages the moment they were transmitted from Japan. Our top command in Washington knew well they might be a declaration of war, or something very near it.

As they were decrypted, the first and last of the sixteen messages, intended to be instructions to the two Japanese ambassadors then in our capital, came out in the Japanese language and required translation. The fourteen parts of the main message, for the first time during the entire life of Magic, decoded directly into perfect English. In other words, the actual decoded text of the formal break in negotiations between Japan and the United States, as sent to Japan's ambassadors in Washington to be "put in a nicely drafted form," *was in English*. This might be expected of a foreign nation with a strange circumlocutory sort of written language that desired above all to be explicitly understood in a matter of supreme importance. The intelligence community should have taken special note of this extremely significant point.

Unfortunately, the bureaucratic system used by the decoders required all messages to be processed through its recording, translation, and typing sections, and so marked on the secret paper itself. Therefore, no matter how swiftly (or slowly) handled, all Magic, without exception, bore an indication of the time and date "translated." For the crucial fourteen-part message, this meant little more than that the translator had merely okayed and passed on the English parts as they arrived, and no one, apparently, gave much thought to the unusually swift "translations," as indicated by the times the messages were checked out of that section.

This may have been a critical lapse; no previous Purple message had ever decoded into English. All had been intended for Japanese officials only, and being sent in English could only mean that this fourteen-part message was of crucial importance and that Japan wished to take no chance of even a slight change in a shade of meaning a translator in its Washington embassy might inadvertently put into the text. It was intended for study by the U.S. State Department and the U.S. high command. If the intelligence chiefs of the army and navy had noted this important point they might have been more alert to the critical significance of the message itself.

The 1989 British Broadcast Company TV documentary "Sacrifice at Pearl Harbor" portrayed Washington during the week before the Japanese attack and dramatized the confusing information and rumors rife in high government circles at the time. It stated positively that Churchill had information about a Japanese task force at sea headed toward Hawaii and that he shared this with Roosevelt (Rusbridger says he did not); that a number of intelligence officers intercepted a series of messages indicating something radical was going to happen on Sunday the seventh (no doubt of this); that FBI head J. Edgar Hoover and Ambassador Grew had heard as early as the previous spring that Yamamoto was planning an attack on the Hawaiian naval base (Grew reported this, but Hoover apparently did not); and that a special navigation plotting team had been tracking the *Kido Butai* from the Kurile Islands out into the Pacific and knew, on the morning of 7 December, that it was due north of Oahu (this raises the question, which the BBC did not answer, whether the *Kido Butai* observed strict radio silence, as logic would suggest and other information states it did).

The BBC further alleged that all this was deliberately withheld from Kimmel and his staff, and that even intercepts picked up at station Hypo under Rochefort, and elsewhere in the navy complex, were sent only to Washington, where they were buried in the jungle of official paper there. There is no documentary proof of any of this. If indeed it happened as portrayed, the cover-up of all related matter, all clues, was immensely successful—so much so as to be unbelievable. The barest suggestion of these strange things, even today, brings the Roosevelt supporters out in massed emotional formation to defend their revered leader. It is like a religion, to them, to protect him and his memory. The BBC report, not investigated, was at once dismissed as unworthy of belief, and that is the judgment that has stuck in the public mind. Essentially, that is also the reaction to the Rusbridger-Nave book, despite its extensive documentation. Both of these, and all the "revisionist literature"—books and papers galore—have in fact been put aside with virtually automatic castigation as being "poorly researched," "speculative," "not convincing." Few of the allegations have been truly researched; judgment has been rendered against them, in effect without trial, because they raised "possibly damaging and destructive ideas," as suggested by Nietzsche.

This is not to say that the author of this defense of Admiral Kimmel accepts all anti-Roosevelt theories. Nevertheless, witnesses such as those depicted in the BBC broadcast possess some facts (and the presentation causes viewers to guess at more). When there are so many growths of similar shape and color there must be some relationship. They cannot all be spun out of whole cloth, and nearly everyone, even passionate Roosevelt defenders, will agree that there is much that is not known, and probably will never be known, about what went on.

To return to Admiral Kimmel and General Short: Information about the tense state of affairs in Washington during the first week of December would have served, at the very least, to alert them that something unusual was going on. But no such details—not even those intimately related to the welfare of their own official real estate and in some cases even found there—were allowed to reach either one. As Layton succinctly described, Rochefort and the other intelligence analysts were specifically and positively forbidden to pass any information anywhere except through top-secret channels directly to their superiors in Washington, D.C. But Washington's intelligence bureaucracy seems not to have understood that speed and accuracy in the exploitation of intelligence are fully as important as the accumulation of data. William Casey makes this clear in the introductory pages of his book *The Secret War Against Hitler* (Regnery Gateway, 1988).

In his own book, *Admiral Kimmel's Story* (Chicago: Henry Regnery Company, 1955), Husband Kimmel described this imbroglio (p. 79 et seq.):

> The deficiencies of Pearl Harbor as a fleet base were well known in the Navy Department. In an interview with Mr. Roosevelt in June 1941, in Washington, I outlined the weaknesses and concluded with the remark that the only answer was to have the fleet at sea if the Japs ever attacked.

I accepted the decision to base the fleet at Pearl Harbor in the firm belief that the Navy Department would supply me promptly with all pertinent information available and in particular with all information that indicated an attack on the fleet at Pearl Harbor. I knew in general, from my experience in the Navy, of the sources from which the Navy Department might derive such intelligence, including the decoded Japanese intercepted communications. . . . On 25 May 1941 I wrote an official letter to the Chief of Naval Operations [describing] my need for information of all important developments affecting our foreign relations. . . . handed it to the CNO personally, and received his assurance that I would be informed of all important developments as they occurred, and by the quickest secure means available.

A study of Japanese radio intercepts extending over many years permitted the Navy to read many of the intercepted Japanese messages. Information obtained in this manner was referred to as "magic" and was of the greatest value when properly used.

Although the commanders in Hawaii were never supplied with the equipment and trained personnel to decode intercepted "magic" . . . I learned during the investigations [after the attack] that the C-In-C Asiatic Fleet was fully equipped to decode the "magic" intercepted Japanese dispatches as received; also that the Navy Department in Washington . . . supplied the Asiatic decoding unit with copies of important intercepts which the organization failed to obtain with their own facilities. . . . also . . . that a fourth set of equipment designated for [CINCUS] was diverted to the British in the summer of 1941. . . .

The care taken to keep the commander-in-chief of our Asiatic Fleet and the British in London informed of Japanese intentions while withholding this vital information from our commanders at Pearl Harbor has never been explained. . . .

I was never informed of any decision . . . that intelligence from intercepted Japanese messages was not to be sent to me. In July the CNO sent me at least seven ["magic"] dispatches. . . . Dispatches sent to me by the Navy Department in the week before the attack contained intelligence from intercepted messages. On December 1, a ["magic"] dispatch quoted a report [of] a Japanese plan to entice the British to invade Thai. . . . On December 3, a dispatch to me from the CNO set forth an order from Japan to diplomatic agents and expressly referred to this order as "Circular Twenty Four Forty Four from Tokyo." Another . . . referred to certain "categoric and urgent instructions which

> were sent yesterday to Japanese diplomatic and consular posts."
>
> The Navy Department thus engaged in a course of conduct which definitely gave me the impression that intelligence from important intercepted Japanese messages was being furnished to me. Under these circumstances a failure to send me important information of this character was not merely a withholding of intelligence. *It amounted to an affirmative misrepresentation.* [emphasis supplied] I had asked for all vital information. I had been assured that I would have it. I appeared to be receiving it. . . . Yet, in fact, the most vital information from the intercepted Japanese messages was withheld from me. This failure not only deprived me of essential facts. It misled me.
>
> I was not supplied with any information of the intercepted messages showing that the Japanese government had divided Pearl Harbor into five areas and was seeking minute berthing information as to the berthing of ships of the fleet in those areas, which was vitally significant.

It is easy to say that Kimmel and Short, in charge in Hawaii, should have had more information and used it better, but whose responsibility was it to get this vital information to them? Do not their immediate superiors in Washington, who kept it to themselves, bear more responsibility than they? Who, then, is really to blame for the surprise at Pearl Harbor?

5

The Other Key Players

A *brief review of the other star players* of this difficult time may be useful. In addition to Admiral Kimmel these were Adm. J. O. Richardson, Kimmel's predecessor as CINCUS; Adm. Thomas C. Hart, commander in chief of the Asiatic Fleet based at Cavite in Manila Bay; Adm. Harold R. Stark, CNO; Lt. Gen. Walter C. Short, army commander in Hawaii; Gen. George C. Marshall, chief of staff of the army; Gen. Douglas MacArthur, commander of the newly established (July 1941) U.S. Armed Forces Far East (USAFFE); Henry L. Stimson, secretary of war; "Colonel" Frank Knox, secretary of the navy; and a latecomer to this author's analysis, Vice Adm. Richmond Kelly Turner. With the exception of Admiral Richardson, all were in important military command posts on 7 December 1941, and the fates of all were closely intertwined. The last, just added to the list, seems somehow to have been the "eminence grise" whose presence, and personality, somehow appeared at nearly all the moments when difficult (and frequently wrong) decisions were made.

It may be questioned why Adm. Ernest J. King, who took over from Admiral Stark and became a combination CNO, CINCUS, and Commander in Chief (COMINCH), and Rear Adm. Claude C. Bloch, Richardson's predecessor as CINCUS and naval district commander in Hawaii, are nowhere named in this list. Admiral King indeed took on a big part in the tremendous drama of this war, but he was not involved with Pearl Harbor, not assigned to Washington when the Japanese attack took place. He had been commander of the Atlantic Squadron, based in Norfolk, and as the squadron was upgraded to Atlantic Fleet, he went up with it. When Roosevelt and Secretary Knox began to look about them for someone to bring order to the chaos existing in Washington in the aftermath of Pearl Harbor, they fixed on King, and the rest, as the saying goes, is history. Admiral King's own reported comment, on hearing of his appointment, was characteristic of the man: "When they get in trouble, they send for the sons-a-bitches!" But although an unpopular officer, greatly feared by all with whom he came in contact, he was also greatly admired and is considered one of the architects of our victory.

Bloch is an entirely different story. Upon completion of his tour as fleet commander, in January 1940, he went to a preretirement sinecure as commander of the 14th Naval District, the Hawaiian area, with his headquarters in the Pearl Harbor Navy Yard. He was in overall command of the patrol planes provided by the Navy Department for air surveillance of the waters around Hawaii. Figures vary as to the actual number of patrol planes available, but Bloch's testimony states that there were seventy-two, of which twelve were in overhaul and thus not in a flying condition, and twenty-four were at Midway. He had the remaining thirty-six under his direct control in Hawaii and could have called on the army (General Short) for an additional eight B-17s that had been configured and trained for patrol duty. All were plagued by a shortage of spare parts, and the consensus was that continuous flying, as air patrolling would require, could be carried out for but a few days at most. After the attack it was noted that Bloch had not approached Short for assignment of the B-17s, but evidently this was considered beside the point inasmuch as it had been decided not to institute air patrols at all.

Bloch participated in the conference on this subject and in the decision, concurred in by Kimmel and all others involved, to concentrate on training and readying the few planes in the patrol force instead of using them up prematurely in air patrols they could not maintain for more than a few days. The judgment of those present was that until adequate forces were provided—something over which no one in Hawaii had any control (Kimmel had been complaining for months about the shortages)—the commanders in Hawaii had no choice but to depend on receiving the promised "alert" warning from Washington before initiating patrols. Otherwise, the planes and aircrews would quickly expend themselves and be unable to function when truly needed. Bloch, several years senior to Kimmel in the navy list, was now subordinate to him in its rank structure. His advice was, of course, sought and listened to, and his agreement heartening, since he had so recently been commander of the fleet himself. The recommendation of the conference was unanimous, but when to begin air-surveillance patrols was up to CINCUS. Bloch's function was only administrative.

Admiral Richardson was Admiral Kimmel's immediate predecessor in command of the fleet at Pearl Harbor. He had relieved

Admiral Bloch as CINCUS on 6 January 1940 and normally would have been in command on that terrible December morning twenty-three months later. When Richardson took over, the U.S. Fleet was based in Long Beach, California. In April and May of that year it engaged in maneuvers simulating war with Japan. (Such maneuvers were nearly standard; there was no other enemy, or potential enemy, in that ocean.) The fleet maneuvers ended in Pearl Harbor, where a planned rest and recreational stay of about two weeks was continuously extended by directive of Washington.

It was gradually clear that the stay was to become permanent, at least for the foreseeable future. Richardson complained, twice directly to Roosevelt, that the fleet had inadequate logistic support to maintain itself at Pearl Harbor, that its presence in Hawaii could not exercise a restraining influence on Japanese action, and that he, the fleet commander, was not being kept adequately informed about what was going on in Washington. A great deal of improvement was made during the next year in both the Pearl Harbor facilities and the capabilities of the Pearl Harbor Navy Yard, but it is now evident that Richardson was only too right. In reading his own account (*On the Treadmill to Pearl Harbor*), completed in 1958 but not published until after the 1972 death of his old friend Admiral Stark, whom the book criticizes most strongly, one has to recognize the probability that Roosevelt had come to look on Richardson as a bothersome nuisance in the big international game of power politics he had begun playing.

Whether Richardson might have been more alert than Kimmel, and therefore more successful in avoiding surprise, cannot be answered, but a careful reading of his memoirs indicates that he, at least, did not think so. In Kimmel's place, with the information Kimmel was receiving, he wrote that he would have been taken just as much unawares. He went on to say, however, that if he had been CNO instead of Stark, Admiral Kimmel would have had much more of the critically important up-to-date information than he did receive. Clearly stated in several places is Richardson's opinion that Stark failed grossly in his responsibility to CINCUS, his immediate subordinate, and that it was this failure that led directly to the surprise of the attack itself.

Richardson was so vocal with his concern about the untenable position of the fleet at Pearl Harbor, and stated his feelings so strongly to the president himself, as well as in more routine official circles, that he was fired as fleet commander after only a year as CINCUS, ten months before the attack. This was not lost on Kimmel:

he would carry out the president's wishes to the best of his ability, not oppose them. After all, Roosevelt *was* commander in chief of the army and navy and had the constitutional mandate to control them in every way.

Both the bringer and the prophet of disaster are usually almost equally unpopular, along with whoever is perceived as having been invested with leadership of its victims. Most particularly is this true in military organizations. For Admiral Richardson, not quite a prophet of disaster but the closest thing to it at the time, there was no warning that he was about to lose his job, except that he knew he had been unusually forthright in stating his disagreement with the president. He had gone so far as to say that senior officers in the navy had lost confidence in their civilian leadership. This "hurt the President's feelings," the admiral was later told. The axe fell without even a preliminary telephone call from his close friend, the CNO; so it is probable, as Richardson believed, that instructions from Roosevelt himself must have forbidden the courtesy. In January 1941, exactly one year after he took command, he received a dispatch cutting his normal tour in half, returning him to Washington, and directing his replacement by his cruiser force commander, Rear Admiral Kimmel, who was thus jumped from two to four stars.

In Washington, although told by Secretary Knox to expect a call to the White House, Richardson never again saw the president (he had seen him frequently before). Returned to his permanent rank of rear admiral, he was employed in a succession of minor jobs in Washington. He reached the statutory retirement age of sixty-four in October 1942, was put on the retired list, and was immediately recalled to active duty in similar assignments—as before, not connected with the war effort. He was finally retired in 1947 at the highest rank held on active duty: full admiral, in accordance with the official practice. In his book he says, "After Pearl Harbor, Admiral Kimmel received the rawest of raw deals from Franklin D. Roosevelt and, insofar as they acquiesced in this treatment, from Frank Knox and 'Betty' Stark (CNO)." Elsewhere in the same book he wrote, "I believe the President's responsibility for our initial defeats in the Pacific was direct, real, and personal."

He also wrote, "In the impression that the Roberts Commission created on the minds of the American People, and in the way it was drawn up for that specific purpose, I believe that the Report of the Roberts Commission was the most unfair, unjust, and deceptively dishonest document ever printed by the Government Printing

Office. . . . I cannot conceive of any honorable man being able to recall his service as a member of that commission without deep regret and the deepest feeling of shame." These are forthright words, as Richardson meant them to be.

Admiral Hart has already been mentioned. The Purple machine that provided Magic was available to him and General MacArthur via a top-secret special shipment sent in January 1941. MacArthur's claims to Major Clausen—that he saw none of the Magic radio intercepts—are hard to believe, inasmuch as Hart, the other person in Manila authorized to receive them, evidently did so and was not caught napping by the Japanese. Apparently the Asiatic Fleet commander took aboard enough information, either from Magic alone or in combination with his evaluation of Japanese seaborne movements, to be ready for the attack when it came to the Philippines, and MacArthur should have done the same.

Hart disposed of the forces under his command as well as anyone could have in the short time available to him: he sent surface ships south and had his submarines spend daylight hours submerged, lying on the bottom of Manila Bay. He would have done even better, possibly have saved the submarine *Sealion* (in overhaul at the U.S. Navy Yard, Cavite, and therefore immobile) and Cavite's large stock of submarine and destroyer torpedoes, had he had another day's warning. His performance illustrates at least what could have been done in the very minimum of time.

The commander of the U.S. Asiatic Fleet flew his flag from the main truck of the beautiful cruiser *Houston,* his flagship, beloved by Roosevelt, who had made several pleasant cruises in her. Hart was nothing if not a knowledgeable fleet commander, and he planned to maintain his headquarters at Manila as long as the city was in American hands. He was therefore outraged when MacArthur, with no prior warning, announced on 24 December 1941 that he had declared Manila an "open city" as of midnight. This unexpected action, well described by Tolley in *Cruise of the* Lanikai, forced an instant and disorganized evacuation of all base forces and equipment that could be moved to Batavia (now Jakarta) on the island of Java in the Netherlands East Indies, where he planned to set up a new base for operational control. It was a terribly hectic time in Manila. A great deal of irreplaceable equipment and supplies had to be abandoned, as much as possible of it burned, smashed to bits, or dumped in deep water. The submarine force lost hundreds of new Mark 14 torpedoes, a shortage that hampered operations for more than a year.

Hart was to be in Batavia only about six weeks. Initially he was in command of all the Allied naval forces available in that part of the world, but this little fleet, known as the ABDA Fleet (American, British, Dutch, Australian) and intended to function as a unit under the joint command, had never operated together and did not even possess a common signal system. It was clearly to be a sacrifice to the oncoming Japanese forces, which could in no way have been prevented from overwhelming them and the entire little nation (the Dutch East Indies) it had been sent to assist. Our Navy Department no doubt realized his impossible situation. It must, simultaneously, have recognized the risk it was taking with Magic should Hart be captured, as was inevitable were he to stay, and subjected to torture or mind-altering drugs. Peremptory orders from Washington directed him to turn over his little fleet to the senior Dutch naval officer in the area and return home, which he did in mid-February.

Although he must have guessed that he was being protected because of his knowledge of Magic, it no doubt caused Admiral Hart, a dedicated naval officer, much pain to abandon his forces in the summary way he did, in the midst of a faltering sea campaign, fully aware that they were being used as a death offering in support of a cause already known to be lost. The Congressional Medal of Honor posthumously awarded to the commanding officer of the sacrificed *Houston* was truly deserved, as the facts available now, as well as then, demonstrate; but it can never be more than an inadequate symbol of the debt owed to all the men of that forlorn, deserted Asiatic Fleet.

Yet war is never without sacrifice, demanded and given. Before blame and accusation are handed out it is first necessary to decide what were the alternatives to all concerned. Japan, with a warrior class based on a samurai culture, would have had no difficulty with this problem. Its fleet would have been expected to fight to the death for the greater glory of the emperor. Neither, probably, would Nazi Germany, which might, in its own cynical way, have simply ordered its forces to abandon allies it could not help further. Had we abandoned the Dutch East Indies, more of our Asiatic Fleet might have survived and, probably, no more of the Dutch would have died. But the Dutch were our allies, and it would have been hard to predict the judgment of history. Just the same, that fleet, and those men—except for its submarines, eight old destroyers, and the damaged cruiser *Marblehead* that got away—were sacrificed to the expediencies of international political necessity.

Admiral Hart retired from active duty in June 1942. In February 1945 the governor of Connecticut appointed him U.S. Senator on the death of Senator Francis Maloney of that state. Hart did not run for reelection in 1946, and his term expired the next year.

Admiral Stark received considerable unofficial blame for Pearl Harbor, though few then knew anything specific as to the reasons. He was shunted aside by the appointment of Admiral King as COMINCH. All the many investigations of the Pearl Harbor debacle, it now appears, one way or another have faulted Stark for not keeping Kimmel adequately informed. Richardson stated this accusation directly:

> I consider that 'Betty' Stark, in failing to pick up a telephone and give Kimmel a last-minute warning on the morning of Pearl Harbor, committed a major professional lapse, indicating a basic absence of those personal military characteristics required in a successful war leader. I believe his failures in these respects were far more important derelictions than those of any of his subordinates. . . . I cannot conceive of how he could have treated Kimmel as he did . . . unless . . . (it) was due to influence or possibly direct orders from above. . . . His means of communication with Kimmel were equal to, if not superior to, those available to Marshall for communication with Short. He made no effort to warn Kimmel on the morning of December 7, but referred the matter to Marshall.

In his memoirs Richardson said he believed instructions had been given that no one but General Marshall was to send warnings to Pearl Harbor, and this explains why Stark did not send a warning directly. Regarding the lesser matter of simply keeping Kimmel informed, in which Richardson reiterated his criticism of Stark, he made a similar accusation relating to his own service as CINCUS (Stark did not inform him he was to be relieved) and went on obliquely, "I believe also that few, if any, other senior officers in the Navy could have served the President so long and so satisfactorily as did Admiral Stark." He clearly did not consider this enigmatic comment to be one of high praise.

In 1942 Admiral Stark was quietly transferred to England, where he served the United States well during the balance of the war. Nothing was ever done about his failure to notify Kimmel, and he never defended himself against the charge. Richardson sarcastically said, "In view of what happened to our fleet at Pearl Harbor on December 7, 1941, I believe he may have a few regrets as to his part in the matter."

Lieutenant General Short, U.S. Army commander of the Hawaiian Department, is something of an enigma. Like George Marshall, he seems to have held an austere personal outlook on his duty and evidently accepted the disaster to himself as akin to but lesser than the deaths and serious injuries that overtook about 2,300 soldiers, sailors, airmen, and civilians on that terrible day. Holding his dismay, anger, whatever personal guilt he may have felt, and the terrible sorrow within his own breast, he quietly disappeared from the official scene. Except for his testimony when called before the sequence of investigations of the matter, in which he defended himself vigorously, he said nothing and wrote nothing. He had done his duty to the best of his ability and had been caught by a strange combination of Magic, international politics, failure of superiors to discharge their obligations to him, and (very probably) army politics as well.

He believed Marshall to have been his personal friend and apparently could never reconcile Marshall's treatment of him with the earlier memories of their friendship. However, like the samurai who put the intangible greater good of their system above even their own lives, he did not flinch at the penalty exacted of him by the overlords whom he served. After his forced retirement from active duty in March of 1942, he worked for the Ford Motor Company in Dallas, Texas, and quietly found his peace by puttering in the garden he loved. He died in 1949.

General Marshall was another American samurai, one of the authentic heroes of modern American history. He has rightly been revered by the American public, whom he served as chief of staff of the army, then as secretary of state, and finally as secretary of defense. Seldom has one individual so combined the qualities of austere high-mindedness, self-abnegation, seriousness of purpose, and intellect. He was admired by presidents, by the news media, by all who came into contact with him. The nation was singularly fortunate that he was near the seat of power during the extraordinary period that encompassed World War II and its aftermath. So far as is known, during Marshall's entire career there was only one lapse in his superlative stewardship of our country's best interests, and that was on Pearl Harbor Day.

That was the morning when he cut himself off from all official communication and went "horseback riding." Lesser officers bearing important information—the decode of the final section of the crucial fourteen-part message; Admiral Stark's request that a war-warning message be sent to the fleet at Pearl Harbor; the critical, partly intuitive, but as we now know accurate, information about the intentions of the Japanese fleet, which Colonel Bratton, the army's top intelligence officer for Far Eastern Affairs, desperately tried to convey to Marshall—all had to wait until the general could be found.

Marshall never did adequately explain his whereabouts on the night of 6 December or the morning of the seventh. He was reported in the press as having been present on the night of the sixth at a reunion of old World War I comrades at the University Club on 16th street, a few blocks north of the White House, and there were unconfirmed statements—rumors really—that he was seen in civilian clothes in the State Department building on the morning of the seventh.

Marshall was a man of commanding presence and a nearly mystical sense of duty. Absent some overriding reason, there is literally no way he would, or could, have been so derelict in his duties on this all-important Sunday. Other officials—Secretary of State Hull, Admiral Stark, and many lesser ones, in particular those involved with code work—were at their desks or were trying frantically to reach someone in authority with what they considered important information. All were well aware of the critical state of Japanese-American relations. The army chief of staff could not have been an exception.

Admiral Richardson wrote that though he had no proof, he was certain that Roosevelt had directed that only General Marshall could send a warning message to Hawaii. Would the conscientious Marshall have absented himself from his post virtually the entire morning of that terribly important Sunday—on his own? Richardson did not think so. On the contrary, the rest of his life he believed that the president had wanted an attack of some kind to launch us into the war and that Marshall had held the key.

Loyal to the core to his sworn superiors, no doubt believing that it was indeed vital for the United States to get into war with Germany, Marshall had given his word, not only as the senior member of the U.S. Army but also as one of the president's most trusted advisers, to keep the confidence reposed in him. If necessary to protect the United States, or its president, he would sacrifice anything: life itself, or his personal honor.

One possible explanation of his strange actions on that Sunday morning might be that he was actually offering himself as a scapegoat. Should it come down to the specific question of just exactly *who* had failed to send notification where it should have been sent, he would accept blame and permit the president, or the secretary of war, to do with him as they might find necessary. He might, in essence, in such contingency have behaved as General Short was to do.

This was not, however, what he did when the army board of investigation sent up its findings in 1944. According to army regulations, findings of fault in general officers had to be sent for approval to the secretary of war and the chief of staff of the army. No provision existed if one of the generals faulted happened to be the chief of staff himself. It must, however, be remembered that the situation in 1944 was very different from that in 1941. The end of the war, in which Marshall had had such a big hand, was beginning to come in sight: D-Day had already taken place in Normandy, and the slow but inevitable destruction of Nazi Germany was afoot. By this time Marshall had indeed become indispensable to Roosevelt and Stimson too, and it cannot be possible that both men did not fully see and understand the deteriorated, now genuinely precarious, state of the president's health. Marshall went to see Stimson with the board's report and said that its publication, even in secret, would "destroy his usefulness" to the president, the secretary, and the army itself. He would have to resign his post and ask to be put on the retired list.

Stimson's reaction, which he may well have already decided upon after reading his own copy of the report, was to suppress it entirely and to have Clausen, a civilian lawyer, in uniform for the duration, who had functioned as a "recorder" for the board, make a special investigation, for his use alone, to support his intent to refute the board's recommendations. Clausen's version of how he carried out this directive may be read in the book he co-authored with Bruce Lee just before his death, *Pearl Harbor: Final Judgement.*

It will be remembered that H. R. Haldeman, in his posthumously published *Haldeman Diaries* (New York: G. P. Putnam's Sons, 1994), saw himself in somewhat the same light as these pages suggest Marshall may have. Both men were ready to sacrifice themselves for the president. If either had to lie for him, he would lie, but only for the deepest, most important reasons. Neither would ever "rat" on his boss—though it's not yet obvious to what extent the candid disclosures in the Haldeman book will be considered to be "ratting." In this connection it was said of Marshall that he could never write his memoirs, and Marshall himself announced that he never would.

Telling untruths would have been excruciatingly difficult for a man of Marshall's integrity, but for the country and its administration, and the world as he saw it, it may have been something he had to do. In the end he simply "forgot" many things rather than lie about them. It must have been a bad time for him, but neither was he accustomed to flinching under pressure.

Admiral Richardson had the highest respect for General Marshall, and it is obvious he felt that Marshall had little choice but to act as he did.

General MacArthur's USAFFE (U.S. Army Forces Far East) was created on 26 July 1941 when President Roosevelt called the Philippine armed forces into the service of the United States. Initially this force consisted only of the relatively small U.S. Army garrison on Corregidor, augmented by the Philippine Constabulary (the army of the autonomous but not yet fully independent Philippines), and other U.S. Army forces in the archipelago. MacArthur, army chief of staff from 1930 to 1935, already personally wealthy, was now politically powerful as well. As field marshall of the Philippine Army, he had a fabulous apartment at the top of the Manila Hotel, supplied and staffed by the Philippine government, from which he carried out his administrative duties. Although the U.S. Army might have selected someone other than a flamboyant and ambitious retired general, even a former chief of staff, for the post of commanding general of the USAFFE, Roosevelt picked MacArthur, a choice from which there was no audible dissent.

With the arrival of the Purple machine, sequestered with its specially trained operators on Corregidor, MacArthur and Hart had been given access to Magic. Other than the operators of the secret instrument, the two commanders were theoretically the only ones to see the messages. MacArthur's statement to Clausen that he had not seen any Magic cannot be supported. Even if in fact he did not see the messages, it was his duty to see them; so the blame for the failure is the same.

Whatever his sources of information and warning, which were at least as good as those that warned Hart to move his surface ships out of harm's way before the first Japanese aircraft appeared, MacArthur did not do nearly so well as his navy counterpart. He did not lay in an adequate supply of provisions in the Bataan Peninsula, even though an earlier War Plan Orange—and indeed the currently effective plan, Rainbow 5—called for a retreat to that area in the event of invasion. Provisions were fully available, had he directed their deployment to Bataan, and very quickly a retreat to that peninsula did become necessary. MacArthur's plan, however, had made not even contingent preparation for this possibility. It called for fighting the landing on the beaches, where he maintained that the best defense, essentially an *offensive* type of defense, could be mustered. This proved a complete failure, largely because he no longer had an air force to provide his troops with air cover and surveillance of enemy movements. In short order he had to take shelter in the tunnels of Corregidor, and when orders came to save himself, he protested loudly, but he did so nonetheless, along with his family and some of his servants and, presumably, others who might have had contact with Magic. His highly touted army he left helpless, cut off without food or ammunition replenishment supply, on Bataan. Its quick surrender was inevitable, the loss of life terrible.

He had known Roosevelt well for years, had been held over as army chief of staff by presidential order for an extra year after his term expired in 1934, and may have contributed to the president's political career in ways known to no one but the two of them. The last point is speculative; the facts are that despite his failure on 8 December (East Asia date), a failure now judged to have been more costly to our war effort than the Pearl Harbor debacle (it cost us the entire Philippines for nearly the whole war, and it cost the Philippine people an immense loss of life, by some estimates as many as three million people, most of them civilian), he was continued as commander of USAFFE and later appointed supreme commander far east. And although the victory over Japan had clearly been won at sea, MacArthur was given the honor of receiving the Japanese surrender for the United States. The sop to the navy was that Japan's emissaries were obliged to surrender on board the U.S. battleship *Missouri*.

The records show that even after receipt of urgent messages from Hawaii and Washington describing the bombing that had taken place at Pearl Harbor, and after at least one specific directive to carry out the Joint Rainbow-5 plan to bomb Japanese airfields in Formosa at the beginning of hostilities, MacArthur gave no such orders and remained indecisive.

At dawn in the Philippines, fully aware that the war had begun, MacArthur's army air corps commander, Gen. Lewis H. Brereton, sent up some fighter planes from Clark Field on patrol. This was in the early morning of 8 December, east longitude time. By some accounts the first attack on the Philippine mainland had already taken place, at Baguio in the hills north of Manila, but the air corps fliers found no enemy planes and returned to Clark Field to await further orders. No further orders came, although Brereton begged for them several times. He was, on the contrary, directed to hold everything and wait. No one has ever been able to explain away MacArthur's extraordinary dilatoriness, and one simply has to wonder by what mentality of "waiting for orders" Brereton did not order the dispersal of the planes on his own. He might at least have saved the aircraft, as General Arnold is supposed to have stated indignantly over the secure telephone (which now, after Pearl Harbor, was being used almost indiscriminately).

The situation at Clark Field was, of course, different from that at Pearl Harbor. The principal attack by Formosa-based Japanese bombers and fighters, having been delayed by weather, arrived over Clark Field about nine hours after the Pearl Harbor tragedy was complete. In their reports, the Japanese fliers expressed amazement at finding virtually the entire force of U.S. fighter and bomber planes lined up wingtip to wingtip on the ground, not even in revetments for protection against ground strafing. Their destruction was easy, complete within minutes. When the Japanese attack was over, some thirty-six new B-17 bombers and an equivalent number of P-40 combat aircraft designated as their escorts had been totally destroyed.

Some were shot down while desperately trying to take off. Irreplaceable army air corps fliers, some of whom had just arrived in the Philippines, lost their lives in this debacle.

The loss of most of the aircraft and many trained fliers stationed on our newly declared far-western perimeter, the only force available to defend the Philippines and the Asiatic Fleet, touted by Arnold as able to threaten Tokyo by shuttle-bombing flights to and from Vladivostok, was a more severe blow to the United States than the loss of eight obsolescent battleships at Pearl Harbor, six of which were ultimately repaired and returned to action; for with the loss of our aircraft went also any chance of stemming the Japanese advance in the Far East. Historians are united in laying the blame for this at MacArthur's door. How he could have been so derelict has never been satisfactorily explained.

No hint of official blame was ever leveled at MacArthur, nor was any investigation held of his tremendous failure of command. John Costello, in *Days of Infamy,* a carefully researched history of the beginning of the war from the point of view of the Philippines, goes deeply into MacArthur's devious and successful efforts to avoid any attachment of blame. He was a master of self-justifying public relations, and this artistry stood him in very good stead at this time. Costello has furthermore uncovered evidence that suggests a continuing relationship with President Manuel Quezon of the Philippines, plus a shared hope (hardly a credible belief) that Japan might bypass the Philippines if no attack on Japanese forces came from those islands. Thus the dictum that Japan must "strike the first blow" might have carried a special meaning for MacArthur—but like William Manchester's equally tortured suggestion in *American Caesar,* that some kind of "input overload" might have been responsible, this also is pure speculation. No one will ever understand how an experienced officer of the highest rank could, in such an emergency, have handled his forces, and himself, so poorly.

Stimson was in his seventies in 1940 when Roosevelt appointed him secretary of war. A New York lawyer, he was law clerk for Elihu Root, who served as Theodore Roosevelt's secretary of war and from whom he learned many of his ideals of public service. Early on Stimson became known and respected as an excellent trial lawyer and, because of his association with Root, naturally identified with the Republican Party. In 1910 he ran unsuccessfully for governor of New York. In 1911 President Taft appointed him secretary of war. During World War I he left his lucrative law practice to serve in France as a colonel of artillery. Stimson's career followed a pattern of nearly continuous government service, and he became the perfect example of a modern, high-quality statesman, much like Root, the man after whom he patterned his own career. Following a succession of important diplomatic tasks, Stimson became secretary of state in Hoover's cabinet.

Like Marshall, Stimson had an awesome, imposing presence. Alike in many ways, both men radiated integrity and confidence and were seldom at a loss for the right course of action in nearly every circumstance. Roosevelt was said to have appointed Stimson to his cabinet to present something of a bipartisan flavor to his campaign for a third term, and if this was true he could hardly have found a better person.

Stimson was already known for his belligerent views on the war in Europe and toward Japan's ambitions. He had been arguing for giving Great Britain all possible aid short of actually entering the war, and for stiffening our negotiating position with Japan. Students of the last few days before Pearl Harbor consider him to have been one of the strongest supporters of Roosevelt's campaign to get the United States into the war against Hitler. Although he was recorded as pushing for more time to get the army into better readiness, it is almost certain that this position was basically window dressing. His diary's recording of the attack was significant: "We three [Hull, Stimson, and Knox] all thought we must fight if the British fought [in the Far East]. But now the Japs have solved the whole thing by attacking us directly in Hawaii."

Elsewhere he wrote in his diary,

> When the news first came that Japan had attacked us my first feeling was of relief that the indecision was over and that a crisis had come in a way which would unite all our people. This continued to be my dominant feeling in spite of the news of catastrophes which quickly developed. For I feel that this country united has practically nothing to fear; while the apathy and divisions stirred up by unpatriotic men have been hitherto very discouraging.

It is recorded that some weeks earlier Stimson had ebulliently informed Roosevelt that the situation in the Philippines had changed massively for the better, that we now "possessed the capability of bombing Tokyo from the Philippines," and that this would inevitably be "a strong lever toward containing Japan's military ambitions." He was referring to General Arnold's report of the prospective arrival there of the first group of B-17 bombers, for with a three thousand–mile combat range it was indeed possible for them to reach Tokyo, although they would need to fly on to Russian territory in the Vladivostok area to refuel for the flight back to base. Were munitions also to be available, they could carry out a bombing mission in the reverse direction as well. Having outlined this bombing plan, General Arnold even described the bombs he proposed to employ: incendiary types because of the "wood and paper" structure of the vast majority of Japanese houses. It was none of Arnold's concern, as he saw it, to make the necessary arrangements with Russia; these would be a diplomatic, not a military, duty. Apparently Stimson also thought this would present little difficulty, inasmuch as we had already associated ourselves with

Russia against Hitler. The Soviets would presumably be delighted to be our allies against the Japanese as well.

This proposal shows how little Stimson had thought about the realities of our relationship with the Soviet Union, for he should have understood—as everyone now well appreciates—that cooperation from the Soviets was entirely oriented to benefit them in their desperate war against Nazi Germany, and that Stalin would have seen no reason to risk a war with Japan at that time.

Japan had recently revised its campaign plans from a "northern strategy"—a thrust through the Manchukuo puppet, threatening Manchuria's coal and iron resources—to a "southern strategy" involving naval conquest of the southern East Indies and the oil resources there. This permitted Russia to remove troops from its eastern Siberian territories to reinforce its embattled troops around Moscow. Stalin's hope at this juncture obviously had to be that Japan would continue moving south, and Stimson should not logically have entertained any hope of Russian cooperation. The Soviet Union did not, in fact, begin hostilities against Japan until the final weeks of the war, in August 1945, and then only for its own profit. Stalin had promised to enter the Pacific war against Japan ninety days after the defeat of Germany and technically discharged his commitment almost to the day. Our analysis of his move was that by this time we did not need it; Japan was already prostrate, the atom bomb had just incinerated Hiroshima, and we had heard peace feelers from the Japanese through both Sweden and Switzerland. Additional peace overtures had also been made through Moscow, but of these Stalin gave us no information. Instead, he used the opportunity to seize territory from a Japan unable to defend it—and the outcome, in fact, was strenuous diplomatic pressure on our part to make him relinquish the most outrageous parts of the land grab.

Despite Arnold's eagerness, the contingent of planes was in fact insufficient in number to have anything like the effect he predicted. Possibly more could have been made of their presence if the paucity in their number could have been concealed from Japan—hardly likely in the Philippines. The actual outcome, of course, was just the opposite of Arnold's and Stimson's predictions.

Knox, like Stimson a Republican, was named secretary of the navy by Roosevelt on the same day as Stimson's appointment to the army post was announced. Both men were held to be "interventionists" by those opposed to our entry into World War II. Both had achieved prominence before World War I and had left their gainful posts, out of conscience, to fight in France when we entered the "Great War." Knox had owned and managed several newspapers by 1924, when he ran for governor of New Hampshire. Defeated, he was "ready to retire" soon thereafter but accepted an attractive offer from the Hearst papers instead. Declaring his independence from Hearst a few years later, he bought his own paper, the *Chicago Daily News.*

As publisher, Knox was uncompromising in his constant crusades for reform, was known as a "big navy" man, was strongly anti–New Deal, and became the Republican nominee for vice president in 1936. Not long after the Republicans lost that contest he began to support some of Roosevelt's international moves. Shortly after the beginning of World War II he was advocating all possible help to the Allies and must have seemed a natural bipartisan appointment to the post of navy secretary.

The overall performance of Knox as secretary of the navy is to a large degree overshadowed by the more prominent career of his undersecretary, James Forrestal, who succeeded him. Knox was known, all the same, as an effective secretary, one of the few officials able to bridle Admiral King, the difficult COMINCH. In 1943, in a moment of cool relations because of King's advocacy of Navy Department reorganization, King sent Knox a memorandum recommending "no book or article dealing with our submarine combat operations be published." Knox, recognizing his opportunity, responded with a directive immediately canceling any orders King had given concerning public relations. "To put the matter bluntly and briefly," he wrote, "I know I have the authority and I know I have the experience to handle, without assistance, the question of Public Relations of the Navy [except for] questions of security. . . ." Paolo Coletta, who noted this episode in *American Secretaries of the Navy* (Annapolis: Naval Institute Press, 1980), went on to say that although differences between Knox and King remained, for the rest of his tenure King deferred to Knox on public-relations policy.

Knox resembled Stimson in his dedication to doing his job right and exceeded all cabinet members in his travels to see the actual conditions of the forces for which he was responsible. His decision to visit Pearl Harbor after the Japanese attack was, characteristically, made within hours of his learning of it, and he took off at 8 A.M. the next day. He returned to Washington only a few days later and gave Roosevelt a typed report of many pages that same evening. Unfortunately, this could not be published because it referred to our ability to decrypt Japanese messages, and it evidently was less than pleasing to the president because it stated baldly that the intelligence available in Washington, which would have put Pearl Harbor on alert, had not been sent to the commanders there (Knox had still not gotten to the bottom of Saturday night's missing warning message, about which more will appear in chapter 6). A rewritten version, deleting any mention of Magic, or intelligence that should have been sent to the field, omitting all reference to a missing message, and including a statement that the Roberts Commission was being formed to make a thorough investigation, was released later.

Turner, a member of the Naval Academy class of 1908, was a rear admiral in charge of "war plans" for CNO Stark. No one would ever have applied any other sobriquet to Turner than "Terrible," the title by which he was known for most of his adult life. It was not, however, a nickname. So far as is known, no one ever called him "Terrible" in the same way they might have called Stark "Betty" (granted that only contemporaries, classmates, or friendly superiors had that privilege); "Terrible Turner" was a title, not a name, essentially used behind his back but truly expressive of the man. Terrible he was, probably even more so than the legendary "always in a rage" Admiral King. Turner seemed to be fearless, did not care whom he hurt, and possessed the means of bringing almost anyone to heel.

Numerous descriptions of his operations in old Main Navy on Constitution Avenue, kept in service long past its original demolition date because of its proximity to the White House power center, have come to light. Stark was believed by many to be entirely under Turner's thumb. He depended heavily upon him, turned to him unofficially as well as officially (as head of war plans) for advice, and was reported to have said that he always warmed a little when he thought of Turner.

There can be little doubt that Turner expected to become the next CNO after Stark vacated the job, just as there is no doubt that if anyone got it in his place he would have had a terribly difficult time unless, for career reasons such as assignment to a top sea command, Turner might choose to wait one more turn of the "slate," the top-secret projection of the senior flag-officer assignments. By all accounts an exceptionally able officer, articulate, determined, hard-driving, "Terrible" Turner was reputed also to be a hard drinker, if not an alcoholic. This alone should have disqualified him for high rank, especially during time of war. He was in overall command of the amphibious invasion of Guadalcanal, and there were reports that although he was a capable leader when sober, there were times of failure through drink as well. When the four cruisers were sunk at Savo Island during the early morning hours of 9 August 1942, it was said among the junior officers present that the debacle occurred at least partly because Turner was so inebriated at a late-night conference he had called aboard his flagship, the *McCawley,* that the senior officers attending spent their time trying to sober him up instead of attending to business! In this author's opinion, he did not well fulfill the responsibilities of naval or military leadership and should never have been allowed in the high positions he attained.

The opinion that Edwin T. Layton had of Turner is an eye-opener. It was Layton's collaboration with his close friend Rochefort of Station Hypo (both of them were commanders in those days) that gave Nimitz the vital information enabling him to ambush Yamamoto's immensely superior fleet at the Battle of Midway and turn the course of the war. In the 1980s, feeling that he had finally been released from his wartime pledge not to violate the secrecy of Magic and the other intelligence inputs to the successful outcome of the war, Layton began to write about his experiences. He died before he could complete his self-appointed task, but his book was published posthumously in 1985 and has formed a considerable portion of what I have had to say in this one. According to Layton, the arrogant, self-directed, self-aggrandizing Turner may have been more responsible for the Pearl Harbor debacle than anyone else in the military, or even in the entire country. We shall, of course, never know for sure, but what Layton had to say about him early in his book bears repeating verbatim. Describing an incident that occurred in the wardroom of the USS *South Dakota* on the night of the Japanese surrender ceremony in Tokyo Bay, he wrote:

> The war had made "Terrible" Turner a naval legend. As commander of Nimitz's amphibious forces, he had executed all our landing operations from Guadalcanal to Iwo Jima with brilliant distinction. But few who worked closely with him in these operations could forget—or forgive—his stormy temper, overbearing ego, and celebrated bouts with the bottle. From the manner in which he entered the wardroom that evening, it was evident that he was stoked up.

"Did you see the navy department's release about the findings of the Pearl Harbor court of inquiry?" he demanded, his booming voice stopping all conversation. "They said that goddamned Kimmel had all the information and didn't do anything about it. They should hang him higher than a kite!"

Turner continued to hold forth. Time and again he said, "Kimmel was given all that information and didn't do anything about it. . . ."

I sat there stunned. I knew that what he was saying was not only untrue, but a monstrous slur on my former commander-in-chief. . . . Having been Admiral Kimmel's fleet intelligence officer on 7 December 1941, and having testified at all but one of the secret wartime inquiries into Pearl Harbor, I knew that Turner's bald assertions were scandalously untrue.

Responsibility for this failure bore heavily on Turner who, in his capacity as chief of war plans, had been the forceful junior member of the triumvirate who virtually ran the office of naval operations throughout 1941. He had arrogated to himself many of the traditional functions of the office of naval intelligence, and to protect his errors of judgment and conceal the collective culpability of the most senior officers in the navy, Turner had played a leading part in the campaign to pillory a fellow officer and fine commander of the fleet. . . .

For all his lustrous war record as an amphibious commander, Admiral Turner that evening had lived up to his other reputation as an opinionated, stubborn fool. There he was, hanging Kimmel by his fingernails, when the truth—as we both well knew—was that Turner had failed to relay to the fleet commander at Pearl Harbor the vital intelligence that might have averted the disaster. Despite his loudmouthed bluster in the wardroom of the *South Dakota,* the former director of war plans was later obliged to admit under oath that his assertion was wrong [at the JCC Hearings after the war], but he was never to concede his own errors of judgment. . . .

Turner's behavior was unforgiving—and unforgivable. One of the first things I learned on entering the navy was the primary principle of command, that an officer bears personal responsibility for ensuring that his orders are carried out. Turner, instead, blamed his subordinates, maintaining that they had assured him that Admiral Kimmel was "receiving the same decrypted information" available in Washington. A simple check of his own signal logs would have revealed that we had *not*

> received some of the most essential and important pieces of intelligence that became available to the navy department during four months preceding the Japanese attack. . . .
>
> The internal struggle among the CNO staff amounted to a progressive takeover by the abrasive war plans director of many of the functions and responsibilities of Stark himself. "There had grown up in the office of the chief of naval operations a coterie," explained [Captain Arthur H.] McCollum, who as ONI Far East section head observed the struggle at close quarters. "Stark, Ingersoll (the Assistant CNO), and Turner became a sort of 'triumvirate.' Turner would bring in the ideas and the other two would endorse them—frequently without referring to anyone else on the staff."
>
> As in all triumvirates, one member exerted a dominating influence. In this case it was Richmond Kelly Turner, who aggressively promoted his own intelligence evaluations and made arbitrary decisions on their dissemination, knowing that he could count on Stark to rubber-stamp them.

Throughout the thousands of pages of Pearl Harbor testimony the reader will see continual reference to Admiral Turner, and almost every time the context is in reference to his refusal to send warning messages to the Pacific. Basically untrained in intelligence and ignorant of almost everything Japanese, he nevertheless arrogated to himself, because of his high rank and tremendous sense of self-importance, overall knowledge of and interpretation of all intelligence concerning Japan. Whenever someone happened to hold an opinion differing from his own "off the top of the head" ideas, he would not only insist on his way but also on numerous occasions severely discipline those who were in opposition to his views. The record is replete with his positively stated misjudgments, such as the famous one in which he stated unequivocally that Pearl Harbor possessed a Purple machine and therefore "knows everything we know"—a palpable untruth possibly stated under the influence of hard drink. Having been involved in the redirection of Pearl Harbor's Purple machine to Bletchley Park, Turner can only have astonishingly forgotten it, or must otherwise have been speaking untruthfully in a matter of the greatest importance.

The reader cannot help feeling that had Turner not been in the picture, adequate warning might have had some chance of getting to Pearl Harbor. But Turner's ego was so great that he could never see this. Many others seconded Layton's evaluation.

The final principal player who must be considered was the Japanese commander of the Combined Fleet, Adm. Isoroku Yamamoto. Yamamoto's extensive experience in America (studies at Harvard, naval attaché in Washington, member of Japan's delegation to the post–World War I naval treaty sessions) gave him a good appreciation of America's full, if latent, power. This caused him strongly to oppose any move that might bring U.S. strength into full play against his country. In fact, he wrote numerous memos to government officials as well as to his colleagues in the military, in which he both opposed the Tripartite Treaty with Germany and pleaded for restraint toward the United States. Agawa reproduced one of these urgent messages in his biography (page 186):

> A war between Japan and the United States would be a major calamity for the world, and for Japan it would mean, after several years of war already, acquiring yet another powerful enemy—an extremely perilous matter for the nation. If, after Japan and America had inflicted serious wounds on each other, the Soviet Union or Germany should step in with an eye to world hegemony, what country would be able to check it? . . . It is necessary therefore that both Japan and America should seek every means to avoid a direct clash, and Japan should under no circumstances conclude an alliance with Germany.

A year before the attack, however, Yamamoto became reconciled to the inevitability that when Japan's policy makers turned their military attention to the south of China, as opposed to the north on which they had concentrated for the past decade, such a war would result. The debate between proponents of the "northern movement" and those advocating one to the south had occupied Japanese militarists for years and had also separated army from navy, industries primarily in need of raw materials (iron ore, copper, tin, rubber) from those needing mainly fuel (oil and its derivatives), and, indeed, most segments of Japan's industrial, economic, and policy-making population.

A southern movement, defined as a conquest of southern China, Hong Kong, Singapore, and the Dutch East Indies with their oil resources, would involve war with England and Holland, threat to Australia, and almost doubtless, war with the United States. The war in Europe gave Japan's militarist policy makers what they saw as an opportunity to move south at little cost. Yamamoto, contrary to most ambitious naval officers of his time, opposed this, for he correctly appreciated America's tremendous industrial potential, almost light-years ahead of Japan's. Nonetheless, as commander of Japan's Combined Fleet, a post to which he was appointed in 1938, it was his obligation to plan for the contingency.

As Yamamoto saw it, if Japan decided on war with the United States, the best move would be to inactivate the U.S. Fleet for the six months Japan's high command estimated would be needed to settle affairs in the Far East. Then, helped by America's strong isolationist faction, Japan would negotiate peace with a discouraged United States that still wanted peace more than anything else. Shortly after taking over his new post, Yamamoto, therefore, began to apply all his considerable powers, both personal and official, to conjure up a way to put the U.S. Pacific Fleet out of action. His thinking was right so far as it went, and he succeeded in his aim—but he failed to realize that America's reaction to the sort of mortal insult he proposed would not be very different from what Japan's would have been were the situation reversed.

Like all officers of the Imperial Japanese Navy, Yamamoto venerated Admiral Togo, the victor of Japan's naval war with Russia in 1904–1905. Togo had initiated that war by a surprise attack on Russia's Port Arthur, Russia's premier naval base in the Pacific, on the tip of the Kwan-Tung Peninsula at the top of the Yellow Sea. There had been no declaration of war, but the Japanese minister to Moscow two days earlier had delivered a note breaking off relations. While the Czar's staff was still debating what this might portend, the Russian fleet at Port Arthur received the blow from which it never recovered. Togo did not achieve his entire objective, but the damage to Russia's morale and fleet was decisive. It contributed heavily to the 1905 revolution in that country and thus led to the decisive one of 1917.

Yamamoto thought to do the same at Pearl Harbor. Pearl Harbor was, as he saw it, the key to American naval morale in the Pacific, especially with more and more attention going to Europe and the Atlantic war. Knock out the Pacific Fleet and, much like decadent Czarist Russia, an America more concerned with its own problems than those across the huge Pacific Ocean would be happy to cut its losses and leave that side of the world to Japan. It was an egregious error in thinking, but one popular in a prewar society that praised the murder of too moderate officials by zealous young army officers. Early on, before the end of 1940, Yamamoto assembled his most highly regarded staff officers and began planning an attack on the U.S. Fleet in its Pearl Harbor base.

Like Togo, Yamamoto also insisted on an unequivocal rupture of friendly relations prior to the first overt action by his forces, but because of the much greater speed of communication in 1941, he agreed to only a half-hour time lapse between rupture and all-out attack, instead of the two days given Russia thirty-seven years earlier. His statement made soon after the attack—"I fear we have roused a sleeping giant"—one of the most accurate predictions of his life, may have resulted from his discovery that Japan's foreign ministry had failed in this, to him, critically important obligation; but his realization of how terribly the surprise had backfired, how it had fused American determination to destroy the Japan that had brought it about, is its more likely genesis. Whatever hope he might have once held that an end of hostilities could be negotiated before America threw its full weight against his country vanished in 1942, probably with the smothering defeat at Midway. Another still later and equally well remembered remark shows his feeling at this stage: "[To win this war now] we'll have to dictate peace on the steps of the White House!"

Parenthetically, as must have been typical of wars since the beginning, truth was one of the first casualties. I believe I first heard this statement attributed to Yamamoto in January 1942, and the rendition was simple and direct: "We shall dictate peace on the steps of the White House!" It gave us another reason for hating the "Japs" and Yamamoto. The actual quote came from a letter to Yamamoto's rightist acquaintance Sasakawa Ryoichi, in January 1941. According to Agawa, Yamamoto wrote, after some philosophic discussion of unrealistic policies in which he showed himself not at all sanguine about ultimate victory,

> However, if there should be a war between Japan and America, then our aim, of course, ought not to be Guam or the Philippines, nor Hawaii or Hong Kong, but a capitulation at the White House, in Washington itself. I wonder whether the politicians of the day really have the willingness to make the sacrifices, and have the confidence, that this would entail?

Japan was no more immune to the demands of propaganda than we were. The letter was published during the war as a morale builder, minus the final sentence, and was picked up in America for the same reason, with opposite connotations. To us the author was a fanatical warmonger, worthy of the same detestation as Tojo, and not until after the war was over did anyone look up what he had actually said or written.

As the bad news accumulated, the United States announced that it would accept nothing but unconditional surrender from all the Axis powers, most especially Germany and Japan. As the full implications of the "Europe first" strategy sank in, Yamamoto realized that America in 1941 was very different from decadent Czarist Russia in 1904. He began to understand that he had led his country into an irretrievable, first-magnitude disaster.

Togo could have done no better, despite the mythology surrounding his name and attainments. As Yamamoto began to contemplate the magnitude of the oncoming damage to his country and people, he must have started to see that Japan could not win the war he had begun so dramatically. He had hoped for a dispirited America willing to negotiate to avoid more fighting; what he had accomplished, he now saw beyond doubt, was exactly the opposite: an enraged America whose scruples—whatever they might have been—against the total destruction of Japan and everything it stood for, had been wiped out in a single moment of time. A more moderate southern movement, bypassing the Philippines and leaving Guam alone, would have been far better for Japan.

Suicide, the venerated and formal *seppuku* (hara kiri), was the traditional samurai warrior's way to atone to the emperor for such a grievous error. But Yamamoto's position as fleet commander made suicide impossible. Anything of this nature would have been a confession of defeat at a critical time. Americans with little understanding of the samurai ideal ("live every day in readiness to die") have suggested that Yamamoto might have actually arranged his own death "in order not to have to confess failure to the emperor." Such an idea is a simplistic interpretation of the samurai code. A commander would not desert his troops by committing suicide while the battle was still going on. But if he were to be killed himself, in the front line of battle, he might thereby fulfill his duties to the emperor and depart an untenable situation in an honorable way, even in a peaceful frame of mind. This might be especially true if he foresaw a disaster for which he could conceive of no favorable solution.

Some historians lean therefore to the theory that Yamamoto simply ceased to take other than ordinary precautions for his own safety and allowed fate, in the form of enemy combat action, to take its own course. There are those who argue that Horatio Nelson, the great British admiral, may have done something similar 138 years earlier, though for very different reasons.

Yamamoto's biographer Agawa suggests as much—carefully hedged, as all such unproved ideas must be. In the last few pages of Agawa's book, one finds the following:

> Tayui Yuzuru (an old friend of Yamamoto) . . . chief of staff of the China Area Fleet . . . remembers (Admiral) Yoshida Zengo . . . commander in chief . . . telling him one day that he was sure Yamamoto wanted to die, since he had said things in a recent letter that could only be interpreted that way. . . .
>
> According to Matsunaga Keisuke, former aide to Admiral Yonai (who was) then navy minister and . . . well aware how quick Yamamoto had been to sense the way things were going—though Yamamoto's death might not have been suicide, (he) had deliberately set a term to his own life.
>
> "I feel that he set out, if not with the intention of dying, at least quite willing to do so," says Kondo Yasuichiro (pre-war naval attaché to London). "After all, he deliberately threw himself into what, in the army, would be considered the thick of the enemy's fire."

Yamamoto probably did not know how thoroughly the United States had invaded Japan's military codes and may well have thought the one in which his itinerary to Rabaul and Bougainville had been laid out in such detail was secure, but some Japanese historians have their doubts even on this point. In line with his decision to abandon himself to fate he might simply have ceased to concern himself with details (though one should expect an alert staff to handle such matters for him). At all events, no special precautions were taken, and the routine coded message was sent with such high precedence that it got the immediate attention of the code-breakers. An intercepting flight of sixteen long-range P-38s from Guadalcanal arrived over Bougainville at the same time as Admiral Yamamoto's flight was scheduled to arrive from Rabaul. His six escort aircraft were engaged by the twelve interceptors, the designated four P-38s zeroed in on the two transport planes being escorted—and both transports were shot down. All in Yamamoto's plane were killed. His body, in full field uniform, his left hand holding his ancestral samurai sword, was found the next day, still belted into his seat. He had been struck several times by machine-gun fire from the attacking plane and died before the plane hit the ground.

Americans could not appreciate the effect of Yamamoto's death upon Japanese morale, not even by imagining the loss of Admiral Nimitz under similar circumstances, for absent from our culture was the samurai idea of death in combat as a supremely important final message.

In September, as already mentioned, Yamamoto reportedly told Prince Konoye, then prime minister, "If you insist on my going ahead I will give them hell for a year or a year and a half, but can guarantee nothing after that!" As it happened, the year-and-a-half time limit applied to Yamamoto's own life as well. By April 1943 Imperial Japan's hopes of getting anything worthwhile out of the war it had so dramatically started were dead, and so was he.

6

The Night of 6–7 December 1941

The climax came on 6 December. As described in chapter 3, Magic decoded and translated a message informing the Japanese ambassadors in Washington that a "very long" message in fourteen parts, written in English and containing a response to our hard-nosed reply of 26 November to the "A" and "B" proposals, was being sent. It was to be put into "nicely drafted form" and held until delivery was directed. This "pilot" message, as it came to be called, reiterated that although Japan considered all negotiations ruptured, the embassy was to be careful not to give that impression.

The United States had the pilot message in hand before it was delivered to the Japanese ambassadors.

A watch was immediately instituted for the fourteen-part message, and the first thirteen parts were decoded as fast as they came in. The code-breakers instantly noted that the text was in English. Everyone closely clued into the Japanese scene considered that significant, for the only possible explanation must have been to avoid error in an embassy translation. But there was no time, just then, it being already late on Saturday evening, for the thoughtful consideration the unusual situation deserved. The few code-breakers were working at top speed, fully aware of the urgency. War, they knew, might be declared in this very message they were working on.

The thirteen parts did not come in numbered sequence but were identified in their headings. When the first thirteen parts had been collated and it was evident that there was a delay in the fourteenth part, which must therefore be of transcendent importance, the Magic watch officers decided on their own to send out the thirteen parts and follow later with the fourteenth as soon as received.

Each service made its own Magic deliveries. Routine navy deliveries were to the White House, the navy secretary, and the CNO. The extraordinary security surrounding Magic restricted even knowledge that it existed; only persons holding the requisite top-level clearances were permitted to handle it. Therefore, and ridiculously, the translators themselves were required to carry the vitally important intercepts around the nation's capital. Thus it was that on the night of 6 December a physically exhausted Lieutenant Commander Kramer, already some twenty-four hours on the job, enlisted his wife, now genuinely worried about his health, to drive him to the more distant delivery points. It being by this time rather late at night, the deliveries had to be made to local residences instead of government offices (except for Roosevelt himself, it was required that delivery could be made only, and directly, to cleared individuals). The navy's intelligence chief, Rear Adm. Theodore S. Wilkinson, that Saturday night happened to be giving a dinner party at his home. His guests included his opposite number in the army, Brigadier General Miles, the presidential naval aide Capt. John R. Beardall, and two French naval officers. Excusing themselves from the others, the highest intelligence officers of our two services thus simultaneously received the first thirteen parts of this supremely important message before midnight of 6 December, read them together, and exchanged views as to their meaning.

Neither Wilkinson nor Miles saw anything special in the lengthy sequential bloc of messages in formal diplomatic language. By the pilot message they knew there was to be a final fourteenth part yet to come, and they should have noted the statement that all fourteen parts were to be sent in English. This was so contrary to the usual practice that they ought to have suspected a special reason. But Wilkinson and Miles, intelligence chiefs though they were, had only recently been assigned to that post. They had high rank but little experience in the arcane nuances of intelligence. They thought nothing of the fact that Japan *had encoded this lengthy message in the English language, not in Japanese!*

Had they, in navy parlance, hoisted that point aboard, they could hardly have failed to give it far more attention than they in fact did. They even might have made some useful guesses had they noted the unusual smoothness of the language; but one of the criticisms sometimes leveled at Lieutenant Commander Kramer, the navy's top Japanese translator, was that he frequently spent inordinate time in perfecting the texts of messages that were his responsibility, instead of simply passing them along in rougher form. This perception of Kramer's excessive perfectionism, which he of course found unnecessary on 6 December, may have inadvertently closed off one of the avenues by which our top officers might have gained a better sense of warning.

At about 9:15 P.M. on 6 December, Lt. Lester R. Schulz, on duty in the White House, brought the first thirteen parts of the message to the president in a locked pouch. As it turned out, this was several hours before Kurusu and Nomura were even aware of it. Schulz's standing instructions were to keep his eyes on the papers that had been in the pouch, to wait for and make sure that all of them had been returned and locked once more in the pouch, and then to return the locked pouch to the safe in the White House Map Room, to be picked up by the courier who had brought it. Therefore, he remained standing unobtrusively in the president's favorite upstairs study, saw him carefully read the papers, and saw him hand them to Harry Hopkins, the only other person present, who began to read them attentively.

Schulz was very careful with his testimony before the JCC. He heard Roosevelt say to Hopkins something that sounded like "This means war!" Hopkins replied to the effect that, "It's too bad we can't strike the first blow and prevent a surprise." At this point the president supposedly said, "No, we can't do that. We are a democracy and a peaceful people." Then, raising his voice slightly, he said, "But we have a good record!"

It is known that after the lieutenant left the room, in the neighborhood of 10 P.M., the president attempted to reach CNO Stark by telephone but, discovering he was at the theater, directed he not be paged for fear of bringing attention to the fact and worrying the people present. Instead, he directed a message be left at Stark's quarters for him to call the White House when he returned home, which he did, sometime around 11:30 P.M. Surprisingly, Roosevelt did not call General Marshall, despite Marshall's accepted status as his primary military adviser; testimony is clear on this point. Nor, so far as is known, did he call any members of his cabinet, specifically his secretaries of state, war, and the navy.

It was illogical not to call Marshall. Nor is a convincing explanation made of the failure to deliver to the army chief the first thirteen parts of what must have obviously seemed a supremely important message (the Magic operatives thought so, at any rate, but they were not high on anyone's totem pole). Marshall later testified several times that he could not recall where he was on the night of the sixth, thought he must have spent it at home in his quarters, and Sunday morning went for a long horseback ride where no one could find him. Much was made of all this in the JCC hearings, but no one pressed Marshall to explain. This was in marked contrast to the browbeating experienced by Kimmel, Short, and some of their supporting witnesses, most particularly Safford, on nearly every question asked. No satisfactory explanation of Marshall's movements has ever surfaced. No one brought up the story of his having spent much of the morning in the State Department, and this remains only an unsubstantiated rumor.

Marshall, famed for his photographic memory, never explained his extraordinary memory lapse. The 7 December issue of the morning *Washington Times Herald,* however, reported that on the previous evening Marshall was guest of honor for dinner at a reunion of World War I veterans at the University Club on 16th Street, not far from the White House. It is possible that, like Stark, he found a call from the White House waiting for him when he returned home. Or, conscientious and thoughtful person that he was, he might have checked in with the White House on his way home from the University Club. Being but a few blocks away and fully informed of the critical Japanese situation, for him this would have been both logical and easy, and had he done so, the White House Map Room would undoubtedly have suggested that his presence might be needed "upstairs." This is speculative, but it would explain why Roosevelt did not place a call for him.

It is not possible to conceive of the chief executive of any nation not calling an immediate council of his top advisers upon getting the sort of information Roosevelt had just received. Particularly is this true when the potential enemy is known to have started hostilities in the past with surprise attacks upon important bases. It was clearly Roosevelt's duty to assure himself that all was in as good readiness as it could be, and there is testimony (but apparently not good enough testimony to satisfy all historians) that the army and navy chiefs and Secretaries Stimson and Knox joined Roosevelt and Hopkins in the president's study around midnight. The proof is not ironclad, but Morgenstern made reference to the meeting in 1947. So did Toland and Layton, and the principal source of the story was Frank Knox. According to his account, given to his close friend and confidant James R. Stahlman (newspaper publisher, prewar president of the American Newspaper Publishers Association, naval reserve captain at ONI, who described the meeting in writing to numerous persons over the years), he (Knox), Stimson, Marshall, Stark, Hopkins, Captain Beardall, and one or two other aides brought by their superiors gathered at the White House sometime after 9 P.M., and the senior ones (the two cabinet officers and the two chiefs of service, plus the omnipresent Hopkins) remained until nearly 4 A.M. of the seventh, awaiting receipt of the final part of the message from Japan. Some of the principals present expected this to be a declaration of war, but others were said to have argued that such a declaration was contrary to Japan's known policy.

The men had Roosevelt's copy of the first thirteen parts of the Japanese message and a chart of the far Pacific Ocean areas (this chart still exists, bearing penciled notations of the locations of Japanese naval and troop forces on 6 December 1941). There were substantial reports about the movements of these forces, and it appeared certain that Japan would soon strike in Southeast Asia, probably in the area of the most accessible oil. Yamamoto had succeeded in focusing the attention of our leadership away from Pearl Harbor. Stimson and Marshall, as well as Roosevelt, reportedly said several times that hostilities in Southeast Asia would put us into the war and that we must "make sure the Japs strike first." The White House vigil lasted until nearly four in the morning, ending when it seemed that the fourteenth part of the long Japanese reply was not to be forthcoming. Roosevelt, it can be surmised, probably enjoined those present to "forget all about this meeting" and directed that the Secret Service, housekeeping, and White House gate logs be expunged.

Were it possible to confirm that the secretaries of war and the navy, with the senior officers of their two services, had had this reported meeting with Roosevelt, much of the uncertainty about the causes of our unalertness at Pearl Harbor would not exist. Instead of blaming our commanders there because our forces were observing normal Sunday morning routine after strenuous training exercises rather than being at battle stations, responsibility would without question land on Washington officialdom.

There can be no doubt that Roosevelt and his top advisers fully expected war to break out, but there is no proof that any of them expected this to happen with a surprise attack on Pearl Harbor. All the known circumstances point to our expectation of a surprise attack by Japan somewhere early in December. The time was not precisely fixed, but Parker, in *Pearl Harbor Revisited,* found in Admiral Hart's "Narrative of Events, Asiatic Fleet," the comment, "Guess war is just around the corner, but I think I'll go to a movie." The next day Hart wrote in the same diary, "It was no surprise by a matter of 18 hours."

Locationwise, the best guess was the Far East, almost certainly Borneo, where oil fields, producing wells, and refineries would be irresistible to oil-hungry Japan. A major portion of the Japanese fleet was known to be proceeding in that direction already, and there seemed little hope for the Netherlands East Indies and its principal island of Java. The British were afraid for the great harbor and city of Singapore, on the tip of the Malay Peninsula, and had sent two of their biggest and most powerful warships there to reinforce its defenses. They had, unfortunately, no air defense with them; HMS *Illustrious,* the carrier designated to accompany the two big gunships, had run aground and holed her bottom, and was in dry dock in the United States. Quiet talks had, however, been held with U.S. defense officials in the hope of arranging for assistance should Singapore be attacked. For our part, the major concern was the Philippines.

Privately, our military leaders conceded that neither Singapore nor the Philippines could be held against a determined onslaught by Japan. There seems to have been no thought anywhere—not in Washington, not in Hawaii—that Japan's six most powerful fleet aircraft carriers, three-quarters of its entire available force, which had dropped out of sight, could be anywhere but in port, preparing to join in the southward movement of the Imperial Japanese Navy.

And yet, as we've seen, there were indications of unusual Japanese interest in Pearl Harbor. There was the strange "bomb plot" message, and there were stories that officers advocating it be sent to the Pearl Harbor commanders were summarily ordered to stop talking about it, even threatened with disciplinary action for their temerity. Other officers—Admiral Wilkinson was one—were prevented from sending messages they had prepared. Admiral Turner's name is the most frequently mentioned as decisive on this point, as was the raging anger he visited upon anyone who questioned his decision on any subject, even those not under his purview.

Like Marshall, Admiral Stark also "forgot" he had been called by the president on that momentous night, and he so testified before the JCC; but for him, forgetfulness was less easy because after the hearings had been completed his memory was unexpectedly refreshed. On 6 December 1941 the Starks had taken a dinner guest (Cdr. Harold Krick, a former aide with whom he had maintained an abiding friendship) and his wife to the theater. The CNO made no mention of this to the JCC, or of receiving a White House call. The last open hearing of the JCC had been early in April 1946, after which, on 23 May, a pro forma meeting was held to close the record. Only two days later the Kricks again visited the

Starks, and Krick privately reminded Stark that when they had returned to the CNO's quarters (the house now assigned to the vice president), the duty steward had reported the call and Stark had excused himself to return it. This reminder restored Stark's memory, according to his account, and after careful and lengthy thought about it, in the early morning hours of 26 May the former CNO wrote a letter in longhand to the JCC chairman, Senator Alben Barkley, asking permission to correct his testimony.

Because Stark was scheduled to travel to England for an award ceremony in his honor, the JCC was reconvened for him on Memorial Day 1946, the day before his scheduled departure, with only a few committee members present, all of them objecting to the unprecedented reopening of the hearings after they had been closed and to the unusual timing of the reconvening, on a national holiday. (This was, incidentally, the reason for the slightly unusual wording of the record, which reads, "Final adjournment on 31 May.") Stark told of the White House call but could not remember what he said to the president, nor what Roosevelt said to him (he called the president often, he said, sometimes several times a day, and he could not keep in mind all the things they discussed). The JCC, evidently feeling that communications with the chief executive were privileged, did not query him on this point. Whether or not the committee members had heard the rumors about a midnight meeting in the White House, which they must have, no one saw fit to question anyone on this, either. Surprisingly, Krick, the third party, was the one questioned, very gently, about the telephone call. He testified that he knew only that Stark had left the group for a short time and that, while he presumed his superior had gone to call the White House, Stark had merely commented, on his return, something to the effect that "things were heating up a bit."

The fourteenth part was delivered from the code-breakers at about midnight to Lt. Col. Carlisle C. Dusenbury, assistant to Colonel Bratton. Bratton had directed him to wait for it and upon receipt have it immediately delivered to the army chief of staff. The tone of the fourteenth part was sharper than that of any of the previous thirteen but did not seem sensational to the tired Dusenbury, who testified that he made no effort to show it to anyone, simply put it on top of the file, designated a copy for the navy in accordance with procedure, and secured the office. At 7:30 on Sunday morning, 7 December, Colonel Bratton arrived, read the assembled fourteen-part message, according to him "blew his stack" at Dusenbury for not following orders, but decided it was "the formal statement" of what they already knew, not a declaration of war or anything earth shaking after all. Despite his displeasure with his assistant for not having tried to get it to Marshall the previous midnight, now that the morning had arrived he decided routine distribution was adequate. At this moment, Bratton later testified, he was handed the "delivery" message stipulating that the Japanese ambassadors formally deliver the composite response to the secretary of state at 1 P.M. that day.

Like the pilot message, but unlike all fourteen parts of the principal message, the delivery message was in Japanese and had consequently needed translation to English. Bratton was not privy to the motives and objectives swirling in the minds of the men conducting our top-level international diplomacy, but he did see something ominous in Japan's juxtaposition of English and Japanese in this way. It was clear that matters of importance were in the wind. He claimed later that he saw no potential threat to Pearl Harbor, but the unprecedented emphasis on when the message was to be delivered hinted at an attack somewhere in the Pacific at that time, or shortly afterward. That, and the use of English in the main message, galvanized Bratton into action, as he put it.

After his final deliveries on the night of the sixth, Lieutenant Commander Kramer had a few hours of sleep and returned to work, over his wife's strenuous objections, at 7:30 A.M. Sunday. There he found his copy of the fourteen-part message left for him by Dusenbury and immediately made folders for the White House, the State Department, and Admiral Wilkinson (who, he knew, would take care of deliveries to Stark and Knox). His three office drops being only a few blocks apart, he walked and jogged the entire distance—partly, it may be surmised, to reinvigorate himself somewhat, and partly because of the urgency he felt. When he got back to the Navy Department he found the delivery message waiting for him and, like Bratton, saw it must have special significance and should be delivered at once. While more folders were being prepared, he made a time chart of the Pacific, noted that 1 P.M. in Washington would be 7:30 Sunday morning in Hawaii, and observed that this was the time the big ships, just returned from exercises, would be serving their crews a relatively relaxed Sunday in-port breakfast. As soon as the folders were ready he ran

A happy holiday on board. Cdr. Husband E. Kimmel, executive officer of the USS *Arkansas* (BB 33) in 1919, with his two older sons dressed in sailor suits, Thomas, 5, on the left, and Manning, 7, on the right. Manning graduated from the U.S. Naval Academy in 1935 and was lost during the war in command of the submarine *Robalo* (SS 273), when that boat failed to return from patrol near the Philippines. Tom also went to Annapolis, in the class of 1936, also served in submarines, and survived the war. The third and youngest boy, Edward, could not pass the eye exam for entry to Annapolis but did, nevertheless, serve in the navy during WWII. (Courtesy Thomas K. Kimmel)

Captain Kimmel in about 1934, as commanding officer of the USS *New York*. (U.S. Naval Historical Center NH 48589)

Another happy moment. Rear Admiral Kimmel in late 1940 or early 1941, about to ascend to four-star rank and relieve Admiral Richardson in command of the U.S. Fleet, the most prestigious afloat command our navy had to offer. (U.S. Naval Institute)

◀ When Admiral Nagumo's fliers came over the mountains north and west of Pearl Harbor, the clouds parted almost as if the heavens also were on the side of Japan, according to some personal accounts, and the storied base lay exposed and benign before them. The attack signal was given immediately, the separate flights of attacking planes—horizontal bombers, dive-bombers, torpedo planes, fighters—split into their designated sections, started their dives, and Pearl Harbor was peaceful no more. (U.S. Navy)

◀ The torpedo-carrying planes, destined to wreak the most damage to the U.S. Fleet, came in over the submarine base, seen at lower right under the 120-foot-tall escape-training tower, dropped down low to the water as they passed the navy yard, off to the left, and had a clear shot at the battleships moored off Ford Island, upper left in the photo. The torpedoes, specially fitted not to make an initial deep dive, had to be dropped at very slow speed and from a very low height. The configuration of Pearl Harbor facilitated this. (U.S. Naval Historical Center NH 54301)

A photograph taken from a Japanese attacking aircraft at the height of the attack. Shock waves can be seen eddying from the damaged battleships. Oil is spouting from the side of the stricken *West Virginia,* already beginning to list to port. The list was corrected by counterflooding, and the ship finally settled on the bottom, terribly damaged on her port side but on an even keel. Ahead of her, beginning her own fatal list to port, the *Oklahoma* is also gushing oil, while forward of her is the gasoline-laden tanker *Neosho,* fortunately not a target of attack and just beginning to pull clear. At far right of the picture a portion of the hull of the *California* can be seen, also belching oil out of her stricken port side. In the middle distance, smoke from burning aircraft and repair facilities at Hickam Field is visible. This is the photo so thoroughly described by Burl Burlingame in *Advance Force—Pearl Harbor* (see references). At center left are some splashes in the water, and just to their right, silhouetted against its own wash, appears a small, low, black object greatly resembling a Japanese two-man submarine. Wakes in the water emanating from it indicate that it may have fired its two torpedoes at the *Oklahoma* and *West Virginia.* At lower left the *Nevada,* the only battleship able to get under way on that terrible Sunday morning, is still moored to her concrete bollards, and just ahead of her is the doomed *Arizona,* already in the berth she will occupy forevermore. (U.S. Navy)

Adm. Richmond Kelly Turner, whom many modern historians, including this author, suspect to have been the *éminence grise* who was the true cause of many of the mistakes and failure to send warning that were responsible for our being caught flat-footed at Pearl. (U.S. Navy)

Adm. Harold R. ("Betty") Stark, left, in London in 1943. Adm. J. O. Richardson, Kimmel's predecessor at Pearl, a close friend, believed Stark's failure to take the obviously required initiative of telephoning a last-minute warning to Kimmel on the morning of 7 December was the culmination of a ten-day blackout of information as to the true state of affairs in Washington that resulted in the disaster for which Kimmel was held responsible. (U.S. Naval Historical Center NH 93297)

Secretary of War Henry L. Stimson, one of the towering figures of his time. (National Archives 18-HP-79-2)

Secretary of the Navy Frank Knox, shortly before his sudden death in April of 1944. (U.S. Naval Institute)

Lt. Gen. Walter C. Short, commanding general of the Hawaiian Department. Oahu, with its lovely climate and relaxed atmosphere, commodious quarters at Fort Shafter and salubrious situation in general, was expected to be General Short's final "twilight" tour of active duty in the army. It turned out to be exactly the opposite, and may have hastened his death from pneumonia and related stress-worsened disease. (National Archives 208-CN-12408)

down the hall, down a set of stairs, and around two corners for the office of the CNO.

Gordon Prange's account *(At Dawn We Slept)* is the best at this point. All other reviews of what happened at this extraordinary time simply accept the army chief of staff's vague statement that he believed he was at home all night (despite the *Washington Times Herald* story) and that he went for a ride on horseback the next morning, when it would seem the whole army must have been looking for him. All also agree that Stark arrived in his Main Navy office not long after 8:00 A.M. There he met with Admiral Wilkinson and the latter's assistant, Cdr. Arthur McCollum. The two officers were waiting with the complete fourteen-part message, but not the "delivery" message, in Kramer's original folder. A discussion over its meaning took place that lasted long enough for Kramer, the translator-cum-courier, to return to the CNO's office, this time with the "delivery" message. This gave him the chance to point out to these high officers that 1:00 P.M. in Washington, D.C., was half an hour before morning colors in Hawaii and a couple of hours before dawn in the Philippines and the Kra Peninsula, where Japanese landings had been fairly freely predicted. Wilkinson at once urged Stark to telephone warnings first to Kimmel and then to Hart in Manila.

According to Admiral Richardson, this was the moment when Stark should have picked up his special scrambler telephone to make the call that would have alerted Kimmel at about 3:00 A.M., as was his duty. Versions differ on just what Stark did; most accounts say he picked up the phone, hesitated, then decided instead to call the president. When the White House operator said the president was unavailable, Stark did nothing further. Prange and Clausen say he then tried to call Marshall, but the army chief of staff was not in his office. All agree that Stark did nothing at all during the next few hours, as the last opportunity to forestall complete surprise slowly evaporated.

This failure alone should have put Admiral Stark much higher on the list of those "guilty of dereliction" than anyone yet mentioned in this entire account.

Absent anyone else in authority at that precise moment, Stark could have taken it on himself to call Kimmel with at the least a status report on the sudden imminence of a surprise attack somewhere. At the very least, Kimmel could have had his warship crews called to their battle stations and ammunition made ready. (Crew liberty expired at midnight, except for special cases, and all defensive weapons would have been fully manned. The army, likewise, could have been "closed up" and ready.) Ships with double bottoms open for Monday morning inspection could have gotten them closed and watertight.

Richardson stated that he was positive there had been "some directive from higher authority" that only Marshall was to make any such call, but he believed Stark should have done it anyway, and he never forgave him. Richardson was clearly outraged, and the entire navy would have been also, had it known.

Marshall finally arrived in his office at around 11:00 A.M. (some accounts put it even later, around 11:30, but working the clock backward from the most positive time check leads to 11:00 as about the probable time). He is reported to have slowly and painstakingly studied the fourteen-part message his two most senior intelligence officers, Miles and Bratton, laid before him, almost as though he were deliberately killing time (Prange says he read it "with glacial deliberation"). In the meantime Miles and Bratton, with the crucial delivery message virtually shaking in their hands, several times "frantically" tried to bring it to his attention. But Marshall, known for fearsome concentration and forbidding style, refused to be diverted. Finally, with the office clock showing nearly noon, he reached for it. Containing himself as well as he could, Bratton explained that "something was going to happen" at one o'clock. Marshall then wrote out a warning message in pencil in his nearly illegible handwriting, initiated a call to Stark, who had been waiting for more than two hours to talk with him, rebuffed the CNO's offer to have the message sent by more powerful navy radio, added Stark's request that "naval opposites" be informed, and sent Bratton off to get it transmitted by army radio to the Philippines, Pearl Harbor, and the Canal Zone. If there developed a question as to priorities, he said to Bratton, the Philippines should have the highest.

No one has tried to explain Marshall's extraordinarily deliberate procedure at a time when everyone in his immediate vicinity was so urgently pointing to the need for haste. It is almost as though he knew more than they, and as if speed were definitely *not* desired. There are those, of course, who see his delay as fitting the entire pattern of the twenty-four hours now drawing to a close. Roosevelt-haters go even further: while Stark was unsuccessfully trying to reach the president through the White House telephone that Sunday morning, Roosevelt was poring with concentrated interest over his fabled stamp collection in his private study, with Hopkins reclining nearby rumpling "first dog" Fala's ears. Evidently, it being a Sunday, Roosevelt had directed that he not be disturbed. This tableau is probably imaginary. The only known fact is that Stark was unable to reach the president at this time, although he testified he generally had little difficulty in doing so. Marshall evidently made no effort to call the president.

The message General Marshall sent, in the face of a nearly apoplectic Bratton who kept saying, or trying to say, that something very serious indeed was going to happen, now within the hour, was as follows:

> JAPANESE ARE PRESENTING AT ONE PM EASTERN STANDARD TIME TODAY WHAT AMOUNTS TO AN ULTIMATUM ALSO THEY ARE UNDER ORDERS TO DESTROY THEIR CODE MACHINE IMMEDIATELY STOP JUST WHAT SIGNIFICANCE THE HOUR SET MAY HAVE WE DO NOT KNOW BUT BE ON ALERT ACCORDINGLY STOP INFORM NAVAL AUTHORITIES OF THIS COMMUNICATION MARSHALL

Army SOP (Standard Operating Procedure) required then, and still does, that important operational messages be sent by all means available, simultaneously, with appropriate priority precedence. Marshall, who at least theoretically knew all the army rules, made no effort to do this; nor did he place any procedural priority on his emergency message. This was an absolutely amazing gaffe for anyone accustomed to sending or receiving important military messages. He directed Bratton to hand carry the message to the Army Message Center, which Bratton did with alacrity, but in spite of Bratton's urgency, atmospheric difficulties caused the message for Short to go by Western Union; and since it bore no procedural priority, Western Union lumped it with a number of other messages for routine handling.

It was logged out of the Army Message Center at 12:17 P.M., only ten minutes before sunrise in Hawaii, about three quarters of an hour before Hull's one o'clock appointment with Nomura and Kurusu. But Murphy's Law was not done with it yet. In Hawaii it was simply one of several unimportant-looking telegrams given to a motorcycle messenger who took shelter when the attack began. General Short finally got his warning hours after everything was over. Sensing the irony, he meticulously carried out the only specific instruction it contained: he sent a copy to his opposite number in the navy and threw the original in the wastebasket.

Kimmel did the same. Both copies were salvaged by underlings.

As the foregoing shows, the failures in Washington were extensive. None can be proved to have been by intent, despite the accusations of conspiracy mongers who for years have been claiming Roosevelt "set up" our fleet in Pearl Harbor, but cumulatively they were devastating. Secretary Knox, upon arriving at Pearl Harbor two days after the attack for his hurried inspection, exclaimed incredulously to Admiral Kimmel and a number of others at different times, "Didn't you get the message we sent you Saturday night?" There were reports such a message was sent during the course of the early morning White House vigil that Knox attended, but nothing has ever been found to confirm the existence of this message.

The most favored historical explanation in the beclouded circumstances is that Marshall's handwritten message, sent at noon on the seventh, was the only one to which Knox could possibly have referred, but no one has suggested how he might have known of it. Several researchers have proposed the idea that a message might have been composed and somehow discarded during the long White House vigil, but there has been no confirmation of that late-night session. What is clear is that there is no record of such a message either at Pearl Harbor (or anywhere in Hawaii) or in Washington.

It is certainly conceivable that the president and the group theoretically meeting with him had composed warning messages to Pearl Harbor and Manila (and possibly also to the Panama Canal Zone) but, the meeting having terminated for lack of the fourteenth part of the Japanese message, the president had second thoughts about the risk of compromising Magic and canceled the last-minute warning. This scenario is unsubstantiated under the known circumstances, but it does fit the facts we have.

Admiral Stark, on 6 December, is supposed to have commented that further warnings to the Pacific commanders might confuse them, since "we have sent them so much already." Whatever he may have been thinking, the record proves that no tactical warning whatever, and very little of what might be called "strategic warning," had been sent for more than a week to the men on whom the blow was about to fall. Morgenstern, with the benefit of all the hearings before him, including that of the Army Pearl Harbor

Board, which he quotes devastatingly, is very clear on this. As he points out, Washington knew well that something was about to happen, and he even believes that Washington had correctly deduced when and where the blow would fall; but everyone there, from the commander in chief on down, chose to do nothing until after it happened.

Admiral Yamamoto had spent a year in planning the attack. He well knew how covertly it had to be conducted and demanded the utmost secrecy from inception to execution. His precautions against accidental radio signals from the *Kido Butai* were reported by Lt. Gen. Minoru Genda of the postwar Japanese Self-Defense Force (the former Commander Genda of Yamamoto's special planning staff) to have extended to the sealing or removal of transmitter keys from all the ships' radios. Even an innocuous signal was subject to interception by direction-finder stations that might wonder how it had happened to come from an area where no ships were supposed to be; hence, all possibility of the same was eliminated.

General Genda's account is nevertheless incompatible with recent stories alleging there were low-frequency signals intercepted at various places, particularly by the Matson liner *Lurline.* These have been cited by revisionists wishing to prove that Roosevelt knew of the approach of the Japanese carriers across the North Pacific. Now, in the just published NSA study by Parker, it appears that such signals may have emanated from two Russian freighters traveling in that area. This could have been the source of the confusion. Civilian radio operators, no matter how well motivated, cannot be expected to have the special expertise of a trained military intercept operator.

Yamamoto might also have expected the big movement of Japanese naval forces into Southeast Asia to dominate our attention. That move was no feint; but by accident or design, its secrecy did not compare to the absolute blackout imposed on the *Kido Butai,* both during its preparation and finally as it lunged eastward across the North Pacific. The Japanese commander, who always planned in utmost detail, expected the southern movement to attract all our attention, as it did. It would be the height of arrogance on our part to assume that the Japanese success could only have been due to our own failure. Admiral Yamamoto and his advisers had had a great deal to do with it. Viewed purely as a naval operation, immoral though it may have been because conducted outside of war, the surprise attack on Pearl Harbor was a brilliant maneuver, well executed by highly capable, seasoned professionals. Its amorality, however, resulted in the most fearsome retaliation ever in the history of warfare.

During the hours leading up to the attack on Pearl Harbor there occurred several chance events that, if instantly and correctly evaluated, might even at that late moment have enabled our forces to be alerted. At 3:42 in the morning of 7 December the minesweeper *Condor,* one of two sweeping the entrance to Pearl Harbor, sighted what looked like a small submarine apparently headed for the entrance. She immediately notified the destroyer *Ward* (DD 139), on her first day's patrol under a brand-new skipper, Lt. William W. Outerbridge. The *Ward* went to action stations, found nothing, and in due course terminated the search. Since there was no confirmation of the sighting, no report was made of it.

At 6:30 A.M. a PBY patrol plane also in the harbor approach area sighted a midget sub and began dropping smoke signals on it. At 6:45 the *Ward* herself spotted a periscope feather and then another small conning tower (not likely to have been the same one seen three hours earlier) in the water astern of the small repair ship *Antares,* which was about to pass through the open harbor-net gate with a barge in tow. At very close range, the *Ward* hit the submarine's conning tower with her second shot, and the sub disappeared. The old tin can followed with depth charges, the PBY did the same, and nothing further was seen of the submarine except an oil slick of very modest dimension. Postwar assessments of Japanese records confirm the sinking.

Both the *Ward* and the patrol plane sent action reports via priority messages, but these had to be encrypted before being sent (usually by two officers working and checking the procedures) and similarly decoded on the other end after receipt. It took half an hour for the *Ward*'s urgent message to be encrypted, sent, received, decrypted, and handed to a responsible superior. The delay of the PBY's message (with fewer people available to encode it in the first place) was nearly an hour. Admiral Kimmel's duty officer logged in the *Ward*'s message at 7:16, and a telephone call started the admiral dressing to go down to his headquarters instead of to his scheduled early Sunday golf game with General Short.

In the meantime, two army privates, Joseph E. Lockard and George E. Elliott by name, "fooling around" with their intriguing new mobile radar set while awaiting the truck bringing their breakfast, got a radar return from a large group of aircraft coming in from the north. Installation of the radar had not yet been completed, nor had the indoctrination of its assigned personnel. Having not cut off the radar when their drill period was over, as directed—in effect having been playing with it, searching areas and frequencies beyond the scope of their instructions, much as one might today with a new computer—they were concerned over what they should do with their puzzling contact. Finally they decided to report it and chance the possible "chewing out."

Lt. Kermit Tyler, himself brand-new at the job (this was his second day on it), had been informed only that there might be a flight of B-17 bombers from California. Rather pleased with the interest shown by the two privates, Tyler decided that although "the old army" might fault them for not strictly following orders, he would simply overlook their disobedience. Had he checked into their report a bit further, or had one of the young operators thought to describe more fully what they were seeing on their cathode-ray-tube display (anything resembling a modern television tube was far in the future), he might have discovered that this particular contact had a much greater number of planes than the B-17 group was supposed to contain. But he did not think to do this, having no experience with the surprising capabilities of this new device. In short, he paid no attention to the amateurish discovery. One may also wonder how much attention senior officers might have paid to an excited report from a not-yet-dry-behind-the-ears army shavetail.

To add to these signals received but not rightly interpreted, a Japanese scouting aircraft, assigned to check out the Lahaina anchorage immediately prior to the attack, and another at Pearl Harbor, had been seen circling lazily overhead at moderate to high altitude. Yamamoto had been convinced that some last-minute reconnaissance was necessary. Had part of the fleet been at Lahaina, as was often the case, part of the attack force would have diverted to attack it there; and, of course, he was most anxious to destroy our aircraft carriers, knowing even better than we that they were the most valuable of all targets. The spy planes departed as soon as the bombing and torpedo runs started, and the distance in any case was too great for unassisted eyesight, but a few "old China hands" were said to have recognized the Japanese insignia on the wings of the orbiting planes and started toward their machine guns. Whether this was true or not, by this time the bombs and torpedoes were about to drop, and a few minutes' prior notice would have made no difference.

The first bombs fell on Pearl Harbor at 7:55 A.M., Hawaii time (1:25 P.M. eastern standard time), five minutes before morning colors in Honolulu. Two attack waves came in, separated only by how long it had taken the carriers to get the second flight up from the hangar deck and spotted for takeoff. According to Japanese records the two waves had a total of 354 planes, 183 in the first and 171 in the second. When the bombing and torpedoing stopped at last, one first-line battleship had been capsized at her berth, another had blown up, and two more had been sunk where they lay (but the water being shallow, they were resting on the bottom with their upper works showing and months later, refloated, were sent to the States for repair. In 1944 they were back in action at the Battle of Surigao Strait). The only battleship able to get under way, the *Nevada,* received so much damage that she was forced to beach herself on the edge of the entrance channel to avoid sinking in the middle and blocking it. The three other battleships that were at Pearl Harbor that morning happened to be moored where the amazingly effective Japanese torpedoes could not reach them (one in dry dock, two behind sunken sister ships). These three suffered extensive bomb damage nonetheless, would not be able to get under way for weeks, and required lengthy repair periods.

Other vessels of lesser importance had also been sunk, and many more were damaged. Military airfields were also attacked; upwards of two hundred army air corps aircraft at Hickam Field had been caught lined up as if for inspection (they had been so placed to facilitate a guard perimeter against sabotage). Nearly all were destroyed, as were about one hundred navy aircraft in other locations. In return, only some thirty Japanese planes had been shot down, most of them during the second attack.

Pearl Harbor, the principal U.S. Navy base in the Pacific Ocean, had been put out of action, the fleet it nominally sheltered out of action too. The lives lost at Pearl Harbor numbered 2,403, plus 68 unlucky civilians (Prange's figure is 2,403, but some authorities give numbers of killed or missing of all services reaching above 3,000). The wounded were a thousand more. Japan had thoroughly achieved its objective of temporarily knocking the U.S. Navy out of the war.

Nearly simultaneous surprise attacks were made on Guam, Wake Island, the Philippines, the Malay Peninsula, and Hong Kong.

A great fleet was approaching the Dutch East Indies. Japan went on with the remainder of its plan of conquest in Southeast Asia more or less as expected by War Plan Orange (Rainbow 5 by this time). Looking back the half century since, it's clear that the strategy had, in fact, been pretty accurately anticipated, excepting only the lunges at Pearl Harbor and Midway and the great speed with which all was executed. (Nimitz's comment on this point was that everything had been anticipated except the kamikazes.)

The big strategic harbor in the area, after vulnerable Hong Kong, was Singapore (it is even bigger now), and England hoped to be able to hold it. Two important ships had lately been sent to augment Singapore's defenses: the *Prince of Wales* and *Repulse.* But they had no chance at all. Hearing of a landing on the Malay Peninsula only a relatively few miles to the north, and rightly seeing this as presaging immediate problems for the Singapore defenses, their admiral, Tom Phillips, only recently having served as the Second Sea Lord in London, assumed the offensive and sailed to attack the landing force. He had no air cover: the aircraft carrier originally intended to be part of his force had run aground and was far away in a repair yard. He went on anyway, was spotted and reported by the submarine *I-58* according to Japanese records. (Unless number designations were later changed, this would make that submarine one of the few that survived the war: the *I-58* gained notoriety in 1945 when she sank the USS *Indianapolis.*) The two British warships were spotted and reported again the next morning by Japanese search planes based at Saigon, and were attacked by shore-based torpedo planes around noon on 10 December.

Nothing could save the ships. After a spirited but short battle, both were sunk with great loss of life, including Admiral Phillips and the captain of the *Prince of Wales,* Capt. J. C. Leach. The water where they went down is relatively shallow; postwar diving investigations have shown the tremendous extent of the damage they received, particularly the *Prince of Wales.* Her entire keel was bent out of line, two of her propeller shafts were likewise bent, and there were great holes in her bottom. She had been badly damaged early on, reduced in maneuverability, and at the end she was a sitting duck. The *Repulse,* on the other hand, adroitly avoided several salvos of torpedoes launched from the same direction, was finally caught by cross-fire attacks, and was in fact the first to sink.

The disaster, which occurred only two days after Pearl Harbor, was the first time really big warships—capital ships—had been sunk by air attack at sea while presumably able to defend themselves. The famous Billy Mitchell sinking of the former German World War I battleship *Ostfriesland,* by bombing from the air, was of an unmanned ship not shooting back, a point the "battleship admirals" of the day allowed no one to forget. The *Prince of Wales* and *Repulse,* with all their antiaircraft weapons shooting like mad, were sunk by torpedoes (not bombs) from planes beyond the effective range of the antiaircraft batteries. In spite of the lessons of the war in Europe, they simply were not adequately armed.

A personal dramatic touch added to the emotional effect on the American navy of the loss of the two big British ships: Only a few days before, Admiral Phillips had flown to Manila to confer with General MacArthur and Admiral Hart. This took place on 5 December, east longitude date, only days after his arrival in Singapore. Protocol flags were flying as the general and the two admirals discussed mutual support. Hart was said to have been greatly impressed with Phillips; but only five days later the rising star of the former Second Sea Lord was extinguished in the wreck of his flagship, and he and his squadron ceased to exist.

The American battleships at Pearl Harbor were even more poorly outfitted. Their antiaircraft armament was outmoded and inadequate, thanks to a Navy Department and a Congress that saw no need to worry about ships so far from the scene of the European war. Here again, as with the two unfortunate British warships, torpedoes, not bombs, did most of the lethal damage, although it must be remembered that the *Arizona* was sunk by an armor-piercing bomb dropped from high altitude (actually an armor-piercing naval shell converted into a bomb) that exploded her forward magazines. Our ships at Pearl Harbor, having been caught by surprise, were for some minutes unable to shoot back at all, but they had little to shoot back with, despite admiring Japanese reports about the speed and effectiveness with which the antiaircraft weapons were manned and began to return fire.

Our navy—all navies, in fact—had become so bedazzled by the powerful mystique and grandeur of battleships that it had lost sight of their true and original purpose. Just as the Royal Navy in the days of wooden ships had put everything into the mantle of seniority (once attained, it was sacred), so that a "post captain" had secured a status for life, and a post captain commanding a ship of the battle line had the stature of a god, so had we remained enamored of the great ships of the steel battle line with their aura of impregnable strength and prowess.

That these magnificent ships could no longer deliver as they used to, that war had gone so far beyond them that they had degenerated into senior captains' toys and admirals' private yachts, many officers of the prewar navy, aviators and submariners notably excepted, simply could not perceive. Yet it was so, notwithstanding all the honest effort by thousands of earnest people—crew members, designers, builders, strategic planners—to make these ships what we thought they should be. Members of the cult of the battleship had lost sight of the real purpose of their objects of veneration. The battleships, with too much invested in them, simply could not keep up with the breathtaking speed of modern development. When war became three-dimensional, warships able to operate in only two dimensions became passé.

As is always the case, however, our organization of human beings had become wedded to the symbol they had devoted their lives to. We sought ways to show battleships had not diminished. We maintained them carefully and trained religiously to use them and their outmoded weapons, for to do otherwise would be destructive of the mystique we had unconsciously but carefully fostered around them. Battleships, with their low-slung power and their seeming absolute mastery of all they surveyed, were the epitome of the prewar navy.

Had our Hawaii commanders been expecting an attack, it is almost sure that Kimmel would have had his fleet to sea, or at least this was what he said in his book (page 110): he "would have arranged a rendezvous at sea with Adm. William F. Halsey's carrier force and been [in] a good position to intercept the Japanese attack." Unfortunately, this is not likely, or perhaps it would be more accurate to say that it was all time-dependent. Were Kimmel to have had two weeks advance notice—that is, awareness of the oncoming attack and its date—he might have implemented his own plan, O-1, WPPac-46 as it was known officially, or anyway that portion of it having to do with a decisive sea battle two to three weeks after the outbreak of hostilities. He planned to use Wake as a sort of bait; Japan would send a powerful fleet to take Wake Island, and unbeknownst to the Japanese, he would be waiting for them with his entire fleet of battleships. Patrol planes would have alerted him to the Japanese fleet's approach, and his three carriers (assuming the *Saratoga* would by this time have returned from the West Coast) would have been his scouting force. The big problem here was the time it would have taken to go into WPPac-46. Nagumo, on the other hand, already deployed with six topflight carriers, might have greeted Kimmel's deployment with delight and sailed zestfully into a probably successful fleet engagement. Or, since the ascendancy of carriers over battleships had not yet been proved, another option Nagumo might have exercised would have been to decline the proffered battle and use his superior speed to retire. No one can usefully predict what would actually have happened.

But if Kimmel had had only a couple of days advance notice he would not have been able to concentrate his far-flung fleet units and certainly would not have been able to use Wake Island as bait the way he had planned. Had he had only a few hours of warning he would have been lucky to have gotten all his ships out of the harbor. Short's air corps fighters would have taken to the air to help the fleet defend itself; there can be no doubt Japanese losses would have been much greater, but one would have to assume that we would have suffered greater loss of life too, even though there might have been fewer battleships actually sunk—unless, of course, one of the ships thereby saved happened to be the *Arizona,* on board of which 1,100 men died when her forward magazines exploded.

To have had the fleet at sea in any way at all except the one envisioned by Kimmel's main battle plan, and possibly even in that one, would have been to play into Yamamoto's hands.

Our fleet of eight overage battleships, insufficiently armed against attack from the air, even with the assistance of the two aircraft carriers available, would have been overwhelmed by battle-hardened and immaculately trained aircraft from not two but six first-line Japanese carriers. Instead of our Pearl Harbor toll, nearly all hands on all the ships would have gone down, far beyond the possibility of salvage or rescue. Compared with this, we got off easy. We may be glad that it was hypothetical.

The general consensus now is that the destruction of our vaunted battle line catapulted our navy into the carrier warfare that turned out to be the determinant in the Pacific and was therefore, on balance, probably a good thing.

Had we still had a battle line with which theoretically to fight the Japanese battle line, we should inevitably have had an internal navy contest between battleship adherents and the others—the aviators, the submariners, the amphibious types, etc. There is a psychology in weapons as there is in everything else. Our battle line of magnificent but aging battleships would have insisted on having the test it was built and trained for. Even though we had built a few new ones and by the end of the war had built several, it is almost certain that had they gone into action under the circumstances expected—the all-out combat visualized by Mahan, tried unsuccessfully at Jutland in 1916 and hardly ever truly achieved in history—not since Tsushima in 1905 and at Trafalgar a hundred years earlier—the battle would have been a disaster for the United States. This is owing to the great superiority the Japanese had in aircraft carriers, and in the now uncontested fact that their battleships were better built, bigger, faster, and modernized to a far greater degree than we had any idea of. All postwar projections of this fleet action, fought under the actual conditions of readiness existing in the two fleets in 1941, ended in cataclysmic loss by our side.

In hindsight, had we planned the attack on Pearl Harbor to take place the way it did and at the time it did, we could not have done better for our side. The Japanese failed to destroy the fuel tanks easily visible on the hills just behind Pearl Harbor. Destruction of these would have confined our fleet much closer to the shores of the United States and given the Japanese correspondingly freer range. They also failed to attack the submarine base, although how much effect this might have had on the war is problematic. There were only five submarines alongside the docks that morning, and the probability is that the operations of the submarine force would not have been severely affected. Except for the lives lost, that the surprise attack took place upon our fleet in harbor was a most fortunate thing, if the alternative was a strategic surprise at sea; for one must also remember that eighteen thousand other men who would have died remained alive because the deep-sea disaster did not take place. Furthermore, almost as if by magic, years of stultified planning for the wrong kind of naval war were wiped away. With our battle line gone, we had to look to naval aircraft flying from our few carriers, supported by cruisers and destroyers, and submarines operating alone in enemy waters, to carry on.

So it did not strike us as a whole, until Pearl Harbor, that as an icon the battleship was no longer worthy of the worship that we gave it. And Yamamoto, for a time the most reviled man in the history of the U.S. Navy, can be said to have done more to modernize our navy, and its thinking, in his own way and in a shorter time, than anyone in all the annals of sea power. In modest truth, the wooden sailing battleships of Nelson or Farragut would have performed little worse than our vaunted battle line on that sad Sunday morning, for the advent of the third dimension in naval warfare had in nearly equal measure eclipsed them both.

But it was also the inability of the so-called "Gun Club," the Bureau of Ordnance (BuOrd), devoted to huge guns and the magnificent but outmoded ships that we called the U.S. Fleet, to provide the dependable antiaircraft armament that the fleet needed, that was really the cause of the tremendous damage to our side. It was fortunate that after having spent years in "developing" a complicated and usually nonfunctional small AA gun, we finally, just before the war, gave up the effort and simply purchased two fine European-made guns, the 20-mm and 40-mm guns, to supplement our fine 5-inch longer-range AA gun, and they became the backbone of our close-in air-defense weapons during the war.

It is also worthy of note that, aside from a few bomb hits, most of the damage the fleet received, so graphically shown in the countless photographs taken, was done by torpedoes. Our navy had never adequately studied how to minimize their tremendous damage capability, how to launch them in shallow water, or, for that matter, how to design and produce a dependable design for our own navy.

History is full of successful surprise attacks. The paucity of those anticipated is likewise noteworthy. At Pearl Harbor, in a single move, Japan greatly embarrassed us as a nation. It did major damage to our defense establishment, offended our national pride in general, and shattered our self-assurance. The foregoing, or some of them, were among the Japanese high command's objectives. Those Japanese officers wanted to shock us, and they certainly succeeded. Never was a shock more devastating, or more global in scope. Nor was there ever one more destructive to the perpetrator.

Tactically and strategically brilliant, the surprise attack was a terrible blunder, the most colossal mistake the Japanese could have made, something an accurate understanding of American history and culture would never have permitted. One need not be a revisionist to believe that if the war had begun in a less treacherous way it might not have ended with nuclear weapons on Japanese cities.

The attack caused Japan, already a member of the Tripartite Alliance with Germany and Italy, to be assigned the same blood guilt as Hitler's Germany. Japanese atrocities and Nazi atrocities seemed to be cut of the same cloth. U.S. fighting men vowed that they would exact revenge, that before the account could be marked paid there would be full retribution on a national scale. Japan would get every bomb back, with interest.

As for the Imperial Japanese Navy, every ship that could be identified as having participated in the attack would be the special target of our forces and would be sunk without mercy; except for the fleet flagship at the time, HIJMS *Nagato,* this actually happened during the course of the war, and we gloried in the doing of it. Though the *Nagato* survived the war, she was damaged and of no operational value. It was no accident that she was placed near Bomb Zero at Bikini. The personnel of the U.S. Navy, of whom I was one of the younger members, would never forget Pearl Harbor as the culmination of a long series of insults received from Japan. Even while we thought the "Japs" were suddenly ten feet tall, in December 1941 we also dedicated ourselves to visiting an overwhelming destruction upon them.

7

The Investigations

The cost of Pearl Harbor, though great, was not so great as would be that of D-Day in Normandy or the overall campaign to liberate France. Nor, in the Pacific, was it so great as would be the cost of Guadalcanal, of Iwo Jima, or—to Japan—of Hiroshima. We were psychologically ready for all those. What hurt about Pearl Harbor was the shock. We were not emotionally prepared, and our pride was devastated. In addition, those opposed to war in principle found the overwhelming reversal of their thinking terribly difficult to cope with. The explosion in what we now call "the media" was already in full swing, with an active press, hundreds of radio stations, columnists, and pundits of all sorts. Nothing was so apparent to Roosevelt as the national demand for immediate answers. A quick explanation was needed that would satisfy the tremendous pressure for an authoritative illumination of the circumstances. Pearl Harbor—how the war started—had to be put behind us so that we could marshall our strength and win that war. Divisive issues simply had to be put aside.

The thought cannot be avoided that self-interest must also have entered Roosevelt's mind. Not only must he divest himself of any public guilt for the heavy damage and loss of life, he must assuage his own conscience too.

Nine investigations of the attack, beginning with Navy Secretary Knox's flying visit to Pearl Harbor two days after the attack, the last and most comprehensive being the JCC Hearings that were completed in May 1946, submitted reports totaling more than thirty-three thousand pages in forty-one printed volumes. All of them seem to have concentrated on what the army and navy commanders knew, when they knew it, and what they did about it. Few have paid much attention to what they *should* have known, and why they did not, beyond the tautological rationale that officers with "greater judgment" would have "more accurately" interpreted the few warnings they actually did receive. Many naval officers in high-ranking posts asked themselves these questions at the time, and there were no answers then, as there are none today.

In 1942 American public opinion, fueled by a demanding media, had to have an immediate scapegoat for the Pearl Harbor disaster, and despite their strenuous efforts, Kimmel's in particular, the two hapless commanders in Hawaii found this was to be their only contribution to the national war effort. Hurriedly called, the Roberts Commission sat, in Washington and Honolulu, until 23 January 1942. In Washington it operated in a rather relaxed manner, treating the army and navy chiefs with friendly courtesy. But in Hawaii it took testimony in secret, permitted no examination of witnesses, and did not inform either Kimmel or Short that they were defendants or even interested parties to the inquiry (a technical term meaning possible defendant against resulting charges). Kimmel and Short were both badgered by Supreme Court Justice Owen J. Roberts and treated as defendants, nevertheless, before what in fact amounted to a court, but in response to their specific inquiries, both were expressly and individually informed that they were not on trial. The Commission found, nonetheless, that they had been seriously derelict in their duties and so reported to the president. The president directed that this report be given immediate and wide publicity, but not until they read it in the papers were Kimmel and Short aware they had been accused.

It was not fair, but it may have been politic at the time. At the beginning, possibly, the ability to lay blame on someone who could then be put aside may have seemed helpful to the overall prosecution of the war. Under such an overriding circumstance one could perhaps argue for relegating truth to a secondary role, but at the bar of history it must always remain primary.

First Investigation: Secretary of the Navy Knox

First on the scene at Pearl Harbor from Washington, on 9 December, was Secretary Knox, understandably stung by the preliminary reports of the damage the navy had sustained and by congressional criticisms of himself and his administration of the navy. Smoke was still issuing from damaged ships; oil from the ships' ruptured fuel tanks covered the waters and shores of the formerly beautiful bay; bodies of dead sailors were still being found floating in the reeking black water, or fished up from the unimaginable wreckage of once proud warships. Part of the *Oklahoma*'s crew was still alive in the overturned ship and could be heard tapping desperately for rescue. In the still-smoking *Arizona,* her foremast and bridge canted crazily where the explosion of her magazines had ripped out their foundations, over a thousand men were still entombed, now given up for lost. The entire base was a fevered madhouse of people rushing around in the chaos, sometimes with little instruction on which to rely, everyone doing his best with whatever tools and equipment came to hand.

It was an indelible impression upon Knox, all the more so because he had been publicly quoted only a few days before as saying that the U.S. Navy was ready for anything, that it could beat the Japanese anytime, anywhere. When he returned to Washington, he handed over a lengthy typed report, together with verbal and private observations, to the president, noting that the commanders out there "would have to go." Whether guilty of inefficiency or not, they had commanded during a disaster to their forces and could not be continued where they were.

Knox's quick overview of the gutted harbor was completed on 12 December and may be found on pages 1,749–61 in part 24 of the extraordinarily voluminous "Report of Hearings before the Joint Committee of Congress on the Investigation of the Pearl Harbor Attack." During Knox's hurried visit he exclaimed to Kimmel, and repeated the question to several other officers at various times, "Didn't you get the message we sent you Saturday night?" His aide who accompanied him, Capt. Frank Beatty, was directed to discover what had happened to the message but was unable to find any record whatsoever of it anywhere in Hawaii. This is reported on page 1,755, with the following note:

> [17] (2) The Army and Naval Commands had received a general war warning on November 27th, but a *special* war warning sent out by the War Department at midnight December 7th to the Army was not received until some hours after the attack on that date. [Italics in original]

In the copy read by the author, someone had underlined the date, 7 December, in pencil. The date is clearly in error, for midnight of the seventh in Washington, D.C., is eleven hours after the attack took place. Perhaps it should read, "midnight December 6th," but this compounds the confusion about the events in Washington during the twenty-four hours preceding the attack. If "midnight" had been rendered as "just before noon," the passage would agree with the accepted interpretation of the remark, that Knox must have been thinking of the message General Marshall undeniably *did* send, at about 11:30 A.M. on Sunday the seventh. There is, however, no question that Knox said, "Saturday night" when he queried Kimmel and the others, and that such a message was never found, despite a serious search for it. Official references to it therefore always explain that Knox must have misspoken when he said "Saturday night," that he really meant "noon on Sunday." This message, the one sent by Marshall, was addressed to Short (who was directed to share it with Kimmel) and was delivered by a Western Union motorcycle messenger some hours after the attack.

It is possible that before he left Washington Knox had heard about Marshall's message—but while this might explain the confusion over his remark, it is only a theory, as are all other explanations. Knox's hurried departure for Pearl Harbor in the pressured hours immediately after the attack (his plane took off at 8 A.M. on 8 December) gave him little time to consult with anyone. Nonetheless, it strains credulity that he should have so misremembered the timing of a message of such great special importance. The mystery of what he said, or meant to say, has thus never been explained. He said something about it to Roosevelt in the report he delivered immediately after his return to Washington, but whatever he said, or wrote, has been expunged from the record. The usual deduction is that the secretary of the navy simply misspoke a number of times in a period of uncommon stress.

The only other possibility is that he thought a message of some sort had been—or was to have been—sent on "Saturday night," that is, before dawn of the seventh in Washington. This, of course, infers it was decided upon at the reported midnight White House meeting following Lieutenant Schulz's 9 P.M. delivery of the Magic decryptions of the first thirteen parts of Japan's message terminating negotiations.

Second Investigation: The Roberts Commission

The second inquiry was conducted by the Roberts Commission, chaired by Justice Roberts, and was directed to discover "whether any derelictions of duty or errors of judgment [by the Hawaiian commanders] . . . contributed to such successes as were achieved by the enemy. . . ." The members of the Commission held a preliminary meeting in Washington before going to Honolulu, where they met on 18 December 1941. At the outset, the Commission established its independence by refusing to accept quarters on any of the government installations. Instead, it set itself up at the Royal Hawaiian Hotel, then the most luxurious local hotel (it is even more luxurious today, although closely surrounded by other, much taller ones).

Numerous witnesses were called, but the proceedings were more like a congressional investigation, in that the Commission made up its own rules, than they were like the formal investigations specified by army or navy regulations. Adm. William Harrison Standley, a former CNO who had retired from active duty in 1937, was recalled to active service as a member of the Commission and later characterized its proceedings as a travesty of justice to the two officers under investigation. Nonetheless, although he expressed strong reservations at the time he did so, he signed the Commission Report because he felt that doing otherwise might adversely affect the war effort.

To understand how Standley, an officer of the old school and of the highest personal repute, could have brought himself to sign off on something he felt was morally wrong, and contrary to national and naval legal rules as well, one must try to think oneself into the conditions of 1941. Since the turn of the century the navy had been thinking about the conduct of a possible war with Japan. The Naval War College at Newport, Rhode Island, had for years annually war-gamed a war with Japan, and the CNO had often suggested that the game include some fundamental tactic or strategy his War Plans Office was then studying. War Plan Orange, actually a synonym for our Pacific strategy, one of the CNO's long-range responsibilities, grew out of the successive earlier efforts at long-range planning, and long prior to Pearl Harbor was being maintained in the top-secret files of the War Plans section of OpNav, the acronym standing for the CNO's entire organization in the Navy Department. By 1941 the Orange Plan strategy was officially dead, superseded by a series of "Rainbow" plans, most recently Rainbow 5. Rear—later Vice—Admiral Turner was in charge of it as director of the War Plans Division, known then as OP-12, and this, as might be expected, was his ticket to the inner circles he so thoroughly dominated in 1941.

Rainbow 5 and its predecessor, the Orange Plan, were continually changed, upgraded, and restudied in accordance with the immediate situation. Details went down to such fine points as the immediate locations of important ships and sites of fuel, munitions, and provisions for them should it suddenly be necessary to carry out some portion of the strategy, or some analogous order from competent authority. To Standley, a one-time director of the War Plans Division himself and CNO from 1933 to 1937, such considerations about possible war or expeditionary needs were always in the near background of his day-to-day operations. He could not avoid putting himself in Kimmel's shoes on the one hand, but had had nearly four years of experience as CNO under Roosevelt on the other. Indubitably there were personal insights that he had to keep to himself; and just as surely his sense of the rightness and fitness of things, the sworn and nearly sacred principles of honor and fairness in dealing with fellow officers and the enlisted men under his command, were under severe strain. He could not oppose the president of the United States, most especially with the nation suffering such an unexpected shock at the very outset of the war he had studied for so long. He nevertheless harbored unexplainable uncertainties about what had happened in Washington and Hawaii and was truly outraged at the imperious bearing, with respect to Kimmel and Short, of the Commission, its chairman, and some of the members. The Commission's nearly obsequious conduct when it came to other witnesses, particularly General Marshall, also preyed on his mind.

Marshall, who was the first to testify before the Commission, did so in Washington before it departed for Honolulu, and the record shows that he was treated with the greatest deference, as was Stark to a lesser degree. For Kimmel and Short, by contrast, the Commission sessions bordered on harassment. While both were called to testify, neither one was permitted to have a lawyer (or "counsel") with him, nor to have any of the rights of an "interested party" as provided for in both military services and in civilian law also. Nor were they permitted to be present when other witnesses testified, even if the testimony given was prejudicial to them. Kimmel is said to have been reconciled to the necessity of being relieved; he was after all the commander during a major disaster to the forces under his charge. So, essentially, was Short. Neither one, however, had any idea that his own conduct in the discharge of his responsibilities was being called into question, and that charges were being preferred against him.

This, in fact, was so contrary to the legal procedures of both services that when Chairman Roberts solemnly assured each, in specific terms, that he was not under investigation, each took him at his word. On this ground, each was refused the right to defend himself against any accusations. It was a "fact-finding commission," Justice Roberts severely maintained. No one was being accused of anything. Consternation therefore reigned in their minds when they discovered that the report, made in secret to the president and immediately given out publicly, castigated them as having failed in their duty, a court-martial offense.

Returning to Washington, the Commission members worked furiously in their plane during its interminably long flights, in makeshift offices during stops, and after their return, and were able to submit their findings on 23 January. The entire report of hearings is contained in parts 22, 23, and 24 of the JCC Hearings. Its exhibits are in part 25. A portion of part 39 is also devoted to the Roberts Commission. As soon as Roosevelt finished reading the findings, he tossed the papers approvingly on his secretary's desk, saying, "Give this out right away, just as it is!" The press was, of course, avidly awaiting it. It stated bluntly that Admiral Kimmel and General Short were "derelict in their duty," and it received—as was to be expected—the widest national distribution.

Kimmel and Short both immediately demanded trial by general court-martial; this was, and is still, the army and navy way when one is blamed for serious malfeasance—although the accused usually seeks to avoid trial instead of demanding one. The circumstances in this instance, however, were very special. Under military law, any time the conduct or performance of duty of any member of the service comes under question or the possibility of question during an official inquiry or investigation, whether or not that individual has yet been involved in any way in the inquiry, he or she must be informed of whatever information or accusation has been brought against him or her. In navy legal procedure he must then be designated as "an interested party"—technical language that gives him the privilege to be present, to be accompanied by legal counsel, and to prefer questions from that moment onward. The Commission insisted on procedure more akin to that of a congressional investigation than a military one and made up its own rules as it went along. Neither Kimmel nor Short was accorded even his supposed constitutional right to confront his accusers, to know of what derelictions he was being charged, or even to know his conduct was under investigation. They were astounded to discover by reading the newspapers that they had been convicted by "star-chamber" proceedings without the opportunity of defense.

Additionally, both had been earlier disturbed by the poor quality of the stenographic assistance employed by Roberts. When they finally were able to read the transcripts of their testimony (which was allowed after strenuous application), they were appalled by the gross errors they found. Many of these were clear evidence of the civilian Commission-hired stenographers' unfamiliarity with basic military terms and procedures. The two commanders were not, however, permitted to change or revise their own testimony, even when the army and navy terms they had used clearly had been misunderstood or incorrectly set down. Finally, after the most vigorous protest, they were allowed to submit corrected testimony as an addendum to the Commission's proceedings.

Only some time later did they discover that the draft transcripts of the testimony taken from Marshall and Stark, some days earlier in Washington, had been as a matter of course returned to them for correction and approval before inclusion in the record.

Courts-martial in our armed forces are not that far removed from civilian trial courts; there are differences in procedures (the grand-jury system does not prescribe the presence of the accused, for example), and the trial system is different (the president of the court is in effect the judge, but he also sits with members of the court when they consider the evidence and participates in and signs the findings). Both legal systems are, however, identical in their intent to search for the truth and render fair and impartial judgment on the accused.

Neither General Short nor Admiral Kimmel was ever court-martialed, at that time or later, despite the White House announcement, made at the time their directed application for retirement was announced, that such a trial would be held as soon as the exigencies of the war permitted. Neither was ever given any opportunity to defend himself against the accusation of dereliction of duty.

Third Investigation: Admiral Hart's Examination

The third investigation, suggested by the navy judge advocate general and strongly supported by Admiral Standley, now relieved of his uncomfortable duties as a member of the Roberts Commission, was officially called an "examination to prevent evidence being lost by death or unavoidable absence of those certain members of the naval forces who have knowledge pertinent to [the attack on Pearl Harbor and who] are now or soon may be on dangerous assignments at great distances from the United States. . . ." Admiral Hart was designated president. This "examination" was convened on 12 February 1944 and concluded on 15 June 1944. General Short was not involved since it was a naval proceeding and all witnesses were naval personnel. This third investigation in the sequence may be found in toto in part 26 of the JCC Report.

The precept under which Admiral Hart held his inquest, signed by Secretary Knox, went on to specify that Admiral Kimmel was to be notified of the time and place of all meetings pursuant to this directive and be allowed to be present, have counsel, question and cross-examine witnesses—in short, to have all the rights of an interested party, as defined in the *Navy Manual for Courts and Boards.* In his response to Hart's official letter of notification, Kimmel wrote back, in equally official language, asking for a delay to give him time to prepare. In concluding, he wrote:

> 3. Attention is invited to the fact that the stipulation between the Navy Department and me as to the conditions under which the testimony may be used has not been submitted to me as planned.

Review of the proceedings shows that Admiral Kimmel attended none of the hearings of the Hart examination, although he was meticulously informed of all meetings and witnesses, and was not represented there by counsel. His explanation of his absence is contained in the following quotation from his own book, *Admiral Kimmel's Story* (pages 158–9):

> Early in 1944 I was invited by the Navy Department to collaborate in an investigation of the Pearl Harbor disaster to be undertaken by Admiral T. C. Hart. Admiral Hart intimated to me that Secretary Knox was favorably disposed toward me and the investigation would benefit me. An exchange of letters with Mr. Knox developed certain stipulations I must agree to before my assistance would be acceptable. These stipulations placed my fate completely at the mercy of the Secretary. I therefore declined to take any part in the Hart investigation. Admiral Hart took the testimony of numerous naval personnel and gathered much valuable data, the most interesting of which was the testimony of Captain Safford who outlined the information received in the Navy Department through the translation of the intercepted Japanese messages.
>
> When I came to Washington for the naval court of inquiry in the summer of 1944, a copy of the Hart investigation was supplied to me. Safford's testimony provided me with my first authoritative information on this subject. Admiral Hart submitted no conclusions, findings or recommendations.

Kimmel was probably wrong in his avoidance of the Hart inquiry. He had his fellow officer's assurance that the investigation would benefit him and that the navy secretary was favorably disposed toward him. His own statement, written years after the fact, indicates that he did not repose full confidence in the secretary and actually may have believed Knox was duplicitous or planned to be. He could not, on the other hand, have held any such opinion about Admiral Hart, whom, according to his counsel, he felt to have absolute integrity. It was later noted, however, that Hart did not call Admiral Stark as a witness and that Hart appeared as counsel for Stark in the following naval court of inquiry.

Kimmel believed he was not to have the full right of unlimited cross-examination, despite the statement in the precept that he would be accorded this right. He felt that any testimony given was available to be used against him and that his own input thereto, by cross-examination or in any other way, might be deleted or ignored if, or when, someone's testimony was brought up to attack him. Moreover, he was personally committed to protecting Captain Safford from any further harm to his career. To Kimmel, the proceedings smacked too much of the Roberts Commission, which had declared him guilty without trial or opportunity to defend himself, and then made a public announcement of its accusatory findings to the nation. Kimmel had gone to his lawyers on the subject and had their analysis in hand, and it is not hard to understand his terribly hurt and bitter feelings at this point.

One of his lawyers, Edward B. Hanify, writing about this in 1991, described the situation thus:

> Admiral Gatch, Judge Advocate of the Navy, told Senator Walsh that the Navy Department felt Kimmel had been badly advised in his conclusion not to go along with and participate in the proceedings. . . . He had intimations from Admiral Hart that the trend of the proceeding was designed to bury quietly the truth about Pearl Harbor in some kind of official word that he was not to blame. Kimmel had originally determined not to participate in the Hart proceeding, considerably before the conference with Gatch, for two reasons: First of all, there was unlimited discretion in the precept permitting a future Secretary of the Navy to determine which of the deposed witnesses would be made available for personal testimony. Second, in any such proceeding Kimmel might feel compelled to reveal the nature of the revelations he had had from Safford, which would imperil

Safford. Safford was to be encouraged to make such revelations directly to Hart if required to testify (and he did).

Under the circumstances, considering the pressures and suffering he had already undergone, it is understandable that Kimmel may have felt bitter toward those responsible. At the same time, however, giving voice to any such feelings in the political context of that time, which included the nation's heightened cleaving to the president because of the war—and from the sound of the passage quoted he may have done this—could not have been useful to his cause.

The case of Captain Safford is a most unusual one. He was universally praised for having been one of the foremost navy cryptologists and for having, from its smallest beginning, led the formation of our cryptanalysis team. But secrecy was so severe and manpower so low that even Captain Safford often had to make office rounds himself with locked pouches of documents, as did all the other male members of the top decrypting team, and this was a source of disparagement.

There were so few persons with the requisite clearances and capabilities that Safford was forced to maintain a killing pace with his special product, far more than any of the top officials whom he served. Frequently he had to work all night, with little or no time off for personal rejuvenation. His wife was known to have become almost pathologically protective of him, sometimes actually interfering with his own desires toward his duty. After midnight on Saturday night, 6 December 1941, Safford went home exhausted after a succession of eighteen-hour days, convinced that war was coming very soon and that he had done all he could to alert everyone in authority. He announced his intention—cheered by his strong-minded wife—of "sleeping for 24 hours." He was still in his pajamas at 2:00 P.M. the next day, having just awakened when the attack came.

Clausen made much of this in his Stimson-directed 1944–1945 special investigation and in *Final Judgement.* In both places he accused Safford of being asleep when he should have been at work in the Navy Department. A review of Safford's treatment at the hands of the administration during this period leads to the inescapable conclusion that his stature, prestige, and credibility took a nosedive just at this time. He is typified as being addicted to strange work habits, unpredictable in temperament, prone to hallucination, and weak in conviction and presentation. It is difficult to understand how an individual with such personal deficiencies could earlier have achieved so much acceptance in a situation of such national importance. It is as though a concerted campaign to reduce his substance began at about the time of Pearl Harbor.

Whether this is true or not, all possible circumstances and influences to reduce Safford's credibility came to bear just at this time, and it may have happened because he was one of the very few with intimate personal knowledge of nearly all the secret messages that had passed between Tokyo and Washington. When Safford realized how the information he had had such a hand in gathering was being used, how little of it was understood and how much was being ignored, he went to great lengths to develop a dossier of all the data, particularly the Magic messages, of which he had personal knowledge. To his consternation he discovered that many of these, which he himself had carefully and correctly filed away in their designated places, were missing. Terribly dismayed, he reconstituted the entire file—and again it disappeared, although other files in front of it and behind it were still in place.

During this same period he began to expect that there would sometime be a court-martial held on Admiral Kimmel, perhaps after the war, and that the information he possessed was critical to Kimmel's defense. He evidently became much concerned, unquestionably indignant, and finally sometime in 1943 took the unprecedented step and personal risk of seeking out the retired Admiral Kimmel to tell him what he knew. This was, in fact, the first intimation Kimmel had of the degree to which Washington's information had been kept from him. Although he had been aware that the CNO had special sources of information, unknown to him, under the general rubric of "Magic," he believed he had been kept informed of all that was pertinent. Admiral Stark had several times assured him that all information, from whatever source, that related to him or to his force at Pearl Harbor would be regularly sent to him. Safford's revelation of what the powers in Washington had known, and how little they had passed on to Pearl Harbor, was devastating. Kimmel also fully appreciated the tremendous personal risk Safford had run in going to him with the information and promised to protect him. This was the genesis of what one might think was the excessive personal concern Kimmel showed for Safford, as described in attorney Hanify's 1991 letter, quoted above.

Admiral Hart called Safford, and the testimony he gave was so complete and so revealing that it should receive a verbatim transcription. It is therefore reproduced here exactly as given on Saturday, 29 April 1944, beginning on page 387 of the Hart Inquiry, part

26 of the JCC Report, with the single exception that paragraphing has been introduced for ease in reading.

Question: What duties were you performing during the calendar year 1941?

Answer: I was the officer in charge of the Communications Security Section of Naval Communications. "Communications Security" was a covering title to mask Communications Intelligence although we also performed security . . . design and preparation of naval codes and ciphers and general communications security duties; that is, surveillance over their use. . . .

9. Q.: Was the unit at Pearl Harbor kept fully informed of the aforesaid results obtained by the Washington Unit?

A. Only as regards the operations of the Japanese Navy in the Pacific Ocean, with one important exception: On December 1, 1941, the Director of Naval Communications released OpNav Secret 011400; *Urgent,* to CinCAF and Com 16 [Manila]; *Priority* to CinCPac and Com 14 [Hawaii]; indicating that the Japanese were planning (a) landing at Kota Bharu in Malaya. . . .

17. Q.: Did your unit, as engaged upon its specialized endeavor, obtain, during November and December, any definite information which indicated the objectives which the Japanese were preparing to attack?

A. Yes, sir.

18. Q.: Please give, chronologically, with particular reference to dates, a brief summary of that information.

A. Going back to the late Spring of 1941, on May 22, we received positive proof of Japanese plans for the conquest of Southeastern Asia and the Southwest Pacific. On July 24, a high authority in Japan directed the withdrawal of merchant shipping from the Northeast Pacific, Southwest Pacific, and Indian Ocean. On September 4, we received information indicating Japan's determination to carry out her program of southward expansion and to expel the United States and England from China, Southeast Asia, and the Southwest Pacific. On October 15, we received unexpected confirmation of Japan's plans and intentions for the conquest of Southeastern Asia. In October, 1941, the Japanese Consuls were directing and advising the evacuation of Japanese Nationals from the Netherlands East Indies, Malaya, Philippines, Hawaii, America, and Europe. By October 28, this was in full progress.

On November 4, we received important information that the internal situation in Japan, both political and economic, since the American embargo, had become so desperate that the Japanese Government had to distract popular attention by a foreign war or else by bloodless diplomatic victory. On November 12, we received important information that the Japanese Government regarded November 25 as the deadline for negotiations then being conducted between the Japanese and American Governments to end. November 17, we received information from a very reliable source that Japan had no intention of attacking Russia in Siberia or she had changed her plans, if such intention ever existed. At one time, when it looked as if Moscow would fall, there were indications from several sources that Japan would invade Siberia.

On November 24, 1941, we learned that November 29, 1941, Tokyo time, was definitely the governing date for offensive military operations of some nature. We interpreted this to mean that large scale movements for the conquest of Southeast Asia and the Southwest Pacific would begin on that date, because, at that time, Hawaii was out of our minds. On November 26, we received specific evidence of Japan's intention to wage an offensive war against both Britain and the United States. On December 1, we had definite information from three independent sources that Japan was going to attack Britain and the United States, and, from two of them, that Japan would maintain peace with Russia.

On December 4, 1941, we received definite information from two more independent sources that Japan would attack the United States and Britain, but would maintain peace with Russia. At 9.00 p.m. (Washington time), December 6, 1941, we received positive information that Japan would declare war against the United States, at a time to be specified thereafter. This information was positive and unmistakable and was made available to Military [U.S. Army] Intelligence at this same time. Finally, at 10:15 a.m. (Washington time), December 7, 1941, we received positive information from the Signal Intelligence Service [(S.I.S.) War Department] that the Japanese declaration of war would be presented to the Secretary of State at 1:00 p.m. (Washington time) that date.

1:00 p.m. Washington time was sunrise in Hawaii and approximately midnight in the Philippines, and this indicated a surprise air raid on Pearl Harbor in about three hours. Kramer appended a note to this effect to the paper sent over from S.I.S. before presenting it to the Secretary of the Navy. I do not know whether or not a copy of this note was appended to the paper given to Admiral Stark. At this same time, information was also received indicating that Japan was about to commence hostilities against the British Empire. This information was sent over to S.I.S. immediately.

19. Q. Going back over that series, to what officials did your unit transmit the information concerning which you have just testified?

A. My unit transmitted information directly to Signal Intelligence in the War Department and to Naval Intelligence representative (that is, Commander A. H. McCollum, head of the Far Eastern Section, or Lieutenant Commander A. D. Kramer, attached to the Far Eastern Section of Naval Intelligence but actually working in the Communication Intelligence Unit). The further distribution of information within the Navy and to the President normally was undertaken by Kramer in his status as a subordinate to McCollum. Information was distributed daily, as a matter of routine, to the President, to the Secretary of the Navy, to the Chief of Naval Operations, the Assistant Chief of Naval Operations, the Director of War Plans, the Director of Naval Communications, and, of course, the Director of Naval Intelligence.

Within the Army, the Signal Intelligence Service, our opposite numbers, gave information to G-2, or Military Intelligence, and Colonel Bratton, head of the G-2 Far Eastern Section, distributed the information to the Secretary of State, the Secretary of War, Chief of Staff, Director of War Plans, and, of course, to the Director of Military Intelligence. On special occasions, information was disseminated at night or whenever it came in. There was a direct exchange of information between S.I.S. and the Navy Department C.I. Unit; also between O.N.I. and M.I.D.

20. Q. Was the foregoing information communicated to officials in the State Department?

A. It was always given to Secretary Hull and sometimes given to Under Secretary Sumner Welles. In the Spring of 1941, the information had gone further but, after a leak to the German Embassy, it was restricted to Secretary Hull and Secretary Welles.

21. Q. Is there any documentary report which shows the date and hour of delivery of the foregoing information to various officials?

A. There is no documentary evidence.

22. Q. Are you able to state, from memory, the date and hour on which the important information, say, from 1 December onward, was transmitted?

A. I can, from my recollection of Lieutenant Commander Kramer's verbal reports to me.

23. Q. Please give what you recall as regards those dates and hours.

A. The information on December 1, 2, 3, 4, 5, and 6, was disseminated about eleven a.m., within the Navy Department and was then given to the Naval Aide to the President who took it over to the White House, some time in the early afternoon. The "Winds Message" was given a special distribution shortly after eight a.m. on December 4, 1941, and was also included in the routine distribution. The information received late on December 6 was highly important and was distributed as a rush job by Lieutenant Commander Kramer, who left the Navy Department in an official station wagon shortly after nine p.m. and who had reached his last official by eleven p.m. Kramer returned to the Navy Department about one a.m. in the morning to see if there was any further information and then went home. He came down the next morning in time to give Admiral Stark written information at the Admiral's nine o'clock conference.

Much of the December 6 information was distributed over the telephone by Admiral Wilkinson and by Secretary Hull. The following officials were given this information that night: President Roosevelt (via the White House Aide), Secretary Hull, Secretary Stimson, Secretary Knox, Admiral Stark, Rear Admiral Turner, Rear Admiral Wilkinson, Rear Admiral Beardall. Lieutenant Colonel R. S. Bratton, U.S. Army, was given the same information at nine p.m. for dissemination to War Department officials, and we did not know any more, except that he got a copy over to Secretary Hull by ten o'clock. As regards information on the 7th, the same officials had this information by eleven a.m.—some sooner.

24. Q. Was any of the foregoing information, under dates of November and December, 1941, disseminated by the main Washington unit direct to the corresponding unit in the Fourteenth Naval District [Hawaii]?

A. No, sir. That was not permitted by a written order then in force; but there was one exception. On the 3rd of December, I prepared OpNav Secret Dispatch 031855, which was released by Captain Redman, the Assistant Director of Naval Communications. A similar dispatch was released by Admiral Wilkinson and filed at 031850. Admiral Wilkinson's message is referred to in the Roberts report.

Before drafting my message, I called Commander McCollum on the telephone and asked him, "Are you people in Naval Intelligence doing *anything* to get a warning out to the Pacific Fleet?" And McCollum replied, "*We* are doing everything *we* can to get the news out to the Fleet." McCollum emphasized both "we's." In sending this information, I was overstepping the bounds as established by approved war plans and joint agreement between Naval Communications and Naval Intelligence, but I did it because I thought McCollum had been unable to get his message released. OpNav 031855 was addressed to CinCAF and Com 16 [commander in chief Asiatic Fleet and commander 16th Naval District, i.e., the Philippines] for action, but was routed to CinCPac and Com 14 [Hawaii] for information. It was written in highly technical language and only one officer present at Pearl Harbor, the late Lieutenant H. M. Coleman, U.S.N., on CinCPac's Staff, could have explained its significance.

Even here, in sworn testimony, Safford was very careful. The only "highly technical language" used was the single word "Purple," twice repeated. See page 52.

25. Q. Did the unit in the Fourteenth Naval District have any material from which they could have gained this information through their own efforts?

A. No, sir, they did not have the material and they could not possibly have gained this information.

The examining officer did not desire to further examine this witness.

The examining officer informed the witness that he was privileged to make any further statement covering anything relating to the subject matter of the examination which he thought should be a matter of record in connection therewith, which had not been fully brought out by the previous questioning.

The witness made the following statement: The C.I. Unit in Washington had no authority to forward to the C.I. Units in Pearl Harbor or Corregidor, or to the Commanders-in-Chief direct, any information other than technical information pertaining to direction finding, interception, and so forth. The dissemination of intelligence was the duty, responsibility, and privilege of the Office of Naval Intelligence as prescribed in Communication War Plans approved by the Chief of Naval Operations in March, 1940.

On the 4th of December, 1941, Commander McCollum drafted a long warning message to the Commanders-in-Chief of the Asiatic and Pacific Fleets, summarizing significant events up to that date, quoting the "Winds Message," and ending with the positive warning that war was imminent. Admiral Wilkinson approved this message and discussed it with Admiral Noyes in my presence. I was given the message to read after Admiral Noyes read it, and saw it at about three p.m., Washington time, on December 4, 1941.

Admiral Wilkinson asked, "What do you think of the message?"

Admiral Noyes replied, "I think it is an insult to the intelligence of the Commander-in-Chief."

Admiral Wilkinson stated, "I do not agree with you. Admiral Kimmel is a very busy man, with a lot of things on his mind, and he may not see the picture as clearly as you and I do. I think it only fair to the Commander-in-Chief that he be given this warning and I intend to send it if I can get it released by the front office."

Admiral Wilkinson then left and I left a few minutes later. At the time of the Japanese attack on Pearl Harbor, I thought that this warning message had been sent, and did not realize until two years later, when I studied the Roberts report very carefully, that McCollum's message had not been sent. In order to clarify the above statement and my answer to a previous question, it is necessary to explain what is meant by the "Winds Message."

The "Winds Message" was a name given by Army and Navy personnel performing radio intelligence duties to identify a plain-language Japanese news broadcast in which a fictitious weather report gave warning of the intentions of the Japanese Government with respect to war against the United States, Britain (including the N.E.I.) and Russia. We received a tip-off from the British in Singapore in late November, 1941, which was immediately forwarded to the Navy Department by the Commander-in-Chief, U.S. Asiatic Fleet, with an information copy to the Commander-in-Chief, Pacific Fleet. We also received a tip-off from the Dutch in Java through the American Consul General and through the Senior Military Observer. The Dutch tip-off was handled in routine fashion by the coding rooms of the State Department, War Department, and Navy Department.

The Director of Naval Intelligence requested that special effort be made to monitor Radio Tokyo to catch the "Winds Message" when it should be sent, and this was done.

From November 28 until the attack on Pearl Harbor, Tokyo broadcast schedules were monitored by about 12 intercept stations, as follows: N.E.I. at Java; British at Singapore; U.S. Army at Hawaii and San Francisco; U.S. Navy at Corregidor, Hawaii, Bremerton, and four or five stations along the Atlantic seaboard. All Navy intercept stations in the continental United States were directed to forward all Tokyo plain-language broadcasts by teletype, and Bainbridge Island ran up bills of sixty dollars per day for this material alone.

The "Winds Message" was actually broadcast during the evening of December 3, 1941 (Washington time), which was December 4 by Greenwich time and Tokyo time. The combination of frequency, time of day, and radio propagation was such that the "Winds Message" was heard only on the East Coast of the United States, and even then by only one or two of the Navy Stations that were listening for it. The other nations and other Navy C.I. Units, not hearing the "Winds Message" themselves and not receiving any word from the Navy Department, naturally presumed that the "Winds Message" had not yet been sent, and that the Japanese Government was still deferring the initiation of hostilities.

When the Japanese attacked Pearl Harbor, the British at Singapore, the Dutch at Java, and the Americans at Manila were just as surprised and astonished as the Pacific Fleet and Army posts in Hawaii. It is apparent that the War Department, like the Navy Department, failed to send out information that the "Winds Message" had been sent by Tokyo. The "Winds Message" was received in the Navy Department during the evening of December 3, 1941, while Lieutenant (jg) Francis M. Brotherhood, U.S.N.R., was on watch. There was some question in Brotherhood's mind as to what this message really meant because it came in a different form from what had been anticipated.

Brotherhood called in Lieutenant Commander Kramer, who came down that evening and identified that message as the "Winds Message" we had been looking for. The significant part of the "Winds Message" read: "HIGASHI NO KAZE AME. NISHI NO KAZE HARE. The negative form of KITA NO KAZE KUMORI."

The literal translation of these phrases is: "EAST WIND RAIN. WEST WIND CLEAR. NEITHER NORTH WIND NOR CLOUDY."

The meaning of this message from the previously mentioned tip-off was: "War with the United States. War with Britain, including the N.E.I., etc. Peace with Russia."

I first saw the "Winds Message" about 8:00 a.m. on Thursday, December 4, 1941. Lieutenant A. A. Murray, U.S.N.R., came into my office with a big smile on his face and a piece of paper in his hand and said, "Here it is!" as he handed me the "Winds Message". As I remember, it was the original yellow teletype sheet with the significant "Winds" underscored and the meaning in Kramer's handwriting at the bottom. Smooth copies of the translation were immediately prepared and distributed to Naval Intelligence and to S.I.S. in the War Department. As the direct result of the "Winds Message," I prepared a total of five messages, which were released between 1200 and 1600 that date, ordering the destruction of cryptographic systems and secret and confidential papers by certain activities on the Asiatic Station.

As a direct result of the "Winds Message," McCollum drafted the long warning message, previously referred to, which was disapproved by higher authority, but which the Navy Department C.I. [COMINT] Unit believed had been sent. Both Naval Intelligence and the Navy Department C.I. Unit regarded the "Winds Message" as definitely committing the Japanese Government to war with the United States and Britain, whereas the information of earlier dates had been merely statements of intent. We believed that the Japanese would attack by Saturday (December 6), or by Sunday (December 7) at the latest.

The following officers recall having seen and having read the "Winds Message": Captain L. F. Safford, U.S.N., Lieutenant Commander F. M. Brotherhood, U.S.N.R., Lieutenant Commander A. A. Murray, U.S.N.R., and Lieutenant (jg) F. L. Freeman, U.S.N.

The following officers knew by hearsay that the "Winds Message" had been intercepted but did not actually see it themselves: Commander L. W. Parke, U.S.N., Lieutenant Commander G. W. Linn, U.S.N.R., Ensign Wilmer Fox, U.S.N., and Major F. B. Rowlett, Signal Corps Reserve.

The following officers should have some recollection of the "Winds Message":

U.S. Navy - Rear Admiral T. S. Wilkinson, Captain A. H. McCollum, Colonel R. A. Boone (U.S. Marine Corps), Commander G. W. Welker, Commander A. D. Kramer, Lieutenant Commander A. V. Pering, and Ship's Clerk H. L. Bryant.

U.S. Army - Brigadier General T. J. Betts, Colonel O. K. Sadtler, Colonel R. S. Bratton, Colonel Rex Minckler, Colonel Moses Pettigrew, Colonel Harold Doud, and Lieutenant Colonel R. E. Shukraft.

The "Winds Message" was last seen by myself about December 14, 1941, when the papers which had been distributed in early December were assembled by Kramer, checked by myself, and then turned over to the Director of Naval Communications for use as evidence before the Roberts Commission, according to my understanding at the time. Further information as to Pearl Harbor's estimates of locations of Japanese forces in early December, 1941, may be found in the monthly report of Station "H"—in the "Chronology" which was prepared daily and forwarded weekly by air mail. This information was, of course, prepared by and currently available to the Pearl Harbor C.I. Unit but was not received in the Navy Department until a delay of about two weeks.

With his testimony about Pearl Harbor, Safford found himself on the wrong side of the fence and, by consequence, his influence and importance were from then on attacked. Though he had once been called the navy's foremost cryptographer, awarded medals and even a special $100,000 cash award in lieu of the commercial copyrights to which he might theoretically otherwise have been entitled, he was thereafter noted as "erratic," unstable, prone to unexplainable flights of fancy regarding his "pet projects" or any matter of his special concern. From that time onward, his influence was essentially nil in the part of the naval profession to which he had devoted his life, and he retired from service in 1951.

Fourth Investigation: Army Board

Fourth of the inquiries was an army Pearl Harbor board of investigation (of General Short) that met on 20 July 1944 and concluded on 20 October 1944. Its proceedings may be found in parts 27–31 of the JCC Report, and its findings in part 39 ("Reports, Findings, and

Conclusions"). This board was composed of Generals George Grunert, Henry D. Russell, and Walter H. Frank, all contemporaries of Marshall and Short. The recorder was Col. Charles W. West; assistant recorder was Major Clausen. The board saw considerable fault in General Marshall, reporting on pages 175 and 176 of part 39 the finding that he had failed in the following particulars:

> (a) To keep the Commanding General of the Hawaiian Department fully advised of the growing tenseness of the Japanese situation which indicated an increasing necessity for better preparation for war, of which information he had an abundance and Short had little.
>
> (b) To send additional instructions to the Commanding General of the Hawaiian Department on November 28, 1941, when evidently he failed to realize the import of General Short's reply of November 27th, which indicated clearly that General Short had misunderstood and misconstrued the message of November 27 (472) and had not adequately alerted his command for war.
>
> (c) To get to General Short on the evening of December 6th and the early morning of December 7th, the critical information indicating an almost immediate break with Japan, although there was ample time to have accomplished this.
>
> (d) To investigate and determine the state of readiness of the Hawaiian Command between November 27 and December 7, 1941, despite the impending threat of war.

On page 137 of part 39 appears the army board's thorough analysis of the events of 26 November 1941 and conclusion:

> It seems well established that the sending of this "Ten Point" memorandum by the Secretary of State was used by the Japanese as the signal for starting the war by the attack on Pearl Harbor.

The board's analysis of the confusing instructions contained in the "war-warning messages" to the navy and army appears on the following pages, and on page 139 is the following:

> The record shows that from informers and other sources the War Department had complete and detailed information of Japanese intentions. Information of the evident Japanese inten-

> tion to go to war in the very near future was well known to the Secretary of State, the Secretary of War, the Chief of Staff of the Army, the Secretary of the Navy, and the Chief of Naval Operations. It was not a question of fact; it was only a question of time. The next few days would see the end of peace and the beginning of war.
>
> If it be assumed that for any reason the information could not have been given to the Hawaiian Department, then it was a responsibility of the War Department to give orders to Short what to do, and to tell him to go on an all-out alert instead of a sabotage alert.

The army board's report was routinely sent to Chief of Staff Marshall, even though he was one of those severely criticized, and to Secretary Stimson, whose diaries had been extensively quoted. Both men were appalled, and it must be assumed they discussed it privately with the president himself. Ultimately, the board's report was sequestered as being detrimental to the war effort, its findings kept severely under wraps, the reputation and character of its members impugned as being inferior on the one hand, and hostile to Marshall on the other. Stimson did this no doubt with the full support of Roosevelt, to whom Marshall had become essential, and Clausen and Lee rather fully described the effort in 1992 in *Final Judgement.* Fearing the disclosure of some or all of the findings, nevertheless, concerned (not legitimately) for their effect upon himself and Marshall—and (quite legitimately) for their effect on our prosecution of the war—Stimson in 1944 set Clausen up as a private investigator with full powers, reporting only to him.

Marshall was quoted, at this point, as expressing his concern to Stimson that his usefulness to the president might be ended were the army board's report to be circulated, even under the heaviest security restrictions. President Roosevelt placed great reliance on General Marshall and would have been sorely pressed had the report come to light. Clausen had been in civilian life a lawyer in high repute on the West Coast and already had a good insight into the problems through his recently completed function as assistant recorder for the army board. He was not, however, either objective or nonpartisan, as the book he published many years later shows so clearly.

Fifth Investigation: Navy Court of Inquiry

The fifth inquiry was a navy court of inquiry (navy alone) that sat from 24 July to 19 October 1944 and is printed in parts 32 and 33 of the JCC Report, with its findings beginning on page 297 of part 39. The president of the court was Admiral Orin Gould Murfin; the members were Vice Admirals Edward C. Kalbfus and Adolphus Andrews. All three were contemporaries of but senior to Kimmel on the navy lineal list. The findings of this court were divided into two sections because of the overriding requirement of secrecy concerning our ability to intercept and decode Japanese messages. Any reference to Magic, or testimony that by any stretch of Japanese imagination might conceivably lead to a suspicion that we were able to read Japan's most secret codes, had to be protected at all costs. The first and longer section, therefore, was classified top secret and was not intended to be given out. The shorter second portion of the findings was unclassified and completely exonerated Kimmel because he had not been kept fully advised, but it could not specify the information he was deprived of.

The court expected this second part to be given out to the press and was astonished when Secretary of the Navy James Forrestal (Secretary Knox having died the previous April of a heart attack) wrote to its president, simultaneously releasing the letter to the press, that the court had marked all the proceedings and findings "secret" and that, therefore, nothing could be given out. Admiral Murfin immediately sought an audience with Forrestal to tell him that this was not true, that the court had expected the unclassified findings to be publicly released and had submitted its findings in two parts for this reason. Forrestal responded that he had meant to direct Murfin to make both parts secret, to which Murfin replied that the secretary could so classify them if he wished, but that he had no right to say the court had done so.

Forrestal nevertheless refused to release the second part of the findings, and the press, having nothing to go on other than the never-retracted incorrect letter from Forrestal, took its words as accurate. Thus this matter died.

Unfortunately, naval procedure, like the army's, required that the CNO and the secretary of the navy—the navy's top naval and civilian officials—approve the proceedings and findings of courts held on officers of admiral rank, and both disapproved the report of the court of inquiry held on Kimmel. The CNO in 1944 was the redoubtable Admiral King. On the ironic date of 7 December 1944 he informed a thunderstruck Kimmel, in private, that despite his personal sympathies he had signed a prepared endorsement of disapproval of the findings of the court of inquiry without even reading the testimony! He also indicated, without exactly saying so, that higher authority had pretty much dictated what his endorsement would have to be.

Four years later, under a 10 November 1948 dateline, the *New York Herald Tribune* printed an article by reporter James E. Warner to the effect that earlier in the year King had written to the Navy Department to say that he was "in error" when he disapproved the findings of the court of inquiry, and that he desired the milder language of his later letter substituted for the pejorative language in his earlier endorsement. Presumably, he had finally gotten around to reading the testimony.

But King was no longer COMINCH (the office had in fact been disestablished), and the damage had already been done. King suffered a disabling stroke that same year (prior to publication of the Warner article) and was no longer capable of speech. Although his mind was said to be as clear as ever, this is improbable, and he was never able to follow up on whatever he might have intended.

Forrestal had been secretary only since May of 1944, having "fleeted up" from the post of under secretary upon Knox's death. Although he quickly became identified as a man of imperious will in his own right, it can be speculated that at the early stage of his tenure, in 1944, he allowed himself to be influenced by King's uncompromising stand on the court of inquiry endorsement. Forrestal's disapproving endorsement of the court's report quotes King's at length and possibly was written by the same person who wrote King's. Like King's, Forrestal's disapproval was based on Kimmel's not having sent up patrol flights to the north after receipt of the 27 November "this is a war warning" message.

The secretary's endorsement goes a bit further, however, stating (page 361, part 39 of the JCC Report),

> There were sufficient Fleet patrol planes and crews in fact available at Oahu during the week preceding the attack to have flown, for at least several weeks, a daily reconnaissance covering 128 degrees to a distance of about 700 miles. *[This is untrue.]*
>
> The sectors north of Oahu were generally recognized as being the most likely sectors from which a Japanese attack would come, if the Japanese were to attack Pearl Harbor. *[This is untrue.]*

> If a daily distant reconnaissance had been flown from Oahu after 27 November 1941, with the available patrol planes, the northern sectors would probably have been searched. *[Possibly, of course, but according to other statements in the record, north would not have been searched more than any other direction.]*
>
> The Japanese carriers launched their planes from a position 200 miles due north of Oahu. *[This is correct.]*

The foregoing would be, if all true, a devastating indictment of the Pearl Harbor command. The fact is, however, that it is actually false, and it may reveal more about 1944 assumptions (willful or from poor memory) about Washington's thinking on 7 December 1941 than it does about the situation's actual realities. It reads as though written with the intent to present the best case against Kimmel and Short regardless of where the truth actually lay, for the only accurate statement in it is the final one.

However, one criticism is valid: On the morning of 7 December the U.S. Navy had only a single patrol plane aloft, sent out under the nominal orders of Admiral Bloch. The army had none at all. Kimmel, disarmed by staff statements that more were not practicable and that there was no prospect at all of an attack on Pearl Harbor, did not insist on more. His reasoning for not doing so was that his readiness posture was aimed at forcing a decisive fleet engagement at sea soon after the declaration of war, under conditions of maximum advantage to our side. His long-distance air patrols were vital to this plan, for without them there was no way he could protect his own fleet from the surprise he intended to inflict on the enemy fleet, let alone locate and surprise it. For the best chance of success he needed far more patrol planes than he had in fact, and in tiptop shape. He had many times brought to Washington's attention his great deficiency of Catalina PBY-5s, the newest and most efficient patrol planes, and had been promised more, but although these had not yet been delivered, Washington (Stark) had promised him plenty of warning before they would be needed. Based on this assurance, his aviation staff conference, to whom he had referred the question, had unanimously recommended against using up the few Catalinas he had, and their crews, in long patrol flights.

All this he had carefully stated to the court of inquiry, and in the judgment of that body his actions and orders were the proper ones for the circumstances, given that he could not have foreseen the coming attack with the information made available to him. He would have required clairvoyance to have anticipated the right sector (north) and the right days (say 4, 5, 6, and 7 December) to fly his patrols, but had he managed to do so the fatal surprise might not have occurred—or not been so terrible.

As already pointed out, determination that the north sector was the most dangerous was made entirely from hindsight in 1945. Nowhere in 1941 did anyone mention the deduction that prevailing winds being northerly (i.e., from the north), enemy carriers to the north could launch and recover aircraft while speeding away from Oahu and possible pursuit. What *was* stated to Kimmel in conference, and in writing by the often referred to Martin-Bellinger Report (Maj. Gen. Frederick L. Martin, army air corps, and Rear Adm. Patrick N. L. Bellinger, commanding navy patrol planes in Hawaii), was that the only patrol worthy of the name was one with a 360-degree coverage to a range of 700 miles, and that for this, 250 to 270 patrol planes were the minimum necessity.

On 27 November there were just thirty-six flyable Catalinas in Oahu, twenty-four more at Midway, and an additional twelve in lengthy overhaul. The army had eight operational B-17 bombers that could also fly distant patrols if necessary. Mathematically, forty-four planes would have been able to cover about 110 degrees, not 128, to a range of two hundred miles, not seven hundred, on a round-the-clock basis for not more than one or two days. Then crew fatigue and a near total absence of spare parts would have grounded all of them.

It would have been dangerous to institute patrols in only one direction—presumably that of the believed maximum danger—because the enemy could be depended upon to learn the direction of such a patrol and simply avoid it. So reported Kimmel's air advisers, and so had stated the Martin-Bellinger Report. Apparently at one point Admiral Halsey had thought the direct line toward Japanese military bases in the Marshall Islands (southwest) to be the one that should be most patrolled (and in an alert in 1940, Admiral Richardson had set up a short-lived patrol in that direction), but nowhere had Admiral Kimmel received any official estimate, least of all from his own air staff, that any sector was more dangerous than any other.

In spite of the later hindsight, the record shows that in 1941 there was no known or predicted "more dangerous sector." The Pearl Harbor Hearings of 1945–1946 contain testimony from Major General Martin and Rear Admiral Bellinger in which they state their hindsight conviction (in 1945) that north was the most likely direction from which to expect an enemy carrier task force to launch an air attack because the prevailing winds were from the north. Other officers, members of Kimmel's staff associated with naval aviation, testified to the same thing—in 1945.

As the JCC Hearings made clear, however, their testimony did not apply to 1941. Their joint estimate, the Martin-Bellinger Report, which they made for their respective commanders in 1941, went into great detail about the inadequate number of patrol-capable aircraft available to the command. They recommended continuing the current training effort on an urgent basis, and simultaneously continuing the pressure on naval budgeteers in Washington to provide more aircraft and crews.

Additionally, Kimmel's advisers repeatedly and strenuously stressed the necessity for plentiful supplies of spare parts. These were mandatory to keep the planes in the air. The PBY-5 patrol planes, the famous Catalinas, required continuous engine maintenance and were known to have a propensity for damaged air cones, the airfoil-shaped covers that went in front of the propellers, which had to be replaced on a regular basis. Neither the army air corps nor the navy had anything like adequate spares, let alone sufficient aircrews, to keep their planes in the air for more than two consecutive days. Even assuming the crews might have been able to fly for an entire twenty-four–hour period, sleeping in turn as their aircraft droned through the sky, it went against logic to assume they would have been able to fly "for weeks," as Secretary Forrestal's endorsement evidently expected, and it would have been even more illogical to presume that the search they might have been able to carry out would have been worth anything at all. General Martin and Admiral Bellinger would have answered with ironic laughter if they had been ordered to fly the patrols suggested.

Evidently neither King nor Forrestal noted the significant point that although Kimmel had repeatedly asked in the strongest terms for additional patrol aircraft, and that a portion of his request had finally been approved (only 100 planes instead of the asked-for 250, however), not one plane of this group had yet arrived in Hawaii. Nearly 2,000 patrol-type planes had, however, been sent to Britain during the same period, a fact unknown to anyone in Hawaii. Kimmel had held a special conference with all his experts and had decided that with the very few planes and aircrews, and no spares, expending them precipitantly in a two-day search in a single sector would have been counterproductive to the overall war plan that was his responsibility. The decision was made to press for more resources and depend on the promised warning from Washington. The court had found this to be the right decision under the circumstances as then known.

Had Kimmel and Short, or any of their advisers in Pearl Harbor, been made aware in even the slightest degree of the state of tension that engulfed Washington on the night of the sixth and the morning of the seventh, they would have had all their patrol planes in the air in an all-out search, and would undoubtedly have spotted the Japanese task force hours before the attack was launched.

With a comment that they "would have to depend on receiving the promised warning from Washington," Kimmel went along with the Martin-Bellinger recommendation. The naval court of inquiry cited these facts and considerations in its recommended exoneration of the admiral, but COMINCH King disapproved this finding in two lengthy endorsements. The first of these begins on page 335 of part 39 of the JCC Report and was classified top secret. After eight pages of fine print discussing information Kimmel should have received but did not, mainly because Stark failed to apprise him of it, as King held was Stark's duty, King wrote, beginning at the bottom of page 343:

> 4. In the final opinion and summary [page 1,208] the Court finds that no offenses have been committed or serious blame incurred on the part of any person or persons in the naval service, and recommends that no further proceedings be had in the matter. I concur that there is not adequate evidence to support general court martial proceedings, but this does not bar administrative action, if such action is found appropriate.
>
> 5. Despite the evidence that no naval officer was at fault to a degree likely to result in a conviction if brought to trial, nevertheless the Navy cannot evade a share of responsibility for the Pearl Harbor incident. That disaster cannot be regarded as an "act of God" beyond human power to prevent or mitigate. It is true that the country as a whole is basically responsible in that the people were unwilling to support an adequate army and navy until it was too late to repair the consequences of past neglect in time to deal effectively with the attack that ushered in the war. It is true that the Army was responsible for local defense at Pearl Harbor. Nevertheless, some things could have been done by the Navy to lessen the success of the initial Japanese blow. Admiral Stark and Admiral Kimmel were the respon-

sible officers, and it is pertinent to examine the possible courses of action they might have taken.

Admiral Stark was, of course, aware that the United States was primarily concerned with its own possessions, and the most important United States possessions were the Philippine Islands and the Hawaiian Islands. His attention should have been centered on those two places, as the Pacific situation became more and more acute. . . . In my opinion, Admiral Stark failed to give Admiral Kimmel an adequate summary of the information available in Washington, particularly in the following respects:

Admiral Kimmel was not informed of the State Department's note of 26 November to the Japanese *[our ultimatum of that date]*. This note was a definite step toward breaking relations.

Admiral Kimmel was not informed of the substance of certain Japanese messages *[the "bomb plot" message]* inquiring as to dispositions of ships inside Pearl Harbor, which, because of their frequency, indicated a supervening Japanese interest in Pearl Harbor as a possible target.

Admiral Kimmel was not informed of the implementation of the "Winds Message" *[this is true]*. Admiral Stark says he never got this information himself, but it is clear that it did reach Admiral Stark's office. This, together with the handling of other matters of information, indicates lack of efficiency in Admiral Stark's organization.

Admiral Stark failed to appreciate the significance of the "1.00 p.m. message" received on the morning of 7 December, although the implications were appreciated by at least one of his subordinates. It appears that had this message been handled by the quickest available means, and with due appreciation of its significance, it *might* have reached Admiral Kimmel in time to enable him to make some last minute preparations that would have enhanced the ability of the ships in Pearl Harbor to meet the Japanese air attack *[agreed]*.

There is a certain sameness of tenor of such information as Admiral Stark sent to Admiral Kimmel. They [*sic*] do not convey in themselves the sense of intensification of the critical relations between the United States and Japan *[agreed].*

In my opinion Admiral Kimmel, despite the failure of Admiral Stark to keep him fully informed, nevertheless did have some indications of increasing tenseness as to relations with Japan. In particular, he had the "war warning" message of 27 November *[this is true],* the "hostile action possible at any moment" message of 28 November *[this was actually the parallel and very confusing message sent to General Short at the same time by the War Department, which the two commanders discussed before receipt of the subsequent message directing wholesale exchange of marine corps and army troops and planes],* the 3 December message that Japan had ordered destruction of codes *[true],* and the messages of 4 and 6 December concerning United States secret and confidential matter at outlying Pacific islands *[these were greatly "watered down" from the messages originally proposed by Safford and as sent warned of nothing].* These messages must be considered in connection with other facets of the situation, and Admiral Kimmel's statement on this phase of the matter must be given due consideration. After weighing these considerations, I am of the opinion that he could and should have judged more accurately the gravity of the danger to which the Hawaiian Islands were exposed. The following courses of action were open to him:

He could have used patrol aircraft which were available to him to conduct long range reconnaissance in the more dangerous sectors. Whether or not this would have resulted in detecting the approach of the Japanese carriers is problematical. However, it would have made the Japanese task more difficult. *[As explained, with the inadequate resources available, this was an impossible proposal.]*

He could have rotated the "in port" periods of his vessels in a less routine manner, so as to have made it impossible for the Japanese to have predicted when there would be any vessels in port. This would have made the Japanese task less easy. *[This is probably a valid criticism, but Kimmel was driving the battle fleet hard in preparation for the big fleet battle in his approved plan for conduct of the coming war, and in-port periods for crew rest were already being rotated to the maximum. Allowing all eight battleships to be in Pearl Harbor on 7 December proved to be a costly mistake, but by the same line of argument Kimmel should be given credit for the absence of the most important ships, his carriers.]*

If he had appreciated the gravity of the situation even a few hours before the Japanese attack, it is logical to suppose that naval planes would have been in the air during the early morning period, that ships' batteries would have been fully manned, and that damage control organizations would have been fully operational *[only too true].*

The derelictions on the parts of Admiral Stark and Admiral Kimmel were faults of omission rather than faults of commission. In the case in question, they indicate lack of the superior judgment necessary for exercising command commensurate with their rank and their assigned duties, rather than culpable inefficiency. *[Stark's fault was not passing on important information; Kimmel's was not having enough ESP to make up the difference.]*

Since trial by general court martial is not warranted by the evidence adduced, appropriate administrative action would appear to be the relegation of both of these officers to positions in which lack of superior judgment may not result in future errors.

This final paragraph states that despite the accused's demand for a court-martial on the charges placed against him, the evidence seems insufficient to convict. Therefore, a trial was to be denied, and "administrative action" substituted. No defense against the charges would be allowed.

Also to be noted is King's position that although Stark was receiving information he did not pass on to Kimmel because he did not correctly interpret it as foreshadowing an attack on Pearl Harbor, Stark's explanation that he honestly did not see it that way was accepted at face value, but Kimmel, having no chance to interpret any of the information Stark had, should all the same have been better able to foresee the attack headed toward him. Such an argument would convince neither judge nor jury in any American civilian court, nor would it have convinced anyone except someone whose basic inclination toward fairness had been overcome because of other axes to grind.

To be mentioned also is that despite the above criticism, Stark retained his four-star rank of full admiral and served out the war in a post of great responsibility in London. For this he received a decoration from the British government and a third Distinguished Service Medal from the United States. Kimmel and Short, in contrast, were reduced in rank, retired against their will only months after the war began, and never again employed on active duty. So much for "positions in which lack of superior judgment may not result in future errors"! MacArthur, although demonstrably more at fault than Short, Kimmel, or Stark, received the highest reward of all, supreme allied commander in the Pacific, and finally commander of Occupied Japan.

On 7 December 1948, having belatedly become aware of the *Herald Tribune* article about King's change of heart, Kimmel wrote to Secretary of the Navy John L. Sullivan. Noting that he had received a copy of the King letter, dated 14 July 1948, Kimmel continued,

> In Admiral King's letter he withdraws that portion of his endorsement on the record of the proceedings of the Naval Court of Inquiry which stated, with respect to Admiral Stark and me, "In the case in question, they indicate lack of the superior judgment necessary for exercising command commensurate with the rank and their assigned duties, rather than culpable inefficiency."
>
> He also withdraws that portion of his endorsement reading—
>
> > "Since trial by general court martial is not warranted by the evidence adduced, appropriate administrative action would appear to be the relegation of both of these officers to positions in which the lack of superior judgment may not result in future errors."
>
> On August 13, 1945, the Secretary of the Navy entered a directive applicable to Admiral Stark and me of similar tenor to the endorsement which Admiral King has now withdrawn. In my case that directive read:
>
> > Accordingly, I direct (that) Rear Admiral Husband E. Kimmel, USN (Retired) shall not hold any position in the United States Navy which requires the exercise of superior judgment.

The Secretary's directive with respect to Admiral Stark was identical with that just quoted applicable to me.

The action of the Navy Department, which included the award of a distinguished service medal to Admiral Stark, subsequent to and apparently as a result of Admiral King's letter of 14 July 1948, has the effect of rescinding the directive of the Secretary of the Navy in Admiral Stark's case.

Admiral King's letter of 14 July changes his original endorsement with respect to me as well as with respect to Admiral Stark. Accordingly, it appears that considerations of fairness would make equally applicable to me a rescinding of the directive of the Secretary of the Navy of August 13, 1945, which I have heretofore set forth.

Accordingly, it is requested that my record bear the notation that the directive of the Secretary of the Navy of August 13, 1945, to the effect that I was not to hold any position in the United States Navy which requires the exercise of superior judgment is rescinded.

It is requested that I be notified of the action taken with respect to this request.

Yours very truly,

H. E. Kimmel,

Rear-Admiral U.S.Navy Retired

There is no record that Admiral Kimmel ever received an answer to this letter, and the probability is that he expected none, having become accustomed to being ignored. He had not been informed of Admiral King's letter when it was sent, although supporters of Admiral Stark apparently had been, inasmuch as it made possible the award of another Distinguished Service Medal to him. It can be noted also that Kimmel asked only for correction of an invidious entry on his record, not a decoration comparable to the one given Stark.

The realization must long since have sunk into Kimmel's soul that fairness and equal treatment in words and on paper are not the same as what bureaucracy does in fact.

The navy court of inquiry and the later special Hewitt inquiry (of which more later)—and the endorsements of both by Forrestal, King, and President Harry Truman—all laid as much blame on Stark as they did on Kimmel. All clearly stated that Stark's failure to pass on to Kimmel any of the extraordinary information he possessed on 6 December and on the morning of the seventh was one of the primary reasons why the Japanese had so successfully surprised our fleet. Yet Stark retained his four-star rank, remained on active duty until after the war, and was even rewarded with another medal, whereas Kimmel was still a pariah, unworthy even of the courtesy of a reply to his dignified but truly poignant letter asking only for a simple statement that part of the obloquy he had been carrying was lifted.

How many times must he have recalled the spent bullet that struck his chest that awful day, eliciting the remark that it might have been better had it killed him! How many times must he have thought of the way a Japanese officer might have solved it all: ceremoniously, on an immaculate white mat, with only a moment's pain—and then all debts paid and honor restored.

Only family and friends could assuage Kimmel's living hell. The navy, to which he had devoted a life of proud and useful service, which had once pointed to him as an example of all that was good and admirable, now thought of him as beneath even crude notice, if it thought of him at all. It had used him, thrown him aside as a worthless sacrifice, and now would not even look his way. He had a file of hate mail. Maybe that was all there was left.

Sixth Investigation: The Clarke Investigation

Sixth was the Clarke Investigation, held urgently in several places over the period from 4 August to 20 September 1944. It occupies the whole of part 34 of the JCC Report, the thinnest of the many printed paperback volumes. Pursuant to oral instructions from General Marshall, Col. Carter W. Clarke, an intelligence officer with top-secret clearance, received a directive from the adjutant general of the army "to conduct an investigation regarding the manner in which certain TOP SECRET communications were handled." The colonel, also remembered as the officer who carried General Marshall's plea to presidential candidate Thomas E. Dewey not to reveal the existence of Magic in the campaign, confined himself specifically to the directive he had received and made no findings of culpability regarding the execution of plans or directives. His full report, which with enclosures consisted of only some 225 pages, is nevertheless an interesting summary of critical messages received or intercepted, and how they were handled. He stated, for example,

> That between 1 October and the afternoon of 7 December 1941, there were at least 37 coded messages . . . between the Tokyo Government and their embassies in various parts of the world which were intercepted by the Signal Intelligence Service and were decoded. . . . [including] at least one copy of a telephone conversation between the Tokyo Government and the Japanese Embassy in Washington. These intercepted and decoded messages were . . . designated as "MAGIC". . . .
>
> That on 28 November 1941 [a message was decoded that] read as follows:
>
> > From Tokyo
> > To Washington
> > 19 November 1941
> > Regarding the broadcast of a special message in an emergency.
> > In case of emergency (danger of cutting off our diplomatic relations) and the cutting off of international communications, the following warning will be added in the middle of the daily Japanese language short wave news broadcast:
> > (1) In case of a Japan-U.S. relations in danger:
> > HIGASHI NO KAZEAME (EAST WIND RAIN)
> > (2) Japan-U.S.S.R. relations:
> > KITANOKAZE KUMORI (NORTH WIND CLOUDY)
> > (3) Japan-British relations:
> > NISHI NO KAZE HARE (WEST WIND CLEAR)
> > This signal will be given in the middle and at the end as a weather forecast and each sentence will be repeated twice. When this is heard, please destroy all code papers, etc. This is as yet to be a completely secret arrangement.
> > Forward as urgent intelligence.
>
> On the same day, 28 November 1941, Col. Bratton made arrangements for listening for Japanese broadcasts that might include this code. . . . The Federal Communications Commission

did thereafter monitor Japanese broadcasts [to detect] the "Winds" code. I am unable to find that a Japanese message using the "Winds" code was intercepted by the FCC or the Army Signal Corps until after Pearl Harbor.

I find that on 5 December 1941, Col. [Otis K.] Sadtler was informed by Adm. Noyes, Naval Communications Officer, that a Japanese message using the "Winds" code had been intercepted the previous night, [meaning] the Japanese-Great Britain relations were to be broken; that . . . Col Sadtler so informed [various officers] but that Gen. Miles or Col. Bratton never informed Gen. Marshall personally (but having been informed that Commander Rochefort knew about the "Winds" code message, Col. Bratton caused the following message to be sent to his counterpart in Hawaii:)

> CONTACT COMMANDER ROCHEFORT IMMEDIATELY THRU COMMANDANT FOURTEEN NAVAL DISTRICT REGARDING BROADCASTS FROM TOKIO [*sic*] REFERENCE WEATHER.

Colonel Bratton seems to have been one of the few intelligence operatives on our side who was fully alert to the prospect of war with Japan. In the absence of instructions from his superiors, this was an effort to alert the Hawaii commanders. Clausen, in *Final Judgement,* makes considerable reference to this message and to the fact that General Short's intelligence officer, for whom it was intended, took no action and must therefore be declared as having been incompetent in his assigned position.

Colonel Clarke described in detail the search for General Marshall, Colonel Bratton's attempts to get the army into action, and the final result: General Marshall's writing of a warning message to be delivered by the army signal corps. Clarke concluded with the following damning tabulation of times concerning Marshall's message:

	EST	Honolulu Time
Filed War Dept. Message Center	12:00 noon	6:30 A.M.
Sent by Western Union	12:17 P.M.	6:47 A.M.
Received at RCA, Honolulu		7:33 A.M.
[Time of Japanese attack]		*[7:55 A.M.]*
Delivered to Signal Officer, Honolulu		11:45 A.M.
Delivered to AGO, Hawaiian Dept.		2:58 P.M.

Blame would have been cast everywhere, but especially upon Short because one of the traditional and primary duties of any commander is to see to it that his orders are correctly understood and carried out by those for whose performance he is responsible.

In the above list, RCA stands for the well-known Radio Corporation of America. AGO is believed to mean adjutant general's office. The Japanese attack began at 7:55 A.M. Thus, had General Marshall's message been instantaneously passed from RCA Honolulu to General Short, it would have been twelve minutes ahead of the first bomb. Short would still have been studying it when the first bomb fell. It is known that the Western Union messenger, riding with General Marshall's message in his motorcycle pockets along with a number of other telegrams or cablegrams of personal nature, took refuge when the first wave of Japanese attackers flew overhead, thus accounting for about half of the nine hours between the message's origination by Marshall and its delivery to General Short. Had the delay been in the other direction, between the origination of a time-critical message from Short to the War Department and its receipt in the control center in Washington, no amount of explanation could have put it right.

Colonel Clarke gave much attention to the "winds code" messages, as did Captain Safford, but they may not have been of significance to the beginning of the war or the Japanese attack. Safford stated conclusively that such messages were received and that he himself placed them in the secret files designated for them. When he later attempted to retrieve them during the Hart inquiry, searching his own and his department files, he found both sets of carefully deposited messages unaccountably missing. He did not so state, and was not asked, but it is possible to read between the lines that he believed someone with access to those carefully protected files had removed the evidence he sought.

Thus, the paper trail of the "winds code" messages no longer exists, and evidence they were received, other than corroboration from other intelligence personnel, cannot be found. When on 1 December Tokyo sent an official message to all Japanese embassies except the one in Berlin but including the one in Washington, D.C., to destroy all codes and secret papers forthwith, the "winds code" messages became important only in that they might specify who was to be attacked first. It has been suggested that the "winds code" may have been set up as an alternate means of sending this instruction to Japan's foreign embassies if radio transmissions were to break down or be interfered with (the 28 November message cited by Colonel Clarke states this, in fact), but that it was not needed because radio communications continued to be effective. Safford nevertheless continued to believe that such a message had been detected, that we should have interpreted it as indicating a major surprise attack on the United States, and that this could only have meant Pearl Harbor.

In the author's opinion, the search for the "winds code" messages turned out to be an unprofitable diversion of our extremely limited interception and decrypting capabilities. Had Japan intentionally wanted to create a "red herring" on this important point, it could hardly have done better. Many cryptologists, dedicated to their unusual profession and spending hours of overtime at it to the point of physical exhaustion, not to mention mental debilitation, might have far better served us at that critical moment had they never heard of the "winds code." The fact remains, however, that several of them testified that they had indeed seen such a message, or messages, even though all record of them has disappeared.

Seventh Investigation: The Clausen Investigation

Seventh was the Clausen Investigation, which began on 24 January 1945 (in response to orders dated 23 November 1944 from Secretary Stimson) and was completed on 12 September 1945. Its report is contained in part 35 of the JCC Hearings. In *Pearl Harbor: Final Judgement,* forty-eight years later, Clausen faults a number of persons, particularly Kimmel and Short, and lays qualified blame on President Roosevelt. Significantly, he places no fault on either General Marshall or General MacArthur but took pleasure insofar as General MacArthur was concerned in the fortuitous fact that he and MacArthur were both thirty-second degree Masons. As he explains it, this fact itself exonerates MacArthur of any fault.

It is difficult to equate the professional and rather pedantic style of his "Report of Proceedings" with the account of them given in his book, but enough comes between the lines of *Final Judgement* to put all his conclusions in doubt. Stimson said that he had put Clausen onto the job to provide information he might need should future expected Pearl Harbor hearings begin to inquire into his role and that of General Marshall. This is probably true enough, but there was a great deal more than that. Clausen, who came into the army during the war with an already developed reputation for effectiveness in court, both as prosecutor and defense attorney, was clearly given the mission of revising the testimony or injuring the credibility of all witnesses whose versions of the events did not agree with the line Stimson wanted. In this Clausen succeeded very well, managing to cause nearly all those whom he accosted to change their testimony. He was, after all, the direct representative of the man who held the careers of most of them in his hands and carried the power to make or break.

No legitimate judge would have countenanced such proceedings. Witness tampering is a felony.

Only a few witnesses seem to have stood firm against Clausen, among them Safford. But Kramer, from whom Safford had expected corroboration, was evidently not proof against the sort of relentless pressure Clausen was capable of putting on him and changed his testimony between investigations, as did a surprising number of others.

Pressuring witnesses was not Clausen's only technique, of course. Another was to prevent persons about whom he did not feel secure from testifying at all, and many were the surprises in terms of witnesses not called. This was particularly noticeable in the JCC Hearings, where time was working for him. These hearings were so protracted that every committee member was anxious to get them over with. Witnesses deemed inimical to the administration were so terribly browbeaten during their sessions in the chair, and no doubt before they got there, that they dreaded taking their turns and were delighted if lucky enough not to be "needed."

Clausen carefully kept all his records. Shortly before he died he made them available to Bruce Lee, a longtime editor at Morrow and other publishing houses, who became his collaborator. The result was *Pearl Harbor: Final Judgement,* published in 1992, which confirms Clausen's cynical partisanship. The book is extremely valuable if studied with care and discrimination, however, for there is much more in it than meets the eye of a quick reader.

Eighth Investigation: The Hewitt Inquiry

The eighth was the Hewitt Inquiry, conducted by Adm. Henry K. Hewitt, and lasted from 14 May 1945 to 11 July 1945. This investigation was apparently inspired by the same defensive attitude as impelled Secretary Stimson to direct the Clausen investigation and may, because of this similarity, have been directed from the same basic supervisory authority. In his book, Clausen makes several references to the Hewitt investigation, which he typifies as being similar to his own, though differently conducted, and in particular to

John F. Sonnett, who essentially conducted it. Sonnett, at the time special assistant to the secretary of the navy, was assigned to Admiral Hewitt as counsel for the inquiry. Like Clausen, Sonnett was a highly regarded lawyer in civilian life. Several people noted that he carried out most of the interrogations for Admiral Hewitt and that his manner was most often that of a prosecutor, as was Clausen's.

Admiral Kimmel, in his book about his ordeal, had this to say about the Hewitt investigation:

> The Secretary of the Navy, Mr. Forrestal, displeased with the findings of the Naval Court of Inquiry, requested Admiral J.O. Richardson, my predecessor as commander-in-chief of the fleet, to conduct a further investigation of the disaster. Admiral Richardson declined[,] stating in effect that he was not available for that duty because the primary qualification . . . was to have no fixed ideas upon the subject; that he, Richardson, was disqualified because he was firmly convinced that much of the responsibility for the Pearl Harbor disaster rested upon the occupant of 1600 Pennsylvania Avenue and the members of his cabinet and that no testimony that might be adduced would change that opinion.
>
> How many Admirals were approached before Admiral H. Kent Hewitt was designated to conduct the investigation I do not know. . . .
>
> The precept . . . specifically provided:
>
>> Except that the testimony that you take should be taken under oath so as to be on equal status in this respect with the testimony previously taken, *you will conduct your examination in an informal manner and without regard to legal or formal requirements.* [Italics supplied. This may be found on page 360 of part 36 of the JCC Report.]
>
> I wrote immediately to the Secretary and requested that I be permitted to be present with counsel during the investigation and be given the rights of a defendant. The Secretary's reply denied me this right on the plea that time did not permit, which reason I did not accept. I wrote a second letter protesting this decision in strong language. I never received a reply.
>
> Thus once more an Admiral was found who was willing to conduct a star chamber investigation from which I was excluded and to arrive at findings on my official conduct without permitting me to defend myself or to know what evidence he had received. Like the Roberts Commission everything was secret. I

> gathered that Mr. Sonnett in effect conducted the investigation. Captain Safford testified that Mr. Sonnett had attempted to intimidate him and finally to convince him that he, Safford, suffered hallucinations. Some witnesses who testified before the Hewitt board changed the testimony they had previously sworn to.

The report of the Hewitt investigation covers 124 pages of small print in part 39 and 1,332 pages in parts 36 and 37 of the JCC Report. It goes over all the old ground in great detail, for Admiral Hewitt plainly wanted no criticism of his performance of this difficult duty. Despite Kimmel's somewhat disdainful reaction to him, understandable in the circumstances, there is no indication that Hewitt was less than objective in his report. His criticisms are muted; doubtless Kimmel's inability to be present to defend himself against testimony contrary to his interest had an effect on Hewitt's own sense of investigative justice. Sonnett's interrogations were sometimes sharp and accusatory, and it is known that he and Clausen had a personal liaison, with the knowledge and approval of their respective secretaries.

Clausen, however, had the harder job, inasmuch as Stimson and Marshall had been far more closely connected to the White House inner circle of 1941, and his product, closely held by Stimson, can be said to have had greater influence.

The Hewitt investigation, by contrast, leaves the student with the reaction that it was essentially pro forma. Nonetheless, it gave King and Forrestal moral support in their disapproval of the naval court of inquiry that cleared Kimmel.

Ninth Investigation: The Joint Congressional Committee

Ninth and last of the investigations was that of the Joint Congressional Committee (JCC), which convened on 15 November 1945, adjourned on 23 May 1946 in hopes of being able to enjoy the Memorial Day holiday, but was reopened on 30 May as a courtesy to Admiral Stark to enable him to correct his previous testimony, he being scheduled to voyage to England the next day. The JCC "finally adjourned" on 31 May and submitted its report on 15 July 1946. It was this committee's turgid and massive compendium of data that has provided most of the material for the researchers into Pearl Harbor, but although various specific sections are of great importance, and some have extreme interest because of the way they have been reported, the JCC Report has not the immediacy as a whole that is normally needed to hold a reader's interest. It contains, however, all the testimony, all the reports, all the exhibits, and all the conclusions of all the investigations. The findings alone are in two "parts"—"paperback books" would be a better description—printed in small type, with quotations reproduced in even smaller type. The findings and associated matter alone total 1,072 pages in all, with an estimated word count of 700,000. The forty-one volumes of fine print, the thirty-three thousand pages (an estimated twenty-three million words), and another fifteen volumes of "exhibits" are so daunting that it can safely be stated that no one can have read all of it, not even the workers who laboriously put it together.

Clear evidence of the basic innocence of Admiral Kimmel and Lieutenant General Short of the charges that ruined their lives lies buried in many places in this huge printed work, but few people alive today have any but perfunctory interest in this evidence, except their families and friends and those, like the author of this book, who feel the honor of the United States is something that needs to be protected—or in this case restored. This is understandable when one considers that history has a way of using people to its own advantage. It has been this way from the beginning of time, and seldom can anything change it. Lucky are those, like Churchill, Roosevelt, and Marshall, who happen to fall on the right side of the historical record; unlucky are the ones on the other.

8

Interpretations and Justifications

There is today a great need for historical reappraisal, even at the risk of being labeled a "revisionist." This word is so often used as a pejorative that some historians have developed knee-jerk reactions whenever they hear it, and any suggestion of revisionist thinking causes those advocating a thoughtful approach to become defensive. It is equally indiscriminate, however, to refuse all new ideas or new versions out of hand, without making an effort to verify which, if any, contain useful information.

Partly because of the exalted positions of the players, the preconceived judgment of Pearl Harbor is more solid than that of nearly any other historical subject. It is certainly true that wildly speculative reconstructions of the past are to be avoided, but it does not follow—indeed, it trivializes the meaning of historical research and reflection to suggest—that all substantive reappraisals of the past amount to revisionism and are therefore unworthy of investigation.

Historians studying Pearl Harbor and honestly attempting to render the most unbiased, best informed verdict about it that they can put together have been constrained to adhere to the basic rules of historical evidence—which, in effect, require them to follow the line of accepted, proven fact. But there have been few proven facts about Pearl Harbor that were not obvious from inspection. There is evidence, however, that political considerations may have controlled many of the judgments rendered.

Fifty-year-old disclosures do not ordinarily receive the attention they would have had half a century earlier, when, presumably, they were kept from public view. Emotions cool. Memories fade, or are stilled by death. At the same time, the rules of evidence are always more rigorously applied in the later years than they can be in the immediate aftermath of a historical event, be it a success or a disaster. We all appreciate that history is often written by persons more concerned with the judgments of the future than with objective accuracy. It is the task of students afterward to sift all the evidence, all the official reports, to determine as nearly as possible what actually took place, and it follows that sometimes they have to challenge accepted ideas.

Recently found historical evidence that is in contradiction to accepted belief is, therefore, not necessarily revisionist simply because it does not agree with an earlier version. It may be more substantive, more strongly buttressed; very possibly it continues to be rated "speculative" only because the more rigorous standards of later scholarship have not yet been satisfied. Sometimes there need only be an objective review to sort out such a matter, an adjudication of contradicting merits or demerits in accordance with approved historical procedure. Often, the only missing ingredient for such a change is the necessary energy on the part of someone to whom the matter is of transcendent importance.

It need not be a family matter, although personal relationships can play a part. As for Pearl Harbor, this author, since childhood imbued with naval history and the ideals of naval integrity, sees the honor of our country, and its navy, as being at stake. A perpetuated wrong will not destroy either the nation or the navy, but the correction of such a wrong, whenever we can do it, is necessary to reaffirm the paradigms of virtues we hold dear.

In analyzing Pearl Harbor and attempting to discern responsibility, one must discard all nonpertinent material. The detail brought out on the subject has simply overwhelmed the normal ability to sort through it. To get to any sort of equitable judgment, peripheral items must be laid aside. We have mesmerized ourselves with a mountain of things that have only a small bearing on what happened. Wohlstetter said it best in her 1962 history: "The relevant signals . . . after the event [were] . . . obscured before the event by the surrounding noise." She could have gone on to point out that the "noise" was even greater after the event, and has increased instead of subsiding.

This has happened because, from whatever direction one happens to look, there is the uneasy sense that all things were not as they seemed then, nor as they seem now. Dissonant opinions are still reverberating, but they need not obscure the objective of this book.

In sorting through the "noise" about Pearl Harbor, it is helpful to address three questions concerning President Roosevelt's conduct of his office during that momentous time. They are

1. What were Roosevelt's probable motives for his policy toward Japan, which amounted to coercing Japan into war?

2. What were his possible motives for letting Pearl Harbor go unwarned?
3. What were his possible motives for sacrificing Kimmel and Short?

The first question, already treated at length, has to do with the propriety of joining in the fight against Hitler and the odious new world order he proposed. Despite some thought that England might have been able to hold out for quite some time longer, the common judgment is that it could only have been for but a few months at most. Churchill convinced Roosevelt of the desperation of the British situation at Newfoundland in August 1941.

How to get the United States into the war in the face of the American isolationist movement was something else. The best guess of Roosevelt and his topmost advisers was that a war with Japan could not but bring Germany into the battle. Hitler, already given more than adequate *causus belli* by our active support of England, would not miss the chance to declare war on the United States under conditions of special advantage. This conviction shaped our policy toward Japan and developed alongside our decision that in a two-ocean war, primary effort was to go to the defeat of Nazi Germany. For four uncomfortable days after Pearl Harbor, one of the great anxieties in Washington was that no war yet existed with Germany.

The second question concerns not only the degree of warning the Pacific commanders should have received but also the amount of foreknowledge of the attack that the president possessed.

Some of the more rabid Roosevelt haters believe he had information about the Japanese task force's transit across the northern Pacific toward Pearl Harbor. They seek any and all possible grounds for believing that he withheld warning so that Japan would "strike the first blow" and thus resolve his political problem. This was, to be sure, how the situation played out, but it is only conjecture that FDR withheld vital intelligence. Books espousing this theory, notably *Pearl Harbor: The Story of the Secret War* by George Morgenstern (Devin-Adair, 1947), *President Roosevelt and the Coming of the War* by the well-known historian Charles A. Beard (Yale University Press, 1948), and *Infamy* by John Toland (Doubleday, 1982), have failed to convince, principally because they came out too soon and (especially in Toland's case) mixed speculation with buttressed fact, thereby making themselves vulnerable to persons specially desirous of defending Roosevelt and Marshall. But all the books just cited show strong efforts to be convincing. Morgenstern has 330 pages of text and 80 pages of appendices. Toland's is 331 pages of text long, with 42 pages of notes, bibliography, and index.

On the other hand, certain elements in Netherlands East Indies intelligence insist to this day that their service detected and provided information of a Japanese carrier task force at sea en route to the point where its aircraft would be launched against Pearl Harbor. A recent book by James Rusbridger and Eric Nave, *Betrayal at Pearl Harbor: How Churchill Lured Roosevelt into World War II,* states that both British naval intelligence officers and those of the Netherlands East Indies, Nave participating, had broken Japanese codes, discovered Yamamoto's plan, and even detected radio transmissions that could only have been to or from the attack force as it headed east across the northern Pacific.

All of this is somewhat hard to swallow, particularly in the face of the Japanese account that Yamamoto (logically indeed) decreed absolute radio silence in the attacking force. Rusbridger works hard on the thesis that Churchill deliberately kept this vital information from Roosevelt—an idea that is even more difficult to swallow. These are two of the principal reasons why this book has not been as well received as it should have been. Nave, a retired officer of the Royal Australian Navy, was eighty-nine at the time it was published and died shortly afterward, but was said to have been of entirely sound mind. He had been attempting to put his memories and papers together for some time when he joined forces with Rusbridger, a freelance journalist-author, now also deceased (by suicide). Recognizing that its controversial thesis would encounter strong resistance, however, the authors supported their arguments with extensive photostated documents. The book's thesis is that effective breaking of some Japanese codes, specifically the JN-25 code as distinguished from Purple, took place in the Netherlands East Indies, Singapore, and Australia. Nave wrote that he participated in the effort from his position in Australia and that the decodes were definitely sent to England and (he was positive) from England to America. Rusbridger argued that Churchill withheld this information from Roosevelt. Nave also claimed that decodes were sent directly from Batavia to the Dutch embassy in Washington and given to the U.S. State Department.

Nave had access to many old records that were reproduced in the book, and the result is impressive. The book is bound in 303 pages, with 152 pages of text (plus 28 pages of front matter including acknowledgments and glossary), 65 pages of photocopied appendices, and 56 pages of notes, bibliography, and index. There is, however, no sign that any of the cited information reached either national leader; so we are left with conjecture only. But it is more than merely a small seed, for the same, or similar, stories crop up constantly.

Though no proof can be found that any of this material was ever seen in Washington, those who claim to have sent it are adamant that it was sent. Similar positions are taken by all the other intelligence operatives who believed they had done their duty but were somehow disregarded. And it is noteworthy that William J. Casey, who worked up to the post of chief of Secret Intelligence for the OSS in Europe during the war and was director of the CIA for President Reagan until 1987, authored a posthumously published book, *The Secret War Against Hitler,* in which he baldly stated (p.7), "The British had sent word that a Japanese fleet was steaming east toward Hawaii." He went on to state that Gen. William J. Donovan, head of OSS, was denied access to Magic, and explained the anguished cry of William Friedman, one of our foremost code-breakers, credited with the principal breakthrough against Japan's secret codes, on learning of Pearl Harbor, "But they knew! They knew!" with the following words:

> The fact is that Friedman knew, but those with the responsibility and power to act had received only an accumulation of raw intercepts. No one had put the pieces together for them and told them of their momentous implications.
>
> . . . Of course such limitations had fateful consequences. The broken Japanese diplomatic cipher gave us minute details of Japanese movements toward Singapore and the Dutch East Indies. . . . Our analysis of radio traffic had the various bits of the Japanese fleet accurately pinpointed most of the time. . . . Unhappily, all the data thrown up by this vast information network never landed in one place at one time where the facilities existed to analyze the facts and project their implications. . . . On November 1 and December 1, Japan made changes in naval call signs so unusual as to hint strongly at preparations for some offensive. The changes were followed by the sudden "disappearance" of the Japanese aircraft carriers. . . . diplomatic reports from Tokyo pointed to approaching political deadlines, first on November 25 and then on November 29, on which something could happen. Coded messages from Japanese agents in major ports, which we intercepted and read, told us what information Tokyo's warlords wanted to have about U.S. defenses.

Their sudden stepped-up interest in Manila and Honolulu should have been hard to miss.

But no one put together any coordinated analysis linking diplomatic reports, changes in call signals, and the disappearance of the carriers, all signs that a Japanese fleet might be steaming somewhere under radio silence, and that the "somewhere" might well be Hawaii or the Philippines. All the pieces were available in Washington, but no one put them together in a mosaic that might have cushioned, if not avoided, the blow against Pearl Harbor.

To be a "revisionist" these days means that one believes Roosevelt deliberately exposed our fleet at Pearl Harbor to "lure the Japanese to attack," had full knowledge of the approach of the six-carrier task force across the north Pacific for that purpose, and refrained from alerting our forces in Hawaii in order that Japan's "first blow" would be so devastating that it would coalesce our entire national political spectrum into support for entry into the war. While this approximates the facts of what happened, there is no proof that it was intentional or deliberate on his part.

The author of these pages will admit to being what might be called a "second-class revisionist" in that he feels that Roosevelt was convinced by mid-1941 of the necessity of our entry into the war and did all he could to bring it about, shifting from "deterrence" of Japan to an ultimatum that became the proximate cause of war. (Semanticists claim our 26 November proposal, which Japan called "humiliating," was not a "true ultimatum" because it didn't threaten war if refused.) The author also believes sincerely that whatever the president did was in the large sense necessary, that anything less would have allowed England to be destroyed and conquered, China and Southeast Asia likewise, and left the United States isolated in a fearful Western Hemisphere to await the next blow. Only the most rabid revisionist holds to the idea that our president "deliberately" plotted all the events of 1941. No genius plotter could have done that. And while the author does think that Roosevelt had cause, possibly at the last minute, to expect our fleet at Pearl Harbor somehow to be attacked in a hit-and-run fashion, he had no conception of the all-out power of Yamamoto's naval effort, no idea of how much damage his aircraft could do.

He had no idea that it included everything the Japanese admiral could put together in a year of careful planning, and that it would result in the destruction of the naval battle line which he himself had done so much to create.

So what should the Pacific commanders have been told? A few hours notice of the true state of affairs in Washington would have caused a general alert, possibly even actual battle stations, to take the place of the scheduled Sunday morning observances. In the hills around the harbor, the army would have kept its best search-radar watch standers on duty instead of securing them for breakfast and would have had sufficient plotting-room personnel and experienced evaluators at their posts to have made sense of the two radar trainees' sudden report of incoming aircraft due north of Oahu.

The U.S. Navy Department in Washington, D.C., the War Department, the civilian and military chiefs of both military services, and the commander in chief of all the armed services did possess information that could have made possible such a warning. It would not have been as positive as a sighting of the incoming armada by a patrol plane, but it would have alerted our forces and had them ready at their battle stations. Why was nothing sent from Washington? To argue, as was done, that a vaguely worded "war warning" on 27 November, ten days before the surprise attack, should have been sufficient to have had everyone at the same state of readiness as would have been achieved by an alert at 2:00 A.M. of the seventh is ridiculous to anyone who has experienced the stress of war.

There are two possible reasons why no special warning was sent. The first has to do with Magic, correctly recognized as of extraordinary value. Were Japan to realize that its most confidential codes had been penetrated, that the United States was able to read its most precious secret messages, the damage to our war effort, and the cost in lives of our servicemen, would have been beyond calculation. Were an attacking Japanese force at any time to recognize that our defense was ready and lying in wait, in effect prepared to ambush, it was feared that a deduction of code penetration could almost be assured. To protect Magic, no specific warning could be given to Pearl Harbor, certainly nothing that could, even remotely, endanger the great secret.

Perhaps our officials of 1941 were excessively concerned—but it is far from obvious that their worries were overblown. Our memories of Coral Sea, Midway, the invasion of Normandy, and the whole extraordinary spectrum of our war effort enable us to argue that we should not have exposed our code-breaking ability any more than we absolutely had to. Roosevelt and Marshall, if indeed they made the fundamental decision to go the alleged Coventry route with regard to Pearl Harbor and the Philippines, made a most painful one. The writer of this book does not agree with it, on the grounds that to be useful, special intelligence must be exploited, but admits to a degree of empathy with those who may have felt they had to make such a decision.

On the other hand, we used information gained by code-breaking prior to the Battle of Midway, and there is no indication that Japan suspected intrusion into its codes had anything to do with the presence of three carriers, one of them known to have been seriously damaged far to the southwest, at the Battle of the Coral Sea, only a month earlier, in perfect ambush position. And just a year later Yamamoto himself was shot down by a large flight of P-38s, land-based planes that could only have come from Guadalcanal, at the absolute limit of the known flight range of such aircraft. They were the only ones that could have done the job, and at that with an extremely short loiter time on station. The possibility of compromising our code-breaking capability was one of the strongest arguments against permitting the effort; so it was brought to the attention of Washington itself, where the president approved the mission. Again, there was no indication of resulting suspicion that code-breaking had anything to do with the providential presence of our aircraft.

At the same time that Japanese-U.S. relations were nearing rupture, Dönitz's wolf packs were having increasing difficulty in finding the ever more numerous and ever more frequent convoys that were crossing the Atlantic to bring aid to Britain. But Germany did not seem to suspect its codes to have been broken—although we now know the idea had been broached. The Germans believed their encrypting systems were unassailable because they used electric machines with changeable rotors that provided nearly an infinite number of different paths of encryption and therefore nearly an infinite—numbering in the billions—number of different possible encoded results for each letter in a message.

In this sense Magic may have operated to our detriment. Had we been using less esoteric sources of information, there would have been less hesitancy in passing it on to field commanders—and in such a theoretical case an incorrect deduction by Japan that we were indeed breaking into its codes might actually have proved beneficial to our side.

A second reason suggested in some quarters for not better alerting Hawaii (specifically) was that Admiral Nagumo, the attack force commander, might have reversed course and aborted the attack on learning he had lost the advantage of surprise. We would thus have been deprived of the excuse we so badly needed to overcome opposition to our entry into the war. This is not a very plausible explanation, but the idea was broached. Prange neatly disposes of this idea (*At Dawn We Slept,* page 841). Nagumo had no such instructions and would probably have welcomed the chance to sink the U.S. Fleet at sea in deep water.

Abstruse considerations of this nature aside, might it have been possible to give Pearl Harbor a better alert than it did receive and yet not compromise Magic? Could a message like the following have been sent, once Japan had tipped its hand by asking for the one o'clock meeting with Secretary Hull?

> THIS IS A WAR WARNING BEYOND ALL WAR WARNINGS. RELATIONS WITH JAPAN AT ALL TIME LOW. JAPANESE EMBASSY BURNING CODES AND PAPERS. AMBASSADOR ASKING MEETING WITH SECSTATE TODAY, SUNDAY, AT ONE PM SEVENTH EASTERN TIME REPEAT ONE PM EST TODAY. BE READY FOR ANYTHING. JAPAN HAS HABIT OF SURPRISE ATTACKS. ARMY NAVY URGENTLY COORDINATE. ROOSEVELT

Could Stark have telephoned Kimmel on the secure phone, as he was urged to do and apparently considered doing? Either measure would have had crews at battle stations instead of preparing for Sunday services. For that matter, what benefit was there, then, in using a secure telephone instead of an ordinary one, or in sending the warning message in code? From whom were we anxious to keep the secret of the meeting with Hull? The moment the Japanese ambassadors asked for that meeting, we should, and could, have been ready to do something useful with that important bit of unclassified information.

Our conclusion in answer to the second basic question, therefore, is that though it *was* vital to protect Magic, it was *also* possible to send Kimmel and Short a "heads-up" signal that would have given their forces a better chance to render a good account of themselves during the initial moments of the attack. As pointed out already, once the request for a Sunday audience with Secretary Hull had been made, the precedent of Port Arthur was more than enough for all necessary deductions.

The sole value of intelligence, after all, is to use it effectively to help one's country in hours of extreme need. This was not done. Intelligent minds, pondering over how to use critical intelligence information, should have been able to conceive of ways to use it effectively. It is evident that the intelligence operatives themselves had a far better understanding of the imperatives than their superiors, who were placed over them in authority but were nonetheless inexperienced in handling the delicate business in which they were engaged. All of the men surrounding the president subconsciously matched seniority and statutory authority with background knowledge of the subject at issue, and untrained authority won the day even though, as a result, the persons giving orders were not competent because they did not truly understand what they were doing. In their responsibility for the proper discharge of their duty, these senior officers failed utterly and completely. Turner was an example of this, and so were Stark and Marshall, and possibly Gen. Leonard T. Gerow, Turner's counterpart in the War Department.

We see reference after reference to "subtle hints" the Hawaii commanders supposedly received, including headlines in the Honolulu newspapers, from which they were expected to have been able to read more than anyone else, more even than the people in Washington, who had Magic and other sources of special information. In fact, the *only* actual warnings sent from Washington to the Pacific Fleet were the emasculated "war warnings" of 27 November and the 3 December notice that Japanese embassies were burning secret papers.

Not a single hint of the frenetic activity in Washington on the night of 6–7 December was sent out to the commanders who had the most right to know. One can imagine what either Kimmel or Short would have done had they had the slightest idea of what was going on in Washington that weekend. In *Admiral Kimmel's Story,* Kimmel wrote (p. 110),

> Assuming that for the first time *on December 5* I had all the important information then available in the Navy Department, it is my present conviction that I would have gone to sea with the fleet, including the carrier "Lexington" and arranged a rendezvous at sea with Halsey's carrier force, and been in a good position to intercept the Japanese attack. . . .
>
> The dispatch fixing the hour for delivery of the Japanese ultimatum to the United States as 1:00 P.M., Washington time, was intercepted and decoded by the Navy Department by 7:00 on the morning of December 7—7:00 A.M., Washington time, [was] 1:30 A.M., Hawaiian time—nearly six and a half hours before the attack. The translation of this short message from the Japanese was a two-minute job. Not later than 9:00 A.M., the Chief of Naval

> Operations was informed of it. This information was not supplied to me prior to the attack. . . .
>
> Regardless of what arguments there may be as to the evaluation of the dispatches that had been sent to me, I surely was entitled to know of the hour fixed by Japan for the probable outbreak of war against the United States. . . .
>
> Even on the morning of December 7, four or five hours before the attack, had the Navy Department for the first time seen fit to send me all this significant information, and the additional fact that 1:00 P.M., Washington time, had been fixed for the delivery of the Japanese ultimatum to the United States, my light forces could have moved out of Pearl Harbor, all ships in the harbor would have been at general quarters, and all resources of the fleet [would have been put] in instant readiness to repel an attack.

According to our War Plan Orange (or more specifically, WPPac-46, successor to WPO), our strategy was to be offensive, to engage the enemy in a great sea battle shortly after the outbreak of war, which our planners expected would be in the Far East. Yamamoto's Combined Fleet, based in Japan's Inland Sea, would presumably concentrate at Truk, in the Caroline Islands beyond the Marshalls. We planned to bring our slower battleships into a decisive battle with Japan's faster ones somewhere near Wake Island during the third week of the war. Kimmel's war plan, and the intensive training of his fleet, was directed to this end. All of his meager forces (except battleships, in which he held a slight superiority) were committed to that battle. The CNO and his War Plans section had not only approved the plan but had added some fine-tuning of their own.

However, when war appeared imminent, not one official in the nation's capital, no member of the civilian leadership, not the CNO nor the army chief of staff, both of whom should have felt responsible for their men on the firing line, did what their duties required.

The majority findings of the JCC agreed. For instance, the list of majority findings states, in part: "Notwithstanding the fact that there were officers on twenty-four hour watch, the Committee believes that under all of the evidence, the War and Navy Departments were not sufficiently alerted on December 6 and 7, 1941, in view of the imminence of war" (part 39, page 252, item 12).

Additionally, on page 262 of part 39, number 16 in a list of 25 "supervisory, administrative and organizational deficiencies," the JCC had this to say:

> *16. Officials should at all times give subordinates the benefit of significant information*
>
> Before the Committee Admiral Turner testified that he regarded an attack on Pearl Harbor as a 50-50 possibility. Assuming this to be correct, there can be little doubt, considering the position he held as Director of War Plans in the Navy Department, that he could have given the commander in chief of the Pacific Fleet the benefit of his conclusion had he been disposed to do so. As a matter of fact Admiral Turner had the principal hand in preparing the November 27 "war warning."
>
> As has been seen, the orders contained in the war warning necessarily carried the implication of an attack from without; however, the dispatch did not reflect the likelihood of an attack on the fleet with the degree of likelihood manifested by Admiral Turner in indicating to the Committee his estimate of the situation. Admiral Turner's position would be indefensible were his estimate based on any information or intelligence he possessed. It appears, on the other hand, that his conclusion was predicated on a rather long-standing impression in the Navy that an attack on our Pacific Fleet by Japan could be expected at one time or another. It is regarded as unfortunate, however, that Admiral Turner did not see fit to give to the Pacific Fleet the benefit of his conclusions outlined, with benefit of retrospection, in such detail before the Committee.

Despite the JCC's gentle assessment that Turner had made his conclusion regarding the "50-50 possibility" of an attack from "a rather long-standing impression" rather than from intelligence, it needs to be noted that he had seen the "bomb plot" message, the two Japanese "deadline" messages, and the message requiring delivery of the fourteen-part message to the secretary of state at 1 P.M. on Sunday, the seventh of December (the "delivery" message). Turner had plenty of specific information to back up his assessment, even a more dramatic one, but not a word of any of this did he pass over to Kimmel in any manner.

It is inconceivable that so many lapses could all have been accidental, or that the "forgetfulness" of all these professionals could have been genuine. The one real question remaining is whether Roosevelt did indeed, as more than one account says, put a clamp on all information directed to Pearl Harbor. Why would he have done this? True, his reason for the often-repeated dictum "*They* must strike the first blow" is clear enough. The isolationists were a powerful force. Being chary with warnings directly traceable to

Magic, to protect that invaluable source, is understandable too. But if Germany was his real target, as historians generally believe, leading the nation into an all-out war on the other side of the world is a strange way to go about getting a declaration of war on Nazi Germany. The only logical explanation is that he expected a Japanese attack in the Far East to bring on a general conflict that would quickly include Germany, and that Pearl Harbor was as big a surprise to him as to anyone else.

So when the blow he had invited was better conducted and more devastating than expected, he abandoned the high ground, and his bureaucratic administrators covered themselves with the mantle of the emergency they had helped bring about—and offered up, as sacrifices to the recognized demand for a scapegoat, the two commanders at the nearest and most obvious, but by no means the only, point of attack.

The commander in chief of the fleet that had received the most obvious and heart-stopping damage was the primary candidate for being made into a scapegoat, but had he been the only one named the national rage might have been uncontrollable, the consequences unpredictable, the injustice unacceptable. The president's men may have felt slightly more fair-minded when they included as a second, lesser, scapegoat the army commander, an official of less rank and in a far less visible position, but still vulnerable because he was in charge of the army in Hawaii and all the base defenses.

The inequality of treatment in selecting scapegoats is even more obvious when General MacArthur in the Philippines is added to the equation. Compared to the disgraceful treatment of Kimmel and Short, MacArthur's preservation in command despite having been caught by surprise nearly half a day after Pearl Harbor was attacked, and his later elevation, stand in ironic contrast.

So the third question concerns the possible motives and justifications for sacrificing the reputations and careers of Kimmel and Short. The first motive—and all accounts generally accept it as authentic—was political damage control. Richardson, Kimmel's predecessor as CINCUS, gave the case for this. All the top command in Washington, he believed, were expecting an attack somewhere, possibly even on Pearl Harbor, but no one had any conception of how heavy an attack Yamamoto would actually mount. What was clear, with the terrible spectacle of those great, wounded behemoths gushing oil into the water of Pearl Harbor, masts collapsed or akimbo, sunk or bottom up at their berths, with two-thirds of the *Arizona*'s crew and a quarter of the *Oklahoma*'s entombed inside, was that carrier-based air power had opened an utterly new era in naval warfare, and that battleships were poorly equipped for it. "The Fleet" *was* the navy to the U.S. citizenry, and to see it so publicly and devastatingly destroyed was a first-class political catastrophe. Sympathy for the surprised commanders, partly, at least, from Roosevelt's realization of the poor quality of the warnings they had received, must quickly have turned into concern for discovery of Washington's own culpability, and—all too humanly—into anger that, even so, they had not somehow been able to make a better showing. In this author's view, this lay at the background of some of the decisions made regarding them.

Roosevelt, according to Richardson, navy-oriented since youth, knew well that the U.S. Navy had been studying war with Japan for years. Despite the serious inroads his support of England in the Atlantic had made upon the strength of the Pacific Fleet, the president thought Pacific Ocean distances to be so great as to preclude naval action anywhere except in the Far East. Like everyone else, Pearl Harbor caught him by surprise. Stories emanating from the White House reported that Roosevelt was nearly beside himself with despair and fury over the damage to "his Navy." Authoritative stories describing his state of mind have reproduced, probably not verbatim, some of the things he said and advice he received. The damage was so great and so unexpected that he could not ignore it. It must be investigated, fault found, and blame laid. Otherwise, blame would reside in Washington and upon all the leaders there, with sure negative effect on the war effort just beginning. Had the attack not been so devastatingly successful, the carnage and destruction not so great, Richardson believed the president might have ridden out the storm with equanimity; under the awful circumstances, he "ran for cover."

Here lies the principal reason, despite fairly specific testimony to the effect that it did take place, why it has been impossible for most people to believe that the midnight White House meeting could have happened.

As news of the catastrophe spread, the great segment of the population closed ranks behind Roosevelt. It was disloyal to disbelieve him, or to suggest his concealment of anything that might have attenuated the damage, although everyone will readily agree that all presidents must have had secret meetings of one kind or another and that Roosevelt probably held more than most. So far as the midnight meeting is concerned, it is not possible to find an instance when an official who might have been present was directly queried about it. Roosevelt is said to have ordered it "forgotten," and if that was his directive it was well carried out. Not one of the persons supposedly present could remember where he was, or what he was doing, the night before the specially modified torpedoes, with temporary wooden fins to prevent them from diving too deeply at launching, began to splash into Pearl Harbor's shallow waters.

If the meeting did take place—and this author believes it did—it was undeniably the most momentous such meeting, not only in the lives of all participants but of the entire history of our country, concerning not only the fate of a traumatized Europe but also whether we would go to war. Even the topmost stars, and this includes the president himself, must have felt themselves dwarfed under the immensity of the events surrounding them, which they had had a hand in shaping.

Second to the political reason was the "we have to get on with the war" reason. Kimmel and Short both subscribed to this in the beginning as part of their penance for being unalert. To everyone in the armed forces, and to all whom the attack galvanized into spirited action, it seemed a valid, if not fully thought through, argument. Indeed, we did have to get on with the war, but thinking people might then, as some do now, question whether it was a legitimate reason for scapegoating the men in charge, who had been kept in the dark on the developing crisis. If anything it was a non sequitur, not a valid reason but an excuse. The reason might be valid in the abstract, but in the concrete it was highly dubious.

A third possible motive, truly unworthy of consideration but perhaps worth mentioning just to dispose of it, concerns the personal pride and ego among the members of our high command. As anyone knows, to prove a senior wrong, especially a military senior, and most especially of all in a matter of grave importance, can be personally detrimental. How much more devastating must it have been for the two Hawaii commanders, whose very existence, no matter what they did or where they turned, was a reproach to the superiors responsible for the disaster! Better to take them completely out of the picture and never let them back in. The Japanese had a terrible, dramatic, but thoroughly satisfying tradition for solving this sort of embarrassment. Even to impute such a psychology to our national leaders is an affront; and yet to a large extent, and with certain important exceptions, they turned their backs on their next-lower-ranking leaders. Kimmel and Short could never, or almost never, understand this. Short, for example, refused nearly to the end to understand that his once firm friendship with George Marshall was a thing of the past, a sacrifice on the altar of expediency.

To invoke the literary superstition that "to the captain of the sunken ship must go the blame for disaster" smacks of the samurai idea of obligatory self-destruction and only draws a red herring across the path of logic. In our culture, though the captain of the ship may expect to be examined, he or she has the right to defend himself or herself and has no obligation to commit suicide, even figuratively.

In summation, none of these motives for scapegoating Kimmel and Short is acceptable to individuals capable of sincere deliberation. The massive difference between the way they were treated and the way everyone else was treated, especially some who were known to be far more guilty (if anyone was "guilty" under the unusual circumstances), was immoral.

After the attack, the president had to seize the political initiative, and quickly. The upshot was the Roberts Commission, sent to Honolulu under a carefully circumscribed charter to look at Pearl Harbor only, and determine specifically whether any "dereliction of duty" by the commanders there had contributed to the success of the surprise attack. One of the Commission's members, Admiral Standley, later repudiated the Commission's process and findings as a travesty. He justified his signing of the report by the fact that a war was on in which we had suffered a severe initial setback and that we needed all our energies to prosecute it, but he said it was a travesty all the same. All examinations of the Roberts Commission Report, and its proceedings, support the conclusion that it was badly flawed in every respect and could have had but a single purpose, the one stated by Admiral Standley: to quell the public hue and cry and permit the administration to carry on with the war.

It was just what Roosevelt needed (his detractors claimed he had had much more to do with its composition than was ever given out), and he seized the exoneration of himself that was offered by its criticism of Kimmel and Short. He turned the Roberts Commission Report over to the press as soon as he had read it. Neither of the two accused officers had been permitted to read the transcript of his own testimony until strenuous protests were made, and neither had been allowed to see the findings. Thus, Kimmel and Short were astounded to see themselves reported by the press as having been charged with dereliction of duty. They had been specifically informed that the Commission was a fact-finding investigation only and that their performance of duty was not in question before it; their first intimation to the contrary, other than the overbearing attitude of Justice Roberts during the proceedings, was when they read the eagerly awaited newspaper accounts and, of course, heard the radio broadcasts. They were, in effect, convicted in the "court of public opinion" without any opportunity of defense, and this "conviction" and the punishment it brought have hung over them ever since, even beyond the grave.

In only three of the nine investigations of Pearl Harbor were the accused permitted to defend themselves (cross-examination of witnesses was allowed in only two), and only these two, the official army board of investigation and the navy court of inquiry, rendered careful decisions of who bore the responsibility. The remaining investigations, including that of the JCC, made "findings of fact" and in some cases went on with accusations of fault—without providing an opportunity for denial or defense when they were made—upon which no action one way or another was taken, but which, all the same, received considerable publicity. The converse, however, was not equally true. There has been no publicity given to the positive finding of nonfault made by the navy court of inquiry, nor to the less positive but still clear enough message of the army board of investigation that Short was less at fault than his superior, Marshall: just silence, implying that the initial accusations were correct and that, regardless of the right of the matter, there can never be compassion if the president of the United States is involved.

The verdict of the navy court of inquiry exonerating Admiral Kimmel was reversed by a political decision of new Secretary of the Navy Forrestal. The army board, which found Marshall's performance censurable in considerable detail, was likewise reversed by Secretary of War Stimson. In both cases there is the clear suggestion, on the record, that the two reversals were made for reasons "above" those that the two military legal bodies were empowered to consider. Other than that some of the information contained in these two verdicts might harm our war effort, nothing more was given out about either one, and the public therefore continued to believe what it had been told: that the two commanders in Hawaii were guilty as charged. In technical fact, they were never "officially charged" at all, but that did not alter the public's perception. "Charged" with dereliction they had been, and the charges having never been answered, guilty they must be, even though never convicted or "punished." Many people, basically suspicious because of their own or someone else's bias against "the military," went further and insinuated that Kimmel and Short were being "protected" against condign punishment by some Machiavellian organization of the military services of which they were a part.

Measured against the salvation of a free Europe and a free Asia, the sacrifice of a few lives can appear worthwhile to the many served thereby. It is also sometimes argued that the enforced sacrifice of (someone else's) career should be philosophically accepted as less of a penalty than the loss of life—but such arguments always falter on the grindstone of logic. The difference is simply too great to permit this sort of facile comparison.

It is clear today that, among those with responsibility for the Japanese attack, first must be President Roosevelt himself. This is not to say that he knew about Pearl Harbor in advance, or that anyone did except the Japanese, but he had received multiple warnings for days that something was about to happen, culminating in the fourteen-part Japanese message specifying exactly when.

The reconstruction of events confirms the supposition that Roosevelt had determined on war with Japan. Since not once did our policy waver in aiming our major effort eastward, however, against Germany, it must be assumed that war with Japan had become the means of getting into the all-out war with Nazi Germany that the president believed was mandatory, and that he had in fact promised Churchill. Such evidence as we have indicates that he did not expect Pearl Harbor, or did not expect anything like the terrible success of that raid. He was as devastated as anyone when he learned of it. Getting into the war by way of Japan cost far more than he had expected.

Though President Roosevelt can be said to have failed us at this point, his reputation as one of our most effective wartime presidents remains secure. To those who still disapprove of how he engineered our entry into World War II, what Europe suffered is the answer. Compared to *that* horror, our sufferings were minor. We could not, and should not, have stayed out of that war.

Second ranking in the compilation of failure and responsibility for Pearl Harbor goes to General Marshall and Admiral Stark, chiefs of the army and navy, respectively, for having been in on many of the discussions and negotiations, aware of the implications of the Magic disclosures, and failing nevertheless to send adequate warning to their subordinates in the field. Nowhere in history do we have the spectacle of an army chief of staff out riding his horse, nowhere to be found while a surprise attack was flying in, nor of a chief of naval operations dithering for hours in his office over whether or not to send a warning to the commander of his biggest fleet.

Whatever fault may be ascribed to George Marshall has to be compared to the tremendous role he has played in our country's history. He is rightly admired as one of the most capable public servants this fortunate republic has ever had. The Pearl Harbor affair is the only blot on his escutcheon. There is no need to deny his responsibility. His back is broad enough to carry it.

Admiral Stark once very revealingly stated that his conscience was clear because everything he did was in response to orders from higher authority. Although not punished in any degree the way Kimmel and Short were, and indeed decorated for his performance in his next assignment, he was nonetheless held by Secretary Knox and the redoubtable Admiral King to have "failed to exhibit the high qualities of leadership" required by his post. He did not defend himself against the unofficial accusations that came his way. In this sense he somewhat resembles General Short.

Third in responsibility for our failure is Admiral Turner, for having unilaterally arrogated to himself all the functions of intelligence evaluation and dissemination in the Navy Department, overawing everyone by an unbridled temper and vicious career destruction, reporting untruthfully about the availability of Magic to Kimmel and Short, and for no known reason blocking the sending of cogent and badly needed warnings to them. He was one of those most noted for evasion of responsibility afterward.

Fourth in the chain of failure are General MacArthur and his staff, not so much for being responsible *for* the attack, as for being derelict in reacting to it. For nine hours our most precious aircraft sat lethargically on the field, a target for Japan to strike—which Japan did, most successfully, and caught us by surprise long after all the world was fully aware that the war had begun.

Fifth, and far less responsible than all of the foregoing, are Admiral Kimmel and General Short, not because they were derelict in their duties, but merely because they were in command and caught short by the attack. Perhaps they should have been better able to read the signs of approaching disaster, although this continues to be problematic, as it was then, too. They should have discussed Japan's orders to destroy secret papers and coding machines (as noted, this was Kimmel's fault). They should have spent the week prior to the attack in studying the war warning received at the end of November instead of so laboriously refuting the scheme to exchange marines and soldiers.

It is true that a review of any commander's plans and preparations, in an effort to find fault with some detail, will inevitably find something that was not done right, or was not done as well as it should have been; and both Kimmel and Short manfully assigned some blame to themselves for not having been more prescient than they were. They did receive a very general war warning ten days before the attack, but they received less warning than anyone else. Every error on their part pales beside the monstrous fact that Washington knew an emergency would exist somewhere in our armed forces on that day, and almost exactly when, and failed to inform any of them. It was not fair for Kimmel and Short to have been forced to carry all the blame, obloquy, and personal invective the nation heaped upon them. They should not have been made to suffer for the rest of their lives for the deficiencies of others. Once the political need for their sacrifice was over, they should have been rehabilitated.

The national leadership, which had the obligation of keeping our military commanders current with matters of their concern, utterly failed our commanders at Pearl Harbor and then blamed them for their own lack of alertness. To have expected them to be more knowledgeable than Washington, D.C., and therefore more ready, is nonsense.

The JCC Report included the "additional views" of Representative Frank B. Keefe, as printed in part 39, page 266-S. An excerpt follows:

> The record of the high military and civilian officials of the War and Navy Departments in dealing with the Pearl Harbor disaster from beginning to end does them no credit. It will have a permanent bad effect on the morale and integrity of the armed services. The Administration had ample opportunity to record and preserve all the facts about Pearl Harbor, even if their public disclosure needed to wait upon the war's end. This was not done. The policy adopted was to place the public responsibility for the disaster on the commanders in the field, to be left there for all time. The policy failed only because suppression created public suspicion, and the Congress was alert. . . .
>
> With full knowledge of Japan's intentions prior to the attack, Washington had one plain duty to the American people. That duty was to inform them of their peril. That was not done. Washington had a further duty to make sure that our forces were

> ready to meet the attack by furnishing their commanders afield and afloat with all available information, or by evaluating that information and giving them appropriate clear and categoric instructions.

After the attack leaving thousands of dead for us to mourn, we had a war to fight, a national emergency of the highest order. It is understandable, though perhaps not totally excusable, that our normal judgment of fairness and due process should have been forgotten in the national trauma Pearl Harbor created.

Inasmuch as no court-martial was ever held, there has been no official, judicial, hopefully fair finding on this case. The mountain of verbiage has so overwhelmed the facts that it is very likely no legal finding of anyone's specific guilt or innocence can now be made. We are left with the "verdict of history," an overworked and abstract thing at best, but it, at least, seems to be coming through clearly. Since all the actors on the stage of the Pearl Harbor drama are now dead, this judgment, slowly accumulating its weight, may be all the country can hope for, and might also be enough, were it not for an unrelenting corollary.

As the judgment of history now stands, the image of our wartime president, the man who reversed the terrible trend of World War II, is eroding. Under current conditions, books like this one will likely continue to appear, and will continue to contribute to the detriment of Franklin Roosevelt's reputation. Giant of stature though he was, he was sometimes small enough to destroy other men to give himself protection he did not need. That one of our greatest presidents would stoop to such ignoble tactics is idealistically indefensible, and partly for this reason it has been suggested he might, had he lived to see victory, have seized the happy moment to right at least part of the wrong.

As seen, it was because of decisions made in Washington that Kimmel and Short were so drastically ill-supplied with both the information and the tools to do their jobs properly. Yet they were disgraced by official act of the president for having been unable to fulfill an impossible task. We as a people cannot have whole and unstinted respect for any society or organization, our own or another, that will not support its own servants. This is one of the most important attributes of a free democracy. Since the U.S. government officially censured its commanders at Pearl Harbor without trial or fair hearing, it is arguable that the same government has a moral obligation to exculpate them, to the same degree that they were stained, and to do it equally officially. The manner in which Captain Dreyfus of the

French army was officially restored to honor, in front of the same regiment before which he had been officially disgraced, comes to mind. Leaving Kimmel and Short to the mercy of history alone is not enough, for this does not remove the shame from the U.S. government and the Franklin D. Roosevelt administration.

To most of us today, fault for what happened half a century ago is of but passing interest. Were justice and the national honor not also involved, it might be acceptable just to let this sleeping dog lie. But until the betrayal of our Pearl Harbor commanders has been historically recognized, and appropriately expunged, a stain remains on the shield of the United States of America.

9

What Is There to Do About It Now?

This author can remember what may well be the most notorious history seminar ever held at the U.S. Naval Academy. Billed as a panel discussion of "New Evidence on Pearl Harbor," it pitted fervent partisans of Gordon W. Prange and his just published, hugely researched, and heavily promoted book, *At Dawn We Slept,* against British historian John Costello, then involved in researching the little understood dimension of the surprise attack that occurred in the Philippines—and who, it developed, held a less than ecstatic opinion about Prange. Also present on the platform and billed as a panelist alongside Costello was an officer from the Netherlands embassy in Washington. The latter, Robert Haslach, was essentially drowned out by the huge and many-faceted shouting match between Costello on one side and commentator Wayne Cole, billed as a Franklin D. Roosevelt specialist and supported by moderator Joseph Strange of the Air University, on the other. At times the proceedings appeared to have three sides instead of only two, since the reasons for the hostility displayed ran so deep.

It was apparent that a "setup" may also have been involved. Both commentator and moderator were longtime colleagues and admirers of Prange, and they disdained Costello on both personal and scholarship levels. The author felt real regret that Haslach, who seemed to have some useful background about code-breaking in the Netherland East Indies, was not allowed a clear field to present his paper. Most persons in the audience brought away with them only the certain knowledge that there was still a great deal of deep feeling over the subject, and wondered why that should be, inasmuch as all the participants were long dead. At this stage, we should be serving history, not personalities.

In November 1987 Secretary of the Navy James Webb asked CNO Adm. Carlisle Trost to review the Kimmel record in response to the petition of the two surviving Kimmel sons that their father be restored posthumously to the rank of admiral. The CNO requested an opinion from the director of Naval History and received an unfavorable reply, in part as follows:

> . . . Admiral Kimmel had been charged by an investigative body headed by Supreme Court Justice Roberts with "dereliction of duty" for failing to take adequate steps to safeguard the Fleet at Pearl Harbor against a possible attack. In 1944, Admiral Ernest J. King also made an administrative decision on Kimmel's responsibility. [In an endorsement disapproving the naval court of inquiry into the case, he] stated in part: "The derelictions on the part of . . . Admiral Kimmel . . . indicate lack of the superior judgment necessary for exercising command commensurate with [his] rank."
>
> . . . Other investigations into the Pearl Harbor debacle place generally lesser amounts of blame on Admiral Kimmel than did the Roberts Commission and the King endorsements. Nevertheless, historians have by no means reached a consensus that Admiral Kimmel was entirely blameless or a mere "victim of circumstances."
>
> . . . I have given my personal views of Admiral Kimmel's conduct in *Eagle Against the Sun* and in the New York Times January 1986 (copies attached as appendix "A") and I see no reason to alter them at this time.

The King and Forrestal endorsements to Kimmel's court of inquiry, in nearly identical language, state that Kimmel's failure to institute air patrols to the north and northwest, from which direction the attacking planes came, was his "most grievous failure." The director of Naval History, in the *New York Times* review that he attached to his disapproving memorandum, says: "There is also the written evidence of an official report on Hawaiian air defenses, completed in March 1941 [the Martin-Bellinger Report], which, as the Prange book *The Verdict of History* points out, predicted that an air attack was most likely to come from the north or northwest."

Unfortunately for the truth in this overplowed area, the Martin-Bellinger Report makes no such statement, and the King and Forrestal endorsements, once again demonstrating that elevated rank or position do not substitute for knowledge of a subject, display absurd ignorance of the realities of protective air-surveillance procedure.

Edward S. Miller, in *War Plan Orange,* points out that many high-ranking officers, Halsey among them, thought the critically important direction from which a raid on Pearl Harbor might come was most likely to be the southwest, where lay Japan's bases in the Marshall Islands. But this was never a part of any of the war plans, inasmuch as no war plan assumed there would be a raid on Pearl Harbor. Halsey, in common with many others, simply applied common sense: the nearest Japanese base was southwest from Pearl, thus it was the most likely direction from which an attack might be expected. But since the actual attack came from the north, the hindsight judgment that north was the most logical direction received undue credence, and the fact that this judgment was years late was overlooked.

Nevertheless, as a consequence of the report from the director of Naval History, Trost wrote back to Secretary Webb, "I believe that we should not attempt to reverse the actions of our predecessors or second guess their intentions unless there is compelling evidence that there was an injustice done. In this case, there is no such compelling evidence."

Dr. Michael Gannon, professor of history at the University of Florida and recent author of the authoritative and extremely well received *Operation Drumbeat* (New York: 1990), having studied certain aspects of Pearl Harbor in depth, has concluded differently. His article "Reopen the Kimmel Case," published in the U.S. Naval Institute *Proceedings* for December 1994, makes mincemeat of one of the principal arguments against Admiral Kimmel, this argument being the following: informed by his air officers that north was the direction of most danger because of prevailing winds, he nevertheless did not institute air-surveillance patrols. The naval court of inquiry held on Kimmel in 1944 soundly disposed of this issue. Danger from the north was hindsight, not stated until 1945. There had been no advance prediction of this in 1941. All information received by Kimmel, most specifically the Martin-Bellinger Report already cited in these pages, stated categorically that air patrol in any single direction would inevitably be discovered and avoided, and that therefore the only useful patrol was one flying around-the-clock and covering 360 degrees around the island of Oahu. To maintain such surveillance would have required 250 patrol aircraft instead of the 49 (44 by another count, depending on overhaul status) available to Kimmel. Were the 49 to have been sent out for sixteen-hour patrols every day, they might have been able to cover a 9-degree arc for three or four days (not 78 degrees as stated by some unknowing optimist), but would then have been out of commission due to breakdowns and crew fatigue.

With the concurrence of his air staff and all others involved, Kimmel had therefore made the decision to conduct no patrols in advance of the specific warning from Washington that CNO Stark had stated in writing he would receive. Short-lived surveillance in any special direction would have been a sham, and would with near certainty have denied Kimmel use of the patrol planes when, according to the war plan he was following, they would have been most needed. The court found that this was the proper decision under the circumstances, noting at the same time that Kimmel's request for 250 aircraft with flying and maintenance crews, made the previous summer, had been reduced to 100 aircraft, but that these had never arrived, even though more than 1,000 had been sent to England since then. Nevertheless, it was on the grounds of not having patrolled to the north on the fifth and sixth of December that Kimmel's major accusation of dereliction was based.

Gannon makes it crystal clear that the putative northern danger was hindsight only and should not have been used in the accusation against Kimmel. He says, citing the actual wording of the Martin-Bellinger estimate of March 1941, which was the "official report" mentioned by the director of Naval History to Trost, "there were no known or predicted 'more dangerous sectors' . . . in any of the official estimates provided to Admiral Kimmel prior to the attack." In courtesy to Trost, now retired, Gannon sent him a copy of his article and the pertinent documents for review.

After careful study of the papers, Admiral Trost has retracted his 1988 disapproval in unequivocal language. He has written to the present secretary of the navy, under date of 4 October 1994, asking that the case of Admiral Kimmel be reopened. "I believe such action is owed to the Admiral," he wrote, "to his sons, and to the Navy. No mistake should be allowed to stand in this sensitive matter, and I personally disavow my unwitting support of one."

There are two additional late-breaking developments to note. The book by John Costello, *Days of Infamy,* already mentioned in these pages, has just come out. Massively researched and carefully documented, it points out in detail the intraservice squabbling, bureaucratic bungling, and political decisions that put the Pearl Harbor commanders out of the loop for both the intelligence and the resources with which to meet the oncoming Japanese attack.

In late November 1994 the American press was titillated by reports from Japan that its Foreign Ministry had found it necessary to apologize to its people for the shame it had brought upon them by beginning the war against the United States prior to the declaration of hostilities required by international law, specifically Article 1 of Hague Convention III. Its Foreign Office had burdened its Washington embassy with the requirement of preparing a lengthy eleven-page document (the famous fourteen-part message that terminated negotiations) for submission to the U.S. Secretary of State "when directed," but had failed to allow enough time for the inevitable problems the embassy might encounter in carrying out the instructions.

Even had the fourteen-part "memorandum" been delivered on time, however, it did not qualify under international law as a declaration of war. It did not even sever diplomatic relations, which were technically in effect until the moment the first torpedo was launched and the first bomb fell.

All fourteen parts of the memorandum were sent in English, circumventing the need for translating its involved language and, of course, shortening the embassy's time problem. But in specifying that only top-level officials could work on the document—ordinary typists with low clearances were prohibited from even knowing about it—the thought had apparently not occurred to Tokyo that diplomatic officials of high rank were not likely to be proficient with an English-language typewriter. The main purpose of sending it in English had been to ensure that the United States received a precisely worded message; that this would make things easier in Japan's Washington embassy must have occurred to the Foreign Office, but time lost in amateur typing and retyping to achieve "clean" copy was too much for the officials pressed into this important service.

The fourteenth and final part of the message, transmitted in English though it was, had been deliberately held back as an extra security measure until early Sunday morning. Japan had no hint that we had broken its most secret diplomatic code, but "Persons familiar with cryptographic work know that other difficulties could arise, and that garbles in transmission, or mistakes made in the encryption/decryption process, would inevitably cause cumulative delays in the lengthy, hand-done, procedure," according to Dr. Robert J. C. Butow, currently professor emeritus of History and East Asian Studies at the University of Washington in Seattle. In his recent article, "Marching Off to War on the Wrong Foot," (*Pacific Historical Review,* 1993), he says, "Officials in the Foreign Office needed to anticipate the worst possible scenario attendant upon the delicate procedure they were contemplating."

They intended, of course, that the official suspension of negotiations take place some twenty minutes before the attack burst upon Pearl Harbor. Because of their unrealistic time schedule, however, negotiations were theoretically still going on for an hour after the attack had begun.

The Pearl Harbor attack, therefore, was made during a time of peace. Negotiations were still going on, even though Japan had decided to terminate them days before (upon receipt of our uncompromising note of 26 November). As our 1994 press reports described Japanese culture, anyone doing wrong is perceived as bringing shame upon all other members of his or her group. A Japanese factory worker who robs a bank, for example, brings shame upon all the personnel of the factory. Thus the Pearl Harbor attack, a crime under a clause of international law to which Japan was signatory, was seen as deeply embarrassing to the entire nation and properly the subject of a governmental apology to its people half a century later.

Japan also expressed regret at having enforced prostitution of Korean and Chinese women for the benefit of its soldiers, and has now engaged itself in some efforts at restitution. And while on this subject, it is to be noted that the United States has likewise apologized, and made restitution, to American citizens of Japanese extraction who were illegally interned in concentration camps during the war.

But the surprise does not end there, for in 1993 Butow discovered two other messages that might have been sent to Secretary Hull on that fateful December afternoon, but were not. These messages were found in a collection of Foreign Office records microfilmed for the Library of Congress between 1949 and 1951. The first was what Japan termed a "statement" (as opposed to the eleven-page, or fourteen-part, "memorandum" that it actually sent). It was also composed in English but was about half the length of the memorandum, less than six pages. This statement, evidently written by the same person or persons who composed the memorandum, ends by saying that Japan had "girt on the sword of justice," thus implying the beginning of hostilities without actually saying so. The other message, likewise undelivered, was a one-page letter composed as though it had been written by Ambassador Nomura, which could have stood alone or been used as a covering letter to either the "statement" or the "memorandum" that was actually sent. It contains the fateful words "consequently, there now exists a state of war between (our) two countries."

Neither the statement nor the cover letter was used.

Both were written in English, and Butow even debates whether the English text or the Japanese text of the three documents came first. (He suggests they were originally composed in Japanese, but the Japanese Diplomatic Record Office believes the reverse.)

Had either of the two shorter documents been transmitted to Nomura and Kurusu for delivery to our Secretary of State, the Japanese envoys would have had a far greater chance of being on time. Furthermore, as Butow lucidly points out, any doubts the memorandum might have allowed to remain regarding Japan's decision for war would have been dissipated, although our high command would still not have known when and where the blow would be struck.

Top officials in our army and navy could not, however, have avoided sending immediate and most urgent warnings to all our outlying posts—but then comes the conundrum: We intercepted and deciphered the memorandum quicker than even the Japanese embassy. Hours before the attack actually took place our officials would have been able to read that Japan had "girt on the sword"—or even the declaration of war contained in the covering letter. It would have been impossible not to recognize the meaning of either message. There would have been no possible grounds for the assertion of ambiguity, as was claimed about the memorandum. Failure in Washington to pass this bit of warning information to the commanders in Pearl Harbor and the Philippines would have been so clear-cut that it cannot be imagined. It would have been sent; Pearl Harbor and Manila would both have been warned. Tactical surprise would have been averted, but nothing could have averted the strategic surprise.

As Butow points out, the letter alone would have fulfilled Japan's obligation under international law to give prior notification of war. Had it been given to Secretary Hull only minutes before the attack, Tokyo could have insisted that the legal requirements had been met even though the attack aircraft had already been en route for several hours when Nomura and Kurusu telephoned the State Department for their appointment with Secretary Hull. There might therefore have been no grounds for Japan's apology, but this is only technical. American rage over the surprise attack would have been very little allayed by this specious, if punctilious, fulfillment of international law. The intent behind Japan's apology to its own people would still be valid, technicality or no.

The publication of the Roberts Commission Report informed the public that Kimmel and Short were derelict. No one knew that they had had no opportunity to defend themselves. They were pilloried publicly and vilified privately. Both received hate mail for having, in the view of some, actually *caused* the disaster. Distraught citizens, some no doubt reacting to the loss of or danger to loved ones at Pearl Harbor, sent vituperative suggestions that the two accused commanders should be jailed or executed, or "have the guts to commit suicide," as a Japanese commander would have.

No thought was given to the deeper implications of what was taking place. Having been accused in effect of a monstrous transgression, magnified by unthoughtful emotion on the part of some American citizens, the Pearl Harbor commanders were punished far above and beyond what they should have had to suffer.

Although the controversy over justice for the Pearl Harbor commanders has always coupled Admiral Kimmel and General Short, and in truth they should be dealt with similarly (although, surprisingly, the army seems in general less willing to forgive than the navy), they themselves behaved in rather different ways. General Short defended himself vigorously in all the investigations to which he was subjected, but then, samurai-like, apparently accepted the verdict, indefinite though it may have been. He retired to his home in Dallas, Texas, took a job as a branch manager with Ford Motor Company, and disappeared from public view. His neighbors rarely saw him, and few of them knew him by sight, or, for that matter, were even aware that the "Mr. Short" whose hobby was growing roses in his backyard had been the army commander at Pearl Harbor. He died in 1949, a quiet self-sacrifice to the last.

Admiral Kimmel was very different. Where General Short apparently resigned himself to the realization that his contribution to the war effort was to be the target of blame for Pearl Harbor, in effect to "gather all the arrows" into his own breast, Admiral Kimmel was never so resigned. He fought to vindicate his name for the rest of his life, and there is no question that this became essentially an obsession with him. He died in 1968, maintaining to the last that he had been misused by history, and in effect begging his compatriots to give him a fair hearing.

With the sole exception of these two, all officers who served in the war were ultimately retired at the highest rank held, even though they might, subsequent to a higher rank, have been employed in a lower one. It is evident that this difference was not accidental but a vestige of the blame placed on the military commanders at Pearl Harbor by the Roberts Commission.

To restore their good names to Admiral Kimmel and General Short will cost us nothing, but doing it will symbolize something our country holds very dear. The two officers should, by official action of the president, be advanced posthumously on the retired lists of their respective services to the highest ranks in which they served. Restoration of the rank would be symbolic of restoration in the national esteem. There need be no funds involved, nor much in the way of ceremonies (but it would be proper to have an appropriate public notice at least equivalent to the public notice with which they were unjustly disgraced). The records would simply show, by the restoration, that these two officers, long wrongly blamed by their country, had been restored to good favor. In effect, the obloquy of the disaster at Pearl Harbor would be lifted from their shoulders. Those who hold personal and national honor as something important could feel that blame had been lifted at long last, and the matter laid to rest.

Needed are no new revelations. We need only reinterpret and to some extent correct the record. It can be assumed that little additional information will come to light unless and until there is some breakthrough in the transcripts of the Churchill-Roosevelt telephone conversations of 1940 and 1941. There is indeed some indication that things may be moving in this direction, but it is not even known for sure how many of the relatively frequent telephone conversations were recorded. Persons in controlling positions, equipped with all the sensors of their time and well aware of the certainty that future historians will be probing everything they can find to look into, can be expected to destroy all records they do not wish ever to have come to light. It must be assumed that only what they are willing to have discovered, or, hopefully, may have overlooked, will be available to researchers.

This is why personal diaries, letters hidden in obscure places, and hidden voice recordings are golden to the lucky finders. Although Richard Nixon unaccountably failed in this respect, one can be sure that Franklin D. Roosevelt and Winston Churchill, masters of history themselves and well aware that researchers would be indefatigable, took care to protect everything they wanted to remain forever unknown.

The half century since Pearl Harbor has seen hordes of earnest scholars poring over every scrap of available evidence. A mountain of facts has been turned up, and a mountain of books has resulted. And the public is still interested in every question surrounding the event, even though the sudden discovery of "smoking guns" can no longer be expected.

Perhaps such ongoing interest is merely an indication that the American public feels the weight of responsibility for having condemned Kimmel and Short without having given them a chance to defend themselves. More than anyone in our history, Kimmel and Short have been solely before the bar of public opinion—and that deep, finely ground judgment is already resounding, nationwide, with the verdict that they have suffered enough.

Rear Admiral D. M. (Mac) Showers, a veteran of thirty years of naval intelligence, sums it all up in a recent letter to the editor (*Washington Post*, 14 January 1995):

> It is now conclusively established that (Kimmel) was not furnished with the crucial intelligence then available to the Navy Department in Washington that would have enabled him to (avoid surprise). . . . The facts . . . and their denial to him are now well known. This is the basis for appeals . . . to remove the stigma from Adm. Kimmel's name and to restore his rightful position.

The suggestion to posthumously restore the ranks the two officers once held is not comparable to a presidential pardon but to the righting of a wrong that has gone on too long. Restoring the two final casualties of Pearl Harbor will heal a running wound in the national body and even a cognitive sore in the stature of our wartime president. It is little enough to do, will require only a few drops of ink and a bit of compassion, and the honor of our nation demands no less.

Who is to be the judge of this? You are, dear reader, and I, and all those who feel likewise. This charade has gone on long enough. No money is involved. Personal justice is all that is wanted now. It is all we can do, and all of America should insist that it be done. There was an opportunity to do the right thing at the half-century anniversary of Pearl Harbor, but it was passed by. Now there will be another appropriate moment, on the fiftieth anniversary of peace in the Pacific. We should make the announcement at Pearl Harbor on 2 September 1995 at the flood tide of the commemorative ceremonies on board the sunken, shattered USS *Arizona.* We should invite representatives of the government of Japan, and if they can be found, we should also invite members of Admiral Yamamoto's family to help symbolize the healing.

The time approaches. There is only one way to handle this simple, but important, restoration of our national honor, symbolic though it may only be. We should, this time, do something right.

References

***Report of the Joint Congressional Committee*, 1946**

This is by far the most exhaustive and thorough compilation of material relating to the Pearl Harbor attack. Printed in thirty-nine volumes, plus a fortieth containing its final report, it includes the full proceedings, verbatim testimony, and complete findings—the entire reports, in other words—of all eight prior government investigations. It is, however, far too long and much too political. This massive compendium of pertinent and irrelevant information, some of it hearsay and some patently incorrect, if not false, suffers from the basic infirmity of all legislative hearings: namely, of itself, it contains no proof of the validity of the testimony given. The original concept of a "hearing" is just what the word means: a congressional committee would "hear" all sides and then reach a decision as to what sort of legislation, if any, it should recommend. Committee members would act, in effect, as a panel of judges over the proposals submitted to it. Those who would appear before it would commonly be restricted to testifying in support of or in opposition to the subject before the committee. Only members of the committee, and its counsel if permitted, would be allowed to ask questions, or cross-examine witnesses. Thus, witnesses would be totally at the mercy of the committee and its counsel and, contrary to trial procedures in a court of law, would be unable to question other witnesses or, if the committee so rules, even hear adverse testimony.

The cross-examination is one of the most valuable tools of a trial lawyer. Without it, weaknesses in testimony can only be shown by other testimony, or brought home to a jury in closing arguments, and the procedure is carefully stated in law.

Committees of Congress, however, make up their own rules. Usually they will permit a witness to be accompanied by counsel who can give him or her quiet advice but who is not permitted to address the committee or ask questions. Apparently this system has worked well enough when it has concerned legislation, but when Congress broadened the scope of committee work to include adversarial proceedings, questions of procedure arose that are still unresolved. An individual wishing to contest a statement made in testimony can have a question asked, for example, only if a member of a committee is willing to ask it, thus losing the immediacy that is a skillful lawyer's principal strength. And even if a committee member is willing to do everything counsel for a witness may ask, the skill, or lack of skill, of the questioner will often cause the result to be of doubtful value. Facts set forth in this manner are therefore often questionable, and in particular they usually fail to safeguard the rights of persons whose conduct or performance is under scrutiny. Precisely this issue, combined with the overbearing manner of the committee counsel and chairman, seen on television by the whole country, brought the McCarthy Hearings into national disrepute.

Proceedings in a court of law are very carefully circumscribed with rules to preserve the rights of all concerned, but this is not the case with hearings before Congress.

Since only the committee and its (own) counsel could call witnesses or interrogate them, in the Pearl Harbor hearings not all the important witnesses were called. Numerous comments were made about the numbing effect of the prolonged hearings and the fact that members of the JCC were anxious to conclude them. A number of obvious questions were not asked of important personages who should have had the correct answers at their fingertips. Findings of fact and opinion were entirely too often blurred, almost as if the committee wanted this. No judgment was rendered as to where major responsibility lay for our being caught unaware, despite the well-known expectation that this would be stated in its findings. Nor was there any decision as to the rightness or wrongness of personnel actions, or lack of same, concerning the senior service commanders in Washington or, for that matter, those in Hawaii and the Philippines as well.

Historians in search of information will find a plethora of that here, but it is presented without discrimination, and hard to locate in the huge mass of material. The reader may feel like an appeal reviewer of an important trial in which, for some strange reason, there was no judge to look to for advice, no way to distinguish pertinent evidence from peripheral detail, no guide as to permissible court conduct by prosecutors or jurors (members of the Joint Committee). After reading all one can of the mountain of information presented, with no memory aids of any kind, one is left entirely on one's own. Absent any professional authoritative control, under these circumstances hearsay, political bias, and preconceptions all have free entry into the average person's deliberation, so that a truly fair verdict becomes essentially an impossibility.

Agawa, Hiroyuki. *The Reluctant Admiral.* Translated by John Bester. Harper & Row, 1979. Originally published in Japanese by Shinchoscha, 1969, under the title *Yamamoto Isoroku.*

The best biography of Yamamoto yet to reach this country, this book shows Yamamoto to be a complex, sympathetic, and in many ways contradictory character. In the drama and fury of war, some of his most thoughtful observations were so misquoted, by Japan as well as by our side, that he was, unfairly, one of Japan's most hated leaders.

Burlingame, Burl (William G., Jr.). *Advance Force—Pearl Harbor.* Kailua, Hawaii: Pacific Monograph, 1992.

By his own account, three decades ago Burlingame arrived in Hawaii at age eleven with two goals: to attain Eagle Scout rank in the Boy Scouts organization and to explore Pearl Harbor. He achieved both objectives, and the one relating to Pearl Harbor has never released its hold on him. Now on the staff of the *Honolulu Star-Bulletin,* early on he became interested in the five midget submarines that invaded our naval stronghold on the day of the Japanese surprise attack. Little is known about them, except that all their crew members, save one, died in the attack. None of the little subs returned to its mother submarine; it was in fact understood that they were on a suicide mission, determined to sacrifice themselves in their emperor's noble cause. The much higher visibility of the attacking aircraft brought with it much publicity and many photographs. Of the submarine effort, very little was known then, and no doubt partly because of Japan's wholesale destruction of records just before the surrender, not much has been discovered since.

Yet it was known that a number of midgets succeeded in entering the harbor, for some were sunk there, their shattered hulls recovered later. At least one was sunk outside the harbor by the USS *Ward,* about one hour before the attack began. Burlingame became fascinated with the idea of the untold stories that must lie behind each of the tiny wrecked submarines, the privations endured by their crews, their successes if any, and the grim manner of their deaths.

He discovered that the skipper of one of the little subs had in fact survived. Each boat had a two-man crew, but the Japanese memorial tablet to these godlike heroes, as they were called, showed only nine persons. One had survived to become "U.S. POW number one"; Burlingame sought him out, one thing led to another, and in due course a considerable amount of information began to accumulate on the author's computer. He began researching the exploits of the other submarines involved, the "motherships" of the midgets, and finally searching for the wrecks themselves, using all the late-developing modern techniques available. Some of them he found, as detailed in this book.

The result is an entirely new dimension of the Japanese attack on Pearl Harbor, one bound to interest historians and underwater archeologists for years to come. More of the little wrecks will probably be found, perhaps one more still in the Pearl Harbor area, doubtless some in other places where attacks were made by these innovative craft and their self-sacrificing operators.

One item of immediate interest centers around one of the best-known photographs of the Pearl Harbor attack. Taken from one of the attacking aircraft, it has been widely circulated in the United States. It shows shock rings spreading out from the damaged ships in battleship row, oil beginning to gush from ruptured hulls. The *West Virginia* and *Oklahoma* are listing to port, the *West Virginia* noticeably more than the *Oklahoma,* moored just ahead of her. Torpedo tracks are also visible in the water, two of them parallel to each other, therefore presumably dropped or fired from separate sources, but a third track is coming in (or going out) at an angle from another as though these two might have been fired from the same source, which looks like a tiny black dot in a froth of roiled water near where the two tracks come together. Noting this, Burlingame, curiosity aroused, sought a better quality print and obtained professional imaging help. Enlarging and enhancing the black dot through a photogrammetric process provided virtual confirmation that it is indeed one of the two-man "suicide" subs, depicted at the very moment of torpedoing two of our proudest battleships. It must have penetrated Pearl Harbor early on that tragic December morning, lain doggo for a few hours until the preordained moment of attack, and then fired one of its two torpedoes into each of them.

The book is episodic, concentrating on details of action, and is little involved with broader tactical or strategic concerns. Its value lies in that very limitation, for nearly all history tries, as it should, to give some idea of the big game being played. This one gives the nuts and bolts, and they are valuable too. Page 198 reproduces the photograph referred to, and page 199 has the enhancement.

A comment from the author of the current book: the two torpedo wakes are clearly visible, extend nearly into their targets, and converge at a point near the probable submarine. However, the sub has not advanced into the V of its spread of torpedoes, as it should have if it were still proceeding ahead. For this reason it is suggested that the sub may already have reversed course, which would be a logical move to clear the area for torpedo-launching aircraft coming along.

Butow, Robert J. C. *Japan's Decision to Surrender.* Stanford: Stanford University Press, 1954.

———. *Tojo and the Coming of the War.* Princeton: Princeton University Press, 1961.

———. "Marching Off to War on the Wrong Foot: The Final Note Tokyo Did NOT Send to Washington." *Pacific Historical Review.* American Historical Association, Pacific Coast Branch, 1993.

Dr. Butow, currently professor emeritus of history and East Asian studies at the University of Washington at Seattle, is one of the foremost scholars of Japan and Japanese history in the United States. *Japan's Decision to Surrender* carries a foreword by Edwin O. Reischauer, then a professor at Harvard and a well-known student of Japan and Japanese culture, later a very successful U.S. ambassador to Japan, credited with restoring the comity between our two nations and even with creating much of it. No reviewer's comment can equal Dr. Reischauer's opinion, expressed at the conclusion of his powerful introduction to the book:

> The full record of that decision also makes one of those true stories that so effectively belittle fiction. It is this story that Dr. Butow has told in careful and scholarly detail but also with a verve that does justice to these dramatic events.

Tojo and the Coming of the War, written after the *Surrender* book, is, of course, chronologically in front of it. A considerably longer effort, *Tojo* contains the same carefully crafted analyses Butow so masterfully demonstrates in his first volume. Here he shows how, in 1941, military tentacles of power had spread through the government and the body politic to the extent that they silenced opposition to the "southern movement," made a Pacific war inevitable, and even threatened the relatively recent overthrow of the shogunate rule that had for centuries dominated the emperor himself.

In "Marching Off to War," in the prestigious *Pacific Historical Review,* Butow continues his masterful study of Japan and the war, bringing out that in 1941 Japan had composed not just the fourteen-part diplomatic note with which to terminate negotiations with the United States, but also a second note, half as long, in part very similarly worded, also prepared in English (as was the fourteen-part "memorandum" that ambassadors Nomura and Kurusu delivered to Secretary of State Hull an hour and twenty minutes late that critical Sunday afternoon in December), but differing in one very essential part. This note, which Japan called a "statement," ended with the following words:

> Our patience finally exhausted and our destiny at stake, the nation has risen, as one man, to meet the challenge. Steeped in the conviction that right always will triumph, our hundred million peoples [*sic*] have girt on the sword of justice, anxious to defend the fatherland and eager to vindicate our glorious cause.

There was also a covering letter of transmittal, unsigned and, of course, likewise not used, prepared as though it had been personally composed by Nomura and addressed to "Your Excellency," presumably Secretary Hull. It consists of only three short paragraphs, the first of which states,

> I have the honour, under instructions from my Government, to inform your Excellency that as the hostile measures taken by the United States have seriously jeopardized the security, and therefore existence, of Japan, they have been constrained to resort to measures of self-defense and consequently there now exists a state of war between the two countries.

Neither the seven-part "statement" nor the covering letter of transmittal was used, and thus they have no standing except as items of historical interest, but Butow goes on to point out, in a footnote, that

> When Nomura and Kurusu entered Hull's office at 2:20 that afternoon, the Secretary of State asked the Ambassador why he had specified one o'clock in his request for an interview—a request made by telephone "toward noon" (a postponement of the appointment was later arranged at Nomura's bidding). The Ambassador replied that he did not know, but that was his

> instruction. Looking back on the encounter, Hull wrote: "Knowing the importance of a deadline set for a specific hour, Nomura should have come to see me precisely at one o'clock, even though he had in his hand only the first few lines of his note, leaving instructions with the Embassy to bring him the remainder as it became ready." If Nomura had done this, he might have saved himself some personal embarrassment, but the fact remains that the final note did not sever diplomatic relations between Japan and the United States, did not warn the American government that Japan would consider itself free to resort to any action it deemed necessary, and did not qualify as a declaration of war under international law. All this was Tokyo's responsibility—not Nomura's. Despite Hull's anger in 1941, he did not feel that Nomura and Kurusu were aware, when they came to his office, that the Imperial Japanese Navy had struck Pearl Harbor. "In fact," Hull later noted, "I am satisfied that they did not learn of the attack until they returned to their Embassy."

In the context of recent Japanese "apologies to its own people" for not behaving in accordance with international law when it initiated war with the United States, as covered in the U.S. press late in November 1994, Butow's final paragraph in this article, at the conclusion of a careful review of the newly discovered documents that were prepared but not used, bears repeating:

> Even if the forwarding letter alone had been handed to Hull, only minutes before the attack on Pearl Harbor, Tokyo would have been able to insist that legal requirements had been met. Hostilities would have exploded in the Pacific just as the Imperial Army and Navy had planned, but the people of Japan would have had the satisfaction of knowing that their government had adhered to its treaty commitments. In such circumstances, no one would ever have been able to criticize Japan's leaders for marching off to war on the wrong foot.

Japan's apologies to its own people for the "major source of shame" it had brought on them by the way it conducted the attack on Pearl Harbor would not have been necessary, Butow feels, but I respectfully disagree. The planes had already been on the way for hours; the *Kido Butai* had been more than a week at sea en route to the attack spot. A few minutes of technicality could not square this!

Casey, William J. *The Secret War Against Hitler.* Washington, D.C.: Regnery Gateway, 1988.

A disciple of William J. ("Wild Bill") Donovan of the Office of Strategic Services (OSS), Casey had a natural affinity for the handling of secret affairs and progressed rapidly in power and influence until, two years after entering the OSS, he was chief of secret intelligence for the European theater. He was only thirty-one years old at the time, and he remained at the forefront of secret intelligence for our country until, under President Ronald Reagan, he was appointed head of the Central Intelligence Agency. He died in that post in May of 1987. Published in 1988, this book covers only World War II and is cited because of the bald statement, made on page 7, "As the Japanese storm began to gather force in the Pacific, the most private communications between the Japanese government and its ambassadors . . . were being read in Washington. Army and Navy cryptographers, having broken the Japanese cipher, were reading messages that foretold the attack. The British had sent word that a Japanese fleet was steaming east toward Hawaii." The book cites neither proof nor corroboration for the statement, and it is here brought out merely to demonstrate that many authorities with top credentials believe it to be true. Antirevisionists have yet to prove it is not.

Clausen, Henry C., and Bruce Lee. *Pearl Harbor: Final Judgement.* New York: Crown Publishers, Inc., 1992.

A badly flawed review of the Pearl Harbor attack, mostly written by a lawyer who, half a century later, still maintained unconditional loyalty to his employer of the time. Admirable though this may be in the professional and personal sense, it is so obviously partisan that it cannot stand as objective history. The value of the book lies in its demonstration of the lengths to which the players in this tremendous drama have gone to force history into the form they want, or believe. It does, however, in its appendices contain much important information of use to the historian, and in its very *non-objectivity* adds greatly to the student's understanding of this extraordinary period of our national history.

Coletta, Paolo. *American Secretaries of the Navy.* 2 vols. Annapolis: Naval Institute Press, 1980.

The best and most convenient source for the biography of Secretary of the Navy Frank Knox, as used herein.

Costello, John. *Days of Infamy.* New York: Pocket Books, 1994.

This is without doubt one of the most thoroughly researched and carefully crafted books about the beginning of U.S. involvement in World War II yet to come out. John Costello's ability to develop sources is uncanny, his depth incredible. In *Days of Infamy* he has made the greatest contribution yet to the developing history of this Armageddon of modern times. With this book he will go into the record as one of the outstanding historians, and prodigious writers, of the twentieth century.

Gannon, Michael. *Operation Drumbeat.* New York, Harper & Row, 1992.

———. "Reopen the Kimmel Case." U.S. Naval Institute *Proceedings* (December 1994).

A professor of history at the University of Florida, Gannon became interested in the German U-boat campaign along the Florida coast in 1942 as he was doing research for a history of the state, and from this got into the tangled morass of our early failures in combating the U-boats. His resulting book, *Operation Drumbeat,* has already become the classic tale of our early wartime experience along the U.S. East Coast. In the process of this study, Gannon has written a novel about this period, and in addition became fascinated with the story of how the United States got into the war in the first place, granted that all sides (except the British) were ostensibly trying to avoid our involvement. His *Proceedings* article demolishes the theory that Kimmel had been informed by his aviation experts that north was the most likely direction from which enemy aircraft carriers might launch a surprise air attack because it was the direction of the prevailing winds, and that he should therefore have set up air-search patrols to the north.

Haldeman, H. R. *The Haldeman Diaries.* New York: G. P. Putnam's Sons, 1994.

Bob Haldeman, Nixon's chief of staff, kept a meticulous diary, dictated on tape after hours, mostly at home, in which he explained much of the secret thinking of the White House during his years there. While most of the diaries written by White House staff generally concern internal White House doings, Haldeman's go into the much broader field of the formation of foreign policy. For the purposes of the present book, however, it has been useful primarily for comparison of techniques of control.

Kimmel, Husband E. *Admiral Kimmel's Story.* Chicago: Henry Regnery Company, 1955.

The admiral's personal story, not one that would win awards for literary flight, but, like his own character, a book that concentrates on the job at hand: his defense of his role at Pearl Harbor. This is solidly done, but his defense is not dramatic enough to garner readers for its own sake, which it might have, had he been able to include a better feel for his personal reaction, at the time, to the terrible event that destroyed his career and, in fact, his life. Even though he had been "found derelict in his duty" in the public mind, at that stage something of this nature might have brought him a big enough audience to overturn the national disinterest in reopening his cause. The American public has a built-in natural sympathy for the underdog seeking justice, but very little for the "overdog" who may have experienced misfortune. Had Kimmel been able to show how he had worked his way up in the navy over a forty-year period with no special assistance, how he had idealistically done his assigned duties in every case—so well that he had been put in command of the fleet sooner than anyone expected—how his attainment of high status was in fact the fulfillment of the American dream, he might have been able to overcome the average citizen's prejudice against high rank. Unfortunately, his book did not strike the needed note. The country was not yet ready to listen to a considered defense of the man it believed responsible for our being blindsided at Pearl Harbor. Had he put in some vivid personal accounts to liven the book up for potential readers, he would have had more of them, but this was not the admiral's style.

Kittredge, Tracy Barrett. "A Military Danger: The Revelation of Secret Strategic Plans." U.S. Naval Institute *Proceedings* (July 1955), page 731.

Captain Kittredge, USNR (Ret.) served on active duty in U.S. intelligence staffs in European waters during both world wars and in the historical section, Joint Chiefs of Staff, following the war. The article is an in-depth analysis of German and American strategic planning in the days before and after the attack on Pearl Harbor, and comes up with some unusual, very well thought out, and authoritative insights into German staff thinking in the early days of the war.

Layton, Edwin T., with John Costello and Roger Pineau. *And I Was There.* New York: William Morrow and Company, Inc., 1985.

Admiral Layton was intelligence officer for three successive Pacific Fleet commanders during the most critical period of U.S. naval history: Admirals Richardson, Kimmel, and Nimitz. He gave all three of them his unstinting loyalty, was dismayed when Richardson was summarily relieved of command for disagreeing too forcefully with President Roosevelt as to keeping the Pacific Fleet in Pearl Harbor, indignant at the injustices shown to Kimmel in the wake of the Japanese surprise attack, and proudly supportive of Nimitz, whom he (and everyone else) held to be probably the most fortunate choice for the job that could have been made. Much of what Layton wrote in his memoir has been restated here, for I am in total agreement with his outlook about Pearl Harbor. There is no doubt that internecine warfare among OPNAV and ONI partisans, fueled by personal and illegitimate ambition, played a large part in the failure to pass proper information to the Hawaiian commanders, and that this failure was the basic cause of their unawareness of the proximity of danger.

Lord, Walter. *Day of Infamy.* New York: Henry Holt & Co., 1957.

A classic account of the surprise attack, typically full of the personal vignettes of people caught in it. As an example of Lord's careful research, however, all the specific details tally with official accounts released later.

Manchester, William. *American Caesar.* Boston: Little, Brown and Company, 1978.

Pretty much the accepted popular biography of General MacArthur. The author makes a manful effort to explain the general's amazing laxness during the first several hours after the attack on Hawaii, but the best he can come up with is "input overload"—as good an analysis as any until the publication of the Costello book (see above).

Miller, Edward S. ***War Plan Orange.*** **Annapolis: Naval Institute Press, 1992.**

Absolutely first-class product of eighteen years of personal interest in the development and history of the famed, though little known, U.S. Navy plan for the conduct of a Pacific war against Japan ("Orange"). Miller shows that the war plan was not at all the sort of "plan" that use of the word might lead one to expect. Most important, it was a series of studies, and Admiral Nimitz was obviously exactly right in his comment that "everything except the kamikazes" had been, to a surprising degree, quite accurately predicted. Plans there were too, all right, but they changed frequently, depending on which set of theoretical planners happened to be in the driver's seat. When the war broke out, no one opened a safe and dragged out the "plan" by which the war was fought and won. Our strategy was made as we went along, but it was grounded in solid studies that nearly all our wartime planners had been steeped in for years.

Morgenstern, George. ***Pearl Harbor: The Story of the Secret War.*** **New York: The Devin-Adair Company, 1947.**

One of the first of the so-called "revisionist" histories and one of the best. It is revisionist only in that it tells facts that other histories, favored by the "establishment," either have ignored or have told differently. When two different authors interpret the same information differently, the usual outcome is that both have a right to their own outlooks, and there is often an effort to obtain further information to get at the truth. Not in this case. Pro-administration partisans have concentrated on undermining, or questioning the "believability" of, all evidence apparently supporting misfeasance in office that contributed to the lack of awareness in Hawaii, while former isolationists have tried to argue that the whole thing was a monstrous plot to get our country into World War II. The truth is almost certainly somewhere in the middle: there was clearly a condition of tension and warning in Washington that should have been communicated to the field commanders with far greater urgency than it was, and staying out of the war would ultimately have been far more costly, by all measurements, than getting in it when we did.

But this is an overall evaluation. What Morgenstern shows is what happened and, essentially, how it came to happen. His book cannot be dismissed as simple "revisionism," for it shows that much happened in Washington that was not made known outside of Washington, and that this was the immediate cause of the surprise. Regarding preparedness and alertness, even the Japanese attackers were impressed by the speed with which our forces reacted. They *were* prepared, and they *were* alert, but they were *not aware of how critical the situation had become* and were struck without warning.

Parker, Frederick D. *Pearl Harbor Revisited: United States Navy Communications Intelligence 1924–1941.* Series IV, World War II, vol. 6 of *United States Cryptologic History.* Fort George C. Meade, MD: National Security Agency, 1994.

This is a scholarly, unbiased, carefully researched account of a specific episode of our code-breaking effort. Parker's judgment is impossible to fault. Also considered is the text of an address given by Parker to the Naval Historians Seminar at the Dudley Knox Center for Naval History in the Washington Navy Yard on 17 May 1990. In the book cited (vol. 6 of the *Cryptologic History*), under the heading "Turning Victory Into Defeat," appears the following:

> Hidden in these [JN-25] messages [not Purple] was the full magnitude of the enterprise planned by the Japanese to begin on 7–8 December 1941. Had these messages been read on a current basis, it is possible, even probable, given the analytic skills so evident in these centers—that the early course of the war would have been significantly altered.

In the same section, however, is found the following:

> The actual reading of current Japanese messages before Pearl Harbor was not to be. . . . Thousands of intercepted Japanese Navy messages in JN-25 were not exploited because, as a result of manpower shortages and higher priorities, the underlying code values remained unrecovered.

Prange, Gordon W., with Donald M. Goldstein and Katherine V. Dillon. *At Dawn We Slept.* New York: McGraw-Hill Book Company, 1981.

———. *The Verdict of History.* New York: McGraw-Hill Book Company, 1986.

———. *Dec. 7, 1941.* New York: McGraw-Hill Book Company, 1988.

The first of this trilogy of books was the blockbuster that triggered the current effort to restore the final and unrecognized victims of

Pearl Harbor. Prange made a massive study of the attack, but did not himself live to complete even the first volume. It was left to his assistants and collaborators, Goldstein and Dillon, to put it together and to render the judgments they have essentially capsulized in the appendix titled "Revisionists Revisited." There they were almost able to put their finger on the real problem when they wrote (page 839),

> the threat from the Nazis and the Japanese militarists was immediate. . . . [revisionist] theses tacitly implied that if the United States stood aside while Hitler swallowed the British Empire and the Soviet Union, *der Führer* thereupon would settle down with a contented sigh, and the Third Reich and the United States would coexist like the lion and the lamb. Even the most cursory look at Hitler's record makes this notion questionable.

But then, in considering the theory that Roosevelt "deliberately dragged the United States into the war," they cite Harry Elmer Barnes as

> the leading spirit of the thesis that Roosevelt had planned the whole thing deliberately, knew about the attack on Pearl Harbor in advance, and wanted it to happen. He believed the president guilty of a triple conspiracy. First, Roosevelt needed an attack on this country because of his campaign promise that Americans would not be sent to war unless the United States was attacked. Secondly, to permit such an attack unobstructed, he arranged that Kimmel and Short should receive none of the information available in Washington from Japanese decoded material. Thirdly, he conspired to cover up the failure to warn the Hawaiian commanders.

Quite rightly, Dillon and Goldstein point out that there is no proof whatever of this exaggerated scheme, particularly those portions hinging on intimate knowledge of things no one could know. Nearly all "revisionists" have fallen into the same trap: from a fairly logical reconstruction of what *did* happen, they progress beyond logic, espouse ideas they cannot prove or even support in logic, and in effect shoot themselves in the foot.

Richardson, Vice Adm. David C. "Review and Commentary on the Clausen-Lee book, *Pearl Harbor, Final Judgement.*" *Cryptolog* (Summer 1993).

Richardson says, in the first paragraph, "Were it not for an astonishing amount of bias, faulty judgment and an ignorance of the operational context of the times in which command decisions were being made, Clausen's highly informative inquiries would make the point quite conclusively that screwups in Washington were the major factor in the disaster."

Richardson, Adm. J. O. *On the Treadmill to Pearl Harbor.* Washington, D.C.: Naval History Division, 1973.

In 1956 Admiral Richardson began writing his account of what went on during that critical period at Pearl Harbor, and although he had always been a good friend of CNO Stark, he had so many critical things to say about him in connection with Pearl Harbor that this book, completed in 1958, was held up from publication until 1973, the year after Stark's death (and a year before Richardson's).

Richardson wrote, among other sizzling passages, "I consider 'Betty' Stark, in failing to ensure that Kimmel was furnished with all the information from the breaking of the Japanese dispatches, to have been, to a marked degree, professionally negligent in carrying out his duties as Chief of Naval Operations." Elsewhere he wrote:

> I am impelled to believe that sometime prior to December 7, the President had directed that only Marshall could send any warning message to the Hawaiian area. I do not know this to be a fact and I cannot prove it. I believe this because of my knowledge of Stark and the fact that his means of communication with Kimmel were equal to, if not superior to those available to Marshall for communication with Short. He made no effort to warn Kimmel on the morning of December 7, but referred the matter to Marshall.

Growing fear of inadvertent disclosure of Magic caused less and less of the information gleaned from it to be sent outside the "Magic circle." According to Richardson, Admiral Turner, who had made himself czar over naval intelligence, had falsely informed his superiors that a Purple machine, to produce Magic, was available to the Hawaiian commanders and that therefore "they know everything we know." Amazingly, no one thought to make sure, and the result was that as tension in Washington increased, everyone became frantically busier and worked longer hours—and information going from Washington to Hawaii decreased; so the Hawaiian commanders actually thought the concern expressed in the "war warning" of 27 November had lessened.

No one expected an attack on the fleet at Pearl Harbor, and when it happened Washington panicked, "[Roosevelt] ran for cover," and the Roberts Commission was sent to Hawaii to find out whom to blame there so that suspicion would not land on Washington officialdom. So wrote Admiral Richardson.

Rusbridger, James, and Eric Nave. *Betrayal at Pearl Harbor; How Churchill Lured Roosevelt into World War II.* New York: Simon & Schuster, 1992.

Capt. Eric Nave, RAN (Ret.), an intelligence officer and Japanese linguist before and during the war, wrote the original draft of this book, which was done over and marketed by Rusbridger. The book has received mixed reviews. The corroboration needed by its wholesale accusation of double dealing by the national leaders of Great Britain and the United States is not sufficient to convince. Although, to be sure, Rusbridger claims he encountered obstructionism from official agencies in both countries, he also claims considerable assistance from them. In fine, however, both authors are lone voices shouting in the wilderness. They do not possess the stature to command serious attention.

Nave was eighty-nine at the time it was published, died shortly afterward, but was said to have been of entirely sound mind. He had been attempting to put his memories and papers together for some time when he joined forces with Rusbridger, a freelance journalist-author, now also deceased. The result is a very short book, only 152 pages of text, plus lengthy front matter, and in spite of its controversial thesis it has not been as well recognized as it should be.

Recognizing they would run into this problem, however, the authors buttressed their arguments with extensive substantiating photostated documents. While antirevisionists will never be satisfied they have received sufficient proof in opposition to their set partiality, well-documented arguments, especially when there are no opposing ones, have a right to be heard. The book's thesis is that effective breaking of some Japanese codes, specifically the JN-25 code as distinguished from Purple, took place in the Netherlands East Indies, Singapore, and Australia. Nave wrote that he participated in the effort from his position in Australia, and that the decodes were definitely sent to England and (he was positive) from England to America. He and Rusbridger also claim decodes were sent directly from Batavia to the Dutch Embassy in Washington and handed to the U.S. State Department.

No proof can be found that any of this material was ever seen in Washington, but those who claim to have sent it are uniformly adamant that it was sent. Similar positions are taken by all the other intelligence operatives who believe they had done their duty but were somehow disregarded—and at this late date the only conclusion there can be is that with all that smoke there must have been a fire somewhere.

Spector, Ronald H. *Eagle Against the Sun.* New York: The Free Press, 1985.

Unquestionably one of the outstanding books about World War II, written with verve and understanding and based on many years of research, this book is bound to be considered one of the definitive accounts of the Pacific war. One reviewer (Clay Blair) says, "Mining a warehouse of material with absolute control, Spector has produced a superbly readable, insightful, gripping, unbiased one-volume history of the American-Japanese war that is, at the same time, a glorious celebration of the American spirit and (rare these days) a ringing tribute to the American armed forces." Significantly, the author served with the Marines in Vietnam, wrote his Ph.D. thesis (later published as a book) on the U.S. Naval War College, and spent ten years at the Army Center of Military History in Washington, D.C. He seems to have drunk deeply at the wells of all three services, and indeed, following publication of this book, he served for three years as director of Naval History, with headquarters at the Washington Navy Yard.

It is notable, however, that although three of the five tributes printed on the back of the book's dust jacket are from the army (two generals and an army historian), there is none from anyone in the navy or the marines. The book itself bears out this observation. It is more oriented toward the army than toward the sea forces. Some informal critics have said he should have had a more thorough review of his manuscript by qualified navy types. All in all, however, this is one of the best books yet written about our war with Japan.

Stahlman, James G., to Rear Adm. Kemp Tolley, 26 November 1973.

Stahlman says, in part,

> It has never been my privilege to have known you, but I was intrigued with your story of "The *Lanikai.*" When I started reading it, I couldn't put it down.
>
> You have developed a subject in which I have been deeply interested since the week after Pearl Harbor, dealing with what

> went on at the White House the night before. There have been so many variations and one or two lies told that I am anxious to have what Frank Knox revealed to me totally confirmed, if possible, although I need no confirmation of anything told by Frank Knox. He was my longtime personal friend and fellow publisher. I knew him back in the '30's when he was General Manager of the Hearst Newspaper properties, including overseeing the International News Service which was then headed by my friend, Frank Mason, who later became one of Knox's consultants, along with Adlai Stevenson and Lewis Strauss before he went on active duty.
>
> I went on active 21 January '41 because I felt that the Navy was getting a ranking in that so-called "defense" period, from the standpoint of press and public relations. I had been President of the American Newspaper Publishers Association, '37–39, and knew practically everybody in the newspaper business. I had held a commission in the Reserves since 1926 in Naval Intelligence and Frank Knox was delighted when I suggested to him that I wanted to do something. . . .
>
> I never called him "Mr. Secretary," but always "Colonel." He took great pride in his Rough Rider days under Teddy Roosevelt, whose bust he always kept on his desk. . . .
>
> The Colonel told me that he, Stimson, Marshall, Betty Stark and Harry Hopkins had spent most of the night before at the White House with FDR, all waiting for what they knew was coming after those intercepts. . . .
>
> I wrote our mutual friend Bob Dennison [Adm. Robert L. Dennison, USN (Ret.)] asking him for your address which his secretary has just sent me. . . . under date of November 21, writing him fully about this whole setup, much of which is repetitive of what I have just written you above. . . .

Stahlman is the best known source of the story of the midnight White House meeting on 6–7 December 1941. A close friend and confidant of Navy Secretary Frank Knox, Stahlman, only a naval reserve captain, had entry to his office through the private entrance at any time, much to the dismay (and sometimes resentment) of senior officers whose access was more formally controlled. During the war he served in the Office of Naval Intelligence (ONI), and then became Knox's special public-relations adviser, setting up offices in all the naval districts and under the fleet commanders. He wrote letters to numerous persons detailing what Knox had told him about the midnight meeting, and having received some confirmation was in search of more. In his letters he mentioned having sold his newspaper, the *Nashville Banner,* in January 1972, that he was "separating his files to prevent overlapping," and had been working on two books for about ten years. How much confirmation he received is not known, and the books he was writing have not been published. He died in 1976.

Toland, John. *Infamy: Pearl Harbor and Its Aftermath.* New York: Doubleday, 1982.

A carefully researched review of the events leading up to Pearl Harbor, convincing of most of the facts and deductions laid out, but flawed because unsubstantiated speculation is also included in its arguments. Toland should have realized that accusing our wartime president of misconduct in an issue as broad as this one, that directly affects so many people even to this day, would require impeccable proof of every item. His failure to pass this rigorous test has, in effect, damaged the proud Pulitzer status he enjoyed for a previous book. *Infamy* suffers from its off-the-wall statement that Roosevelt knew in advance about the approaching Japanese task force and did not permit warning to be sent to Hawaii in order that the "first blow" would be so devastating that the nation would be galvanized in righteous anger, stop all talk about isolationism, and gird itself for absolute victory.

This was, of course, what actually happened. These facts are clear; what is not clear, and is unacceptable, is the villainy Toland ascribes to Roosevelt. Of this there is no proof at all; Toland's stature is the one that suffers because he subscribes to it.

It will be noted that this is the post–Pearl Harbor isolationist view: that, even admitting the inevitability of U.S. entry into the "European War" in order to stop Hitler, it should have been done in some other way. No such "other way" has ever been offered, however, and the world must acknowledge its debt to those two masters of the Machiavellian art, Roosevelt and Churchill, who together preserved its culture.

Tolley, Kemp. *The Cruise of the* Lanikai. Annapolis: Naval Institute Press, 1973. Reprinted 1994 by the Admiral Nimitz Foundation.

The first part of this book is a surprise: a thoughtful analysis of the diplomatic offensive by which Roosevelt induced Japan to enter

World War II. It stops short of suggesting the president had advance knowledge of Pearl Harbor, but it leaves no doubt he caused Japan's entry into the war and knew half a day in advance that Japan was about to implement some desperate sort of contingency plan for that event.

Wohlstetter, Roberta. *Pearl Harbor; Warning and Decision.* Stanford: Stanford University Press, 1962.

Wohlstetter deals best with this difficult-to-understand subject, but the thirty-two years that have followed publication of her outstanding book have produced considerably more in the way of recently declassified information than was available when she wrote it. It would be greatly wanting in respect for a truly accomplished historian to suggest that the newest insights might change her outlook on this sensitive matter, but it is exciting, nonetheless, to consider the possibility.

Index

About the Author

Captain Beach, a 1939 graduate of the U.S. Naval Academy, where he was the regimental commander and second in his class, is a retired career submarine officer of the U.S. Navy. During World War II he completed twelve submarine war patrols, beginning with the Battle of Midway, five of them (1943–45) as executive officer and the last in command of his own submarine. This war patrol was terminated by the Japanese surrender as he arrived in his assigned operating area, deep in enemy home waters, and his ship was the last to return from the war zone. He wears ten decorations for gallantry in combat, among them the navy's second-highest decoration, the Navy Cross, for a war patrol in which his commanding officer received the Congressional Medal of Honor. From 1953 to 1957 he was naval aide to President Eisenhower. In 1960 he commanded the nuclear-powered submarine *Triton* in her epic circumnavigation of the world: an entirely submerged, 84-day, 41,000-mile voyage that still stands as the all-time record for submerged endurance (although, according to Beach, it does not compare, in sheer physical endurance, with a 24-hour depth-charging he once experienced at the hands of the Japanese).

In addition to a brilliant naval career, Beach has had outstanding success as a writer on naval subjects. He is author of three novels and seven nonfiction books, four of them national best-sellers, including *Run Silent, Run Deep* (Naval Institute Press Classic of Naval Literature), and has published numerous articles in top-caliber periodicals. He has been awarded the Navy League Alfred Thayer Mahan Award for literary achievement, the Theodore and Franklin D. Roosevelt Prize, the Samuel Eliot Morison Award for Distinguished Service, the Magellanic Premium of the American Philosophic Society, and the Theodore Roosevelt Association Gold Medal for National Defense and Literary Achievement.

The Naval Institute Press is the book-publishing arm of the U.S. Naval Institute, a private, nonprofit society for sea service professionals and others who share an interest in naval and maritime affairs. Established in 1873 at the U.S. Naval Academy in Annapolis, Maryland, where its offices remain, today the Naval Institute has more than 100,000 members worldwide.

Members of the Naval Institute receive the influential monthly magazine *Proceedings* and discounts on fine nautical prints and on ship and aircraft photos. They also have access to the transcripts of the Institute's Oral History Program and get discounted admission to any of the Institute-sponsored seminars offered around the country.

The Naval Institute also publishes *Naval History* magazine. This colorful bimonthly is filled with entertaining and thought-provoking articles, first-person reminiscences, and dramatic art and photography. Members receive a discount on *Naval History* subscriptions.

The Naval Institute's book-publishing program, begun in 1898 with basic guides to naval practices, has broadened its scope in recent years to include books of more general interest. Now the Naval Institute Press publishes more than seventy titles each year, ranging from how-to books on boating and navigation to battle histories, biographies, ship and aircraft guides, and novels. Institute members receive discounts on the Press's nearly 400 books in print.

For a free catalog describing Naval Institute Press books currently available, and for further information about subscribing to *Naval History* magazine or about joining the U.S. Naval Institute, please write to:

Membership & Communications Department
U.S. Naval Institute
118 Maryland Avenue
Annapolis, Maryland 21402-5035

Or call, toll-free, (800) 233-USNI.